JOY IN
DIVINE
WISDOM

OTHER BOOKS BY MARVA J. DAWN

*The Sense of the Call: A Sabbath Way of Life for
Those Who Serve God, the Church, and the World*
(Eerdmans, 2006)

Talking the Walk: Letting Christian Language Live Again
(Grand Rapids, MI: Brazos, 2005)

Unfettered Hope: A Call to Faithful Living in an Affluent Society
(Louisville: Westminster John Knox, 2003)

How Shall We Worship?: Biblical Guidelines for the Worship Wars
(Carol Stream, IL: Tyndale House, 2003)

Joy in Our Weakness: A Gift of Hope from the Book of Revelation,
Rev. ed. (Grand Rapids, MI: Eerdmans, 2002)

*Morning by Morning: Daily Meditations from the
Writings of Marva J. Dawn,* edited by Karen Dismer
(Eerdmans, 2001)

Powers, Weakness, and the Tabernacling of God (Eerdmans, 2001)

The Unnecessary Pastor: Rediscovering the Call
(co-written with Eugene Peterson) (Eerdmans, 1999)

*A Royal "Waste" of Time: The Splendor of
Worshiping God and Being Church for the World*
(Eerdmans, 1999)

I'm Lonely, LORD—How Long?: Meditations on the Psalms
Revised edition (Eerdmans, 1998; 1st in 1983)

Truly the Community: Romans 12 and How to Be the Church
(Eerdmans, 1992; reissued 1997)

Is It a Lost Cause?: Having the Heart of God for the Church's Children
(Eerdmans, 1997)

To Walk and Not Faint: A Month of Meditations from Isaiah 40,
Second edition (Eerdmans, 1997; 1st in 1980)

*Reaching Out Without Dumbing Down: A Theology of
Worship for This Urgent Time* (Eerdmans, 1995)

Sexual Character: Beyond Technique to Intimacy (Eerdmans, 1993)

Keeping the Sabbath Wholly: Ceasing, Resting, Embracing, Feasting
(Eerdmans, 1989)

JOY IN DIVINE WISDOM

Practices of Discernment
from Other Cultures
and Christian Traditions

Marva J. Dawn

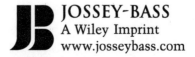

JOSSEY-BASS
A Wiley Imprint
www.josseybass.com

Published by Jossey-Bass
A Wiley Imprint
989 Market Street, San Francisco, CA 94103-1741   www.josseybass.com

Unless otherwise noted, Scripture quotations are from New Revised Standard Version (Iowa Falls, IA: World Bible Publishers, Inc., 1989). Division of Christian Education of the National Council of the Churches of Christ in the United State of America.

Scripture quotations marked NASB are from the New American Standard Bible (Carol Stream, IL: Creation House, Inc.) copyright The Lockman Foundation 1960, 1962, 1963, 1968, 1971.

Scripture quotations marked "The Message" are from Eugene H. Peterson, *The Message: The Bible in Contemporary Language* (Colorado Springs, CO: NavPress, 2002).

Jossey-Bass books and products are available through most bookstores. To contact Jossey-Bass directly, call our Customer Care Department within the United States at (800) 956-7739, outside the United States at (317) 572-3986, or via fax (317) 572-4002.

Jossey-Bass also publishes its books in a variety of electronic formats. Some content that appears in print may not be available in electronic books.

Library of Congress Cataloging-in-Publication Data
Dawn, Marva J.
  Joy in divine wisdom : practices of discernment from other cultures and
Christian traditions / Marva J. Dawn.
      p. cm. (Enduring questions in Christian life series)
   Includes bibliographical references and index.
   ISBN-13: 978-0-7879-8100-6 (cloth)
   ISBN-10: 0-7879-8100-1 (cloth)
   1. Discernment (Christian theology) 2. Decision making—Religious
aspects—Christianity. I. Title.
   BV4509.5.D295 2006
   248.4—dc22   2006012330

Printed in the United States of America
FIRST EDITION
HB Printing   10 9 8 7 6 5 4 3 2 1

ENDURING QUESTIONS
IN CHRISTIAN LIFE™

David P. Gushee
SERIES EDITOR

Only Human:
Christian Reflections on the
Journey Toward Wholeness
David P. Gushee

Living the Sermon on the Mount:
A Practical Hope for Grace and Deliverance
Glen H. Stassen

Joy in Divine Wisdom:
Practices of Discernment from
Other Cultures and Christian Traditions
Marva J. Dawn

CONTENTS

The purpose of the Enduring Questions in Christian Life series is to offer thoughtful reflections on important issues that emerge at the intersection of faith and everyday life. The idea is to bring together the rich resources of Christian thought with the kinds of personally important questions that people (and not just Christian people) have always asked.

This book by Marva J. Dawn—*Joy in Divine Wisdom: Practices of Discernment from Other Cultures and Christian Traditions*—is the third in our series. I think you will find here a work that meets you where you are but at the same time takes you to some wonderfully and revealingly unfamiliar places in its quest for moral wisdom.

The "enduring question" that this book tackles is this: how do we make wise decisions in our lives? How do we "discern" the right thing to do (or the right way to be, or the right path to take)? This is surely an enduring question for human beings, and a vexing one. Human life is filled with uncertainty, and making choices is an inescapable part of the human experience. Most of us face key moments in our lives in which we simply must choose, but we just as simply have no clear sense not just of what to do but of *how to find out what to do.* We must leap, as if into the dark.

And yet that darkness scares us. So we turn and look for help before we leap. In part, this is a book about the rather stark limits of the resources that most people think that they have available to them as they make that turn for help. I'm not just talking about the foolishness of horoscopes, advice columns, and 1-800-PSYCHIC hotlines. Marva Dawn shows us that even Western Christians who take the Bible seriously also overlook resources for discernment that could be available to them but are missed because they somehow do not fit our cultural grid. She introduces Western Christian readers to entirely different ways of discerning reality and making choices. These are available in other world cultures if we just know where to look. The author helps us see them.

It took a particular kind of person with a particular set of experiences to write this book. I certainly could not have done it, because like most people I do not have anything approaching the extensive international experience that Marva Dawn has brought to the writing of this work. She is truly a global Christian, and it is very clear as one reads this book that she travels around the world as a humble listener—even if she is the one invited to speak and teach and preach! It is clear that in her experiences on most of the world's continents, and then through continued dialogue with people she meets on her travels, Marva has imbibed rich wisdom that we desperately need in our cash-rich and yet spiritually poor Western societies.

As you read, you will notice various themes working their way through the book: grace, community, honesty, humility, wholeness, forgiveness, simplicity, suffering, trust, and faith are among them. It turns out that you cannot write about discernment in isolation from a broader vision. Discernment does not occur as some kind of impersonal or rationalistic mechanism. It is instead a deeply human process rooted in the character, the values, and the vision of life that the decision maker brings to the table before any decisions are made at all. And Marva Dawn is quick to remind us that even the paradigm of the "decision maker" wrestling it out on his or her own is deeply flawed. She says early in her book that we "know ourselves . . . genuinely by means of those to whom we belong." Those to whom we belong are those who love us. And ultimately the One to Whom we most deeply belong is the gracious God of the universe, Father, Son, and Holy Spirit, Who is Love. So in the end a book about moral discernment becomes a book about trusting in this God of Love.

One of the themes that runs through this book is conversation. Marva Dawn has learned much by sitting quietly around kitchen tables with people from all over the world. She listens. She speaks quietly. *Joy in Divine Wisdom* is like a conversation over tea. You will not be shouted at in this book. You will not be cajoled, coerced, or manipulated. You will instead be invited to sit with someone for a while and talk about what she has learned on her journey. I think you will be very glad you did.

David P. Gushee
Series Editor

To Connie Johnson,
whose kidney has given me new life,

and to our husbands,
Rob Sachs and Myron Sandberg,
for their constant support
for the transplant
and in every endeavor.

This is a book about the pronoun *we*, a word often tragically absent from contemporary U.S. society's vocabulary. It is missing these days in other cultures, too, but I live in the United States and will be writing from here, with the hopes that what I write will be useful elsewhere.

The biggest anguish for most people in our culture is the question "What is the meaning of my life?" or "Why do I exist?" or, put more spiritually, "How do I discern God's will for my life?" Usually, we ask these questions by ourselves, or, if we ask them of others, we eventually try to figure it out on our own with a little bit of input from others. We decide that it's our own personal job to decide who we are and how to live.

Perhaps we could learn from our forebears and from other cultures throughout space and time to ask first instead, "To whom do I belong?" and then, "How could I find meaning for my life because I am part of such a people and have such a God?" These questions would move us away from the anguish and unanswerability of existential questions to the security and recognizability of our identity as persons enfolded in the love of others, especially the love of God.

I'm asking the alternative questions of the previous paragraph because of what peoples from around the world and across the centuries have taught me. Folks encountered in my work as an itinerant teacher of assorted subjects have shown me that perhaps my own society's habits and ways of thinking are not necessarily the best. Other cultures demonstrate other customs and traditions that can be more useful for making the best decisions—and, correlatively, for making more godly ones.

Exposure to other cultures came slowly to the small, isolated Midwestern town of my childhood. Not until the fourth grade did I meet my first Hispanic acquaintances because they lived on my newspaper route, though I had seen glimpses of global cultures because of missionaries who visited our church and showed slides (and because my parents loved food from other cuisines). Then when I was twenty, it was my privilege to sing in a college choir that traveled around the world to give concerts and visit churches in Japan, Korea, Taiwan, Hong Kong, Thailand, India, Egypt, the Holy Land, Italy, (what was then) East Germany, and West Germany. We came back from that global tour chastened, mostly aware that our nation was probably too rich for its own good and needed to learn to share its resources with the rest of the world, which was, in many places, mired in poverty.

On the choir tour I was also exposed to all the major religions of the world and observed at their worship Buddhists, Taoists, Shintoists, Hindus, Muslims, Jews, flagrant atheists, searching agnostics, and committed Christians. I stress the last of these because I had grown up a Christian but was not quite sure if I was one simply because of my parents. I came back from that tour more devoted to my own religious beliefs, yet more open to the wisdom to be gained from the rest of the faith traditions.

I write from the Christian tradition, but that perspective is not necessary for reading this book, for my main point here is grace—and grace can be seen everywhere, from all outlooks. I have become convinced for myself that grace is manifested brilliantly in the Hebrew and Christian Scriptures which reveal a God named Father, Son, and Holy Spirit, so from that faith conviction I write and am glad to invite others (but not coercively) to consider that tradition's claims, too.

The most important point I discovered in this project of learning about decision making from other cultures was that we can begin in grace. I almost wrote, "we *must* begin in grace," but that word *must* denies grace by making our action another duty.

Pervasive though it may be, the term *grace* is not well understood because it is a hard idea to get into our psyches. We are so firmly grounded in the habits of proving ourselves, paying our own way, "earning our keep," and chalking up accomplishments that we hardly know what to do with a notion that suggests instead that first we are loved gratis, freely and without any requirement that it be deserved or reciprocated. Yet I am convinced that this is the nature of the universe, that all creation is founded in grace, in the totally incomprehensibly gratuitous love of God. I believe that we make our decisions sometimes in error because we don't start with knowing that we are loved (though often we are loved in spite of ourselves).

In order for us to study the topic of making our best decisions about life, then, this book starts with grace. Chapter One also considers some habits and customs that might equip us to receive grace more thoroughly in our lives. Then we will turn in later chapters to other lessons learned from various cultures about alternate practices and observances that lead to clearer discernment.

We will consider, for example, the importance of a foundational Word or scriptural basis for thinking, of "rectifying the names" or clarifying terms, of cultural virtues and moral priorities, and of an enfolding community for assistance in deliberation. Then we will discuss what it could mean to be part of a culture of welcoming, of reconciliation, of a willingness to suffer, and of celebration. These and other habits and practices could enable us to make better decisions that free us truly to be ourselves and to know ourselves more genuinely by means of those to whom we belong.

Sometimes our wealth and "bottom-line" mentalities, our busy-ness and lists of things to do prevent North Americans from seeing things as clearly as we might want. Often our tendency to operate in isolation compounds the problem. We don't realize that the best decisions are usually those that are made in the midst of a community of discernment. We learn who we are most clearly because we are part of a *we,* the community of saints throughout time and space.

And that is where we began, so this introduction is finished, except for brief words of thanks to Sheryl Fullerton, of Jossey-Bass, and David Gushee, the series editor, who invited me to be part of this book series and who trusted me with this topic. I am grateful to them for their tremendous grace and gentle corrections and for the privilege of writing as part of their community of discernment. Thanks also to all the other good people at Jossey-Bass, who have to compensate for my visual impairments and computer inadequacy and who do such a good job of all the other aspects of turning manuscripts into publicized books.

I am also enormously grateful to the Louisville Institute, a program of the Eli Lilly Foundation, which graced me with a "Sabbatical" and then a "Faith and Life" grant, which enabled me to pursue this project without distraction from any speaking engagements or other workloads and while recovering from a kidney transplant. I also offer here heartfelt thanks to all my acquaintances both in the flesh and by written correspondence who have given me the stories included here and for their gracious permission to use their accounts and wisdom for the purposes of this book.

One special caveat I must stress. The people whose stories I tell in these pages insisted that they spoke from their own perspectives and should not be mistaken to speak for an entire culture. They have observed or participated in the habits they share, but they do not claim that everyone in the culture specified would agree on their descriptions. These are instead samples to invite your consideration, models that we might follow for better discernment, practices that we might adopt so that our lives become more what we hope they can be.

Most of all, I offer thanks to Connie Johnson, to whom I am indebted for my life because she gave me one of her well-working kidneys, which is in the process of revolutionizing my health, and to our husbands, Rob Sachs and Myron Sandberg, who have supported us profoundly in this transforming venture. Talk about grace: I cannot imagine how a person could be so loving as to undergo suffering willingly in order to donate to me her kidney. It is sheer gift, and it will take eternity to express my thanks even remotely adequately!

JOY IN
DIVINE
WISDOM

Starting with Grace

How ironic that when I wanted to get busy and *work* on this project, I couldn't. Though I was eager to get started, nonetheless I simply was too newly recovering from my kidney transplant, still trying to adjust my body's chemistry to all the antirejection medications, yet too weak and with a blood pressure too low, still too tired and stiff to sit long at the computer. There was nothing I could do but rest.

But our culture is so insistent on doing, accomplishing, earning our way, winning approval that we have trouble thinking we're worth much if we can't produce anything. That is why this book is founded on habits from other cultures that are more life-giving and health-producing.

In this chapter's case, I would like to focus on the truly alternative culture of Christianity. Tragically, to my great horror, that faith tradition has recently been too associated with U.S. culture—and the more acquisitive and violent aspects of this culture at that. But faith in the Triune God, the God of Christians, is unquestionably distinct from a culture of wealth, luxury, selfishness, and power. Instead, this God is characterized by self-giving donation, loving self-abandonment, generosity and hospitality, welcoming and reconciliation, and triumph through suffering weakness.

In love God created us all. In love God gave us the gift of the entire, wondrous cosmic creation to enjoy and to care for.

In love God rescued us all from our own selfishness, our desire to make ourselves gods. God delivered us from ourselves most clearly when Jesus forgave us, even while we were helping to crucify Him by our mistaken choices or our apathy or our greed for power or our unwillingness to be more than victims.

In love God dwells within us through the Holy Spirit, Who inspires us, empowers us, strengthens us, guides us. In love God enables us to find who we really are as the Trinity's own beloved.

WHO IS THE TRIUNE GOD?

Previously, I named the God of Christians the *Triune God,* and in the preceding paragraph I used the word *Trinity.* It is important that we sidestep here from the topic of grace to consider exactly (or as precisely as we can, because God is always mystery) to Whom these terms refer, for the nature of the Triune God is essential for all that we will learn about discernment in this book.[1]

Sometimes the idea of "Trinity" is dismissed as an archaic dogmatic assertion no longer necessary in the present postmodern world. However, for Christians the discovery that God is Triune is fundamental, for that is how God has been revealed by Jesus—as Father, Son, and Holy Spirit. Some might be tempted to link those three names with the topics of the three paragraphs just before this section, as if only the Father created, only the Son rescued, and only the Spirit dwells in us, but that is basically to deny one paramount point about the Three in One—that They all Three work mutually in and through and with each other, as if in an intertwining dance.

The early Celtic church captured this intertwining of the Three Persons in its prayers and art. Many prayers from Celtic communities involve verses that name each of the Three Persons in connection with a repeated phrase or that end with concluding trinitarian doxologies or hymns of praise. When we look at the beautiful illuminated texts—books of the Gospels with highly artistic drawings in and around the letters of the texts, such as the famous Lindisfarne Gospels, now on display at the British Museum in London—we see many sets of three, such as three-stranded cords interwoven, three figures of persons or patterns around a circle, three levels of flames, or three hands converging.[2]

In the Hebrew Scriptures (which I call the First Testament so that we don't think it is just "Old" and outdated) we get a hint that God is more than meets the eye (or ear, as is usually the case), for the very first chapter includes these verses:

> Then God said, "Let us make humankind in *our* image,
> according to *our* likeness; and let them have dominion
> over the fish of the sea, and over the birds of the air,
> and over the cattle, and over all the wild animals of the
> earth, and over every creeping thing that creeps upon
> the earth.
> So God created humankind in his image, in the image
> of God he created them, male and female he created them.
> (Genesis 1:26–27, emphasis mine)

Before the appearance of Jesus in the flesh on earth, the Bible already shows that God is a plurality within the Godhead, with the result that human beings had to be created in a plurality in order to image God in their interrelationships. That is the beginning of the *we* that is part of our discernment process (which we will discuss further in Chapter Five).

When Jesus became God incarnate as a human being, He introduced us to His Father and yet revealed, through His authoritative teaching and His miraculous works of compassion that He also was God. For that reason I always capitalize pronouns that refer to Him, so that we keep remembering His dual nature as both human and divine. I will also capitalize pronouns that refer to the Triune God in general so that we don't confuse God with the gender of male, especially because the Father and the Spirit are spirit and not body. Though God has been, and continues to be, most completely revealed in the person of Jesus Christ, the emphasis is not on His maleness, but on His personalness, His intimate love. Though the first Person of the Trinity is named *Father,* this accentuates God's difference from Jesus' mother, Mary, a human being, because divinity and humanity are the two sources of Christ's birth. The name *Father* also highlights the combination of sovereign care with perfect wisdom and comprehensive love that makes God the perfect Parent, in contrast to all the failures of human parents.[3]

After Jesus died on the cross and rose again, He ascended. That is, He moved from being visible in the flesh to being invisibly together with His Father, though that does not mean removal from being close to us. Instead of our being able to see Him and touch Him now, we know that He has again entered into the fullness of the Godhead, from which He voluntarily descended to become fully human, and He will someday consummate His reign over all the cosmos. Meanwhile, He sent His Holy Spirit at Pentecost to remain with us and to dwell in us, to guide us and remind us of the entire Triune Presence in our lives.

Heaven is not some place greatly distant, up there, re-moved from us. Rather, I envision that by God's enfolding grace, heaven already surrounds us and indwells us now. The problem is that hell, or separation from God, is also here in this life. We sometimes separate ourselves. Often our circumstances cause us to forget the nearness of God. Frequently, other people divide us from God. Yet in all these sorts of sep-aration, God always remains close to us and is constantly at work in us to transform us into the likeness of Christ. And someday, at the end of time, the Triune God will bring all the divine work to completion, and heaven will be separated from hell forever. Meanwhile, God desires that all human beings would live in relationship with Him through Christ.

One of the reasons I will stress Trinity in this book is that the triune nature of loving mutuality causes the Three in One to want always to be close to us and to enfold us in God's purposes for humankind and God's actions in the world. The Trinity *wants* us to discern well, to participate in what God is doing for the sake of the well-being of the whole creation. That is the character of the Triune Godhead—God is always open to human involvement in the divine will.

The nature of the God of Christianity is that of a Giver, One Who graces us and sets us truly free by that grace to dis-cover ourselves as loved ones, gifted people, who have a lot to give to others through the same grace. The question of identity—who are we?—has a great answer in Whose we are. The kind of God we have, to Whom we belong, makes an enormous difference in what we discover about ourselves and in our discernments concerning the way to live well. Think how much the Trinity loves us and consider that this God wants to transform us into His likeness. The more we look to this God, the more we will become like the Triune One from one degree of glory to another (2 Corinthians 3:18).

If this is the kind of God to Whom we belong, then why should that God not want us to know the best way to live? Some Christians treat God as if the Trinity were a cynical riddle-hider, taunting us as if to say, "I've got a secret; see if you can figure it out." At least, that is the impression we get when people agonize over "finding God's will" or "trying to figure out what God wants me to do" in a certain situation. Is God mocking us from the wings of heaven in the same way that children tease, "Nyah, nyah, nyah, nyah"?

Or does God want to communicate with us, want us to know the best way to live? We belong to the Triune God by the fullness of divine grace. Doesn't God also gladly invite us into the mysterious workings of that same grace?[4]

THE EXPERIENCE
OF SAINTS ANCIENT
AND CONTEMPORARY

Indeed, God's invitation and welcome have been the experience of saints throughout the ages and around the globe. The writer and Augustinian monk known as Thomas à Kempis (1380–1471), who gathered the wisdom of the monks into *The Imitation of Christ* and *Consolations for My Soul,* realized that sometimes human guides are inadequate, but that God Himself would escort us into whatever knowledge we need to live well. And God wants to bring us Joy as we discover His best will. Put into a modern paraphrase, à Kempis wrote,

> May the Mysterious One Who deliberately fails to cover
> His tracks lead you on a merry chase!
> And now that teacherly types like myself have failed utterly
> and miserably to help you in your quest, may He Himself
> take you in hand and lead you to His Heavenly Home![5]

The saints' awareness that God's future has already broken into the present through Christ's accomplished work has made God's Kingdom a living reality now, though not yet thoroughly culminated. Thus, "Heavenly Home" does not just mean an eternity after death in some other place. Rather, the saints of history, as well as saints throughout the world now, are very aware that heaven can be for believers a present reality, and conversation with God a daily opportunity.

But God speaks with us primarily through the tools and the practices that we will be discovering in the rest of this book by means of the gifts of the community of saints to which we belong, so let's not get ahead of ourselves. Instead, let us look at a tangible lived example of grace in action.

I met George Evans from Nigeria in Bratislava, Slovakia, where he stayed with Dr. Jonathan Sorum, a professor at the Lutheran Seminary, and his wife, Reverend Ann Sorum, a pastor at the English-speaking Lutheran church. Jonathan recorded George's account as a "Story of Martyrdom and Hope," and he and George gave me permission to retell it here.

George was absent from his home several years ago when riots broke out as Muslims in his country protested the Miss World contest, which was to be held in Lagos, the capital. Christian churches came under attack. His father, who was pastor of a church which also housed an orphanage and a school, was killed as he stood before the door while about one hundred children and women escaped through the back door. One of George's sisters was killed as she and her mother stood outside a house they owned, which they were trying to sell to finance their escape.

George's mother hired traffickers—a criminal gang—to take her family to England where one of her brothers lives. They left in February 2003, but the traffickers were abusive. The refugees were fed very little, and George began to feel unwell. At various borders the people were ordered out of the vehicles, and they walked across to other vehicles. Finally, George and his brother were put on a small airplane, with the promise that his mother and sister would be put on the next plane. When the plane landed, George hugged his brother to resist the traffickers' effort to separate the two, but he was knocked unconscious and thrown in the back of a truck. As the truck drove through the countryside, the refugee passengers were dropped off the back, one by one.

When George was dropped, he asked where London was because he assumed that he was now in England. But the city to which he was pointed was Bratislava in Slovakia. On the way he collapsed, but "by grace" (as he recounts it) he was rescued by another African refugee trying to cross into Austria, who stopped instead and helped him. George awoke in a hospital with a bleeding ulcer, but he discovered that he had also been receiving sedatives—which explained why he had felt so unwell during the trip.

After being placed in a refugee camp, George applied for asylum as a victim of religious and ethnic persecution, but his application was refused. This left him in limbo because he had nowhere to go while his court decision was appealed. One day in July while George was straightening up materials in the camp library, he found a copy of an English-language newspaper from Bratislava, which contained an advertisement for an English-speaking Christian worship service in that city sponsored by the Evangelical Lutheran Church in America. The next Sunday George got up at 4 A.M. to take a bus to Bratislava, but he could not find the church in time. The second Sunday he was there sufficiently early. One of the pastors at that time, Paul Hanson, and his wife, Kay, provided George with a weekend stay in their home so that he wouldn't have to get up so early.

Jon and Ann Sorum had room in their nearby apartment, which they offered to George. By December they had secured permission for him to stay permanently with them.

They realized, and we could see upon meeting him, that George has an incredibly deep faith and a profound sense of grace. Furthermore, because he himself is gracious, he developed many friendships, especially with international students. He started a fellowship group for Christian international students, which met in the Sorums' home on Saturday nights. George also volunteered at the library at the Lutheran Seminary and befriended the students there. Meanwhile, he continued his efforts to find his brother, sister, and mother.

The most important working of grace in George's life is best told by Jon Sorum's written account:

> Of course, George sometimes gets discouraged. In January
> and February of 2004, the anniversary of his sister's murder and
> of his horrendous journey, when he lost the rest of the family,
> he was wondering why God brought him to Slovakia. For
> months there had been no progress in his asylum process, and
> his life seemed to be going nowhere. Then, one night, he had
> a dream. He was in a classroom, but there were no other pupils
> in the classroom with him. When the teacher walked in, it was
> his father. His father said to him, "George, remember what I
> taught you." He had this same dream three nights in a row.
>
> On the third day he suddenly realized what this dream
> meant. His father had done ministry with the poor. The
> people in the refugee camps in Slovakia were poor and in
> need of many things. As one who had lived in those camps
> and understood what it means to be a refugee, George felt
> a call to reach out to these people.
>
> Even before he told us about his intentions, he put his
> plan into action. He used the little pocket money he had
> to buy milk and some other groceries, brought them to
> the organization that takes care of the refugees and asked

[members] to bring them to the people in one of the camps.
When he told them his plans to start a ministry with the
refugees, they told him it could not be done. When he told
his friends at the seminary about his plans, they also told him
it could not be done.

Slovaks have very little experience with doing charity
work and, in any case, their experience [from living under
communism] is that the obstacles are so great that nothing
can be done. The assumption is that it is up to the government
to take care of such things. George refused to be influenced
by their skepticism. He solicited contributions from businesses,
schools, churches, and other organizations. Within a few
months he had gathered and shipped nine vans full of used
clothing, school supplies and toys to the camps.

His project is called God's Care and is now an official
ministry of Diakonia, the social service arm of the Lutheran
church. Not only has this project helped hundreds of refugees,
but it has shown Slovaks that something like this can be
done, and with resources from within Slovakia. Many young
people, including students at the seminary, have been very
involved in this project, gaining valuable experience and
learning from George's example how to mobilize resources
in order to meet a pressing need in society. He is a young
man, only eighteen years old, without a passport, not allowed
to go to school or get a job. He is without status, and yet
he has become a leader in Slovakia and an inspiration and
an example for many people, especially young people!

Shortly after Jon wrote this account, George was allowed to study at City University in Bratislava. Three spon-
sors paid for his tuition at this private university. But his
asylum petition was denied by the Slovak court, which accepted only two refugees out of the nine thousand who had
applied two years ago.

Meanwhile, many of us continued to pray with George for his mother, Mary Evans, his brother Victor, and his sister Christiana. Now, two years later, George's mother has a good job, his sister has a scholarship to study medicine in Lagos, and his brother has one to study law. George has married a Slovak woman, and they are looking forward to the opportunity to visit Nigeria to see his family.

What is amazing to me is that in a situation that most of us would find intolerable, George continued to be very aware of the grace undergirding his life and, in response to that grace, was immediately ready to act on his threefold dream and find ways to pass on that grace to other poor refugees. Only grace could empower someone so deprived of his own identity and give him instead a sure sense of call. Furthermore, by grace, George's faithful response to that call inspires many others to care for the needy in their society.

It was my experience, too, in working with people from Eastern Europe, the countries formerly under communist rule, that inertia is strong, and the general attitude is that if anything can be done, the government must do it. That makes George's story all the brighter—that he has been able, by grace, not only to serve so many, but also to overcome strong cultural patterns of communist domination and free the people to act graciously on behalf of the poor.

DREAMS

George's victory over his discouragement came primarily from the impetus of his dreams concerning his father. In my correspondence with translators, health-care workers, teachers, and missionaries in other places in the world, many reported to me that dreams are an important means by which people in these cultures receive guidance. Perhaps dreams are not as useful a tool in U.S. culture because we work too hard at analyzing them.

The early saints—the Celts, for example—and contemporary people in Africa and Latin America take dreams more literally and humbly, as did George when he remembered exactly what his father had taught him and immediately put that into practice. Notice also that George received the same dream three times before he realized how to understand it. In other cases, there is either a multiple reception of the same dream or a community that holds the dreamer accountable in order to confirm the content of dreams.

My friend Carol Barrera, a Wycliffe translator for indigenous people in Guatemala, wrote, "One area [of discernment] I see as different from mainstream U.S.A. is that [the Achí people] find direction in dreams, which they take seriously and seek to interpret regarding calls to service." For example, because of their cultural background the Achí "expect to hear from the world of the supernatural in their dreams," so some people whom she knows "have been convicted of sin" by dreams or have been "warned not to take a particular action that would be spiritually detrimental."

Similarly, at the time of our first correspondence my friend Barbara Robertson worked in HIV/AIDS education, prevention, and testing at Haydom Lutheran Hospital in Tanzania. She reported to me her conversations with African friends from several tribes, including Bantu, who come from West Africa; Iraqw, whose oral tradition places their roots around Mesopotamia and who came to Tanzania via Ethiopia; and Datoga, who are related to the Maasai. These people, too, receive frequent guidance by means of interpretation of dreams.

Barbara herself knows a woman who has exceptionally accurate prophetic dreams. In general, however, she wrote that dreams are especially important for the uneducated and undereducated because these people don't have other resources on which to depend. In some remote areas, Barbara reports, many "rely on dreams as a sort of 'God's telephone' to know what is going on with other loved ones."

Barbara also sent this extensive description of how young people decide about marriage partners on the basis of whether or not they see the other in a dream:

> A young man may be of an age to marry but doesn't
> know who he is to choose. He might go to the church
> elders, asking them to pray with him for insight into which
> woman to ask. Then, he might see a certain person in a
> dream. If so, he will go to her and make a marriage proposal.
> If it comes out of the blue for the girl, she will ask that the
> boy give her a month to decide. Then she will wait to see
> if she sees him specifically in a dream. If he doesn't show
> up in a dream, she will most likely not marry him—if she
> is free to make her own decision [that is, if her father is not
> "exceptionally forceful or influential" on that issue].

Now people in the United States would find it terribly naive to base one's choice for marriage on a dream—or we would psychoanalyze all the subconscious motivations that might cause a certain person to be the subject in a dream—but one wonders whether dreams might be more effective as a means for discernment. After all, the divorce rate in the United States is much higher than that of the cultures where dreams are trusted.

However, my point is not necessarily to advocate that practice here, though I believe we could respect our dreams much more than we do—enough to listen to them more humbly. My concern is primarily to suggest that perhaps all of our analyzing sometimes gets in the way of grace. We rely so much on our own intelligence, our own purposefulness, to find our way in the world that perhaps we are not open to the mysterious workings of grace. Perhaps we miss God's direct leadings, God's own gifts of insights, God's prophetic words to us, because we are not ready to receive them.

I don't say this in a condemning way. I only realize in my own life that my education and training often get in the way of simply accepting God's good gifts of wisdom, in whatever forms those might be given to me.

Just when I got to this point in the writing, I encountered the following anonymous prayer assigned for this day in my regular devotion book featuring lessons from the First Testament, the Psalms, the Epistles, the Gospels, and readings from saints throughout the ages:

> O Thou, who art ever the same yet art known to us through
> constant change, help us to realize Thy Providence and its
> everlasting laws, in whatsoever comes to pass. We see Thee
> within the order which Thou hast made, and we believe
> in the Presence that besets us before and behind, through
> Jesus Christ our Lord. Amen.[6]

Could we all rest in grace enough to trust that God's sovereignly good Providence and Presence are available for us to behold in some of the events that appear in our daily lives? I stress the word *some,* for certainly evil, too, takes many forms in the dire circumstances of our world in these days of terror and violence, injustice and poverty, natural disaster and illness. An immense part of the grace that we need is the gift of discernment to comprehend what things are good and according to divine Love and what things are evil and brought to our attention in order that we might defy, resist, combat, or change them.

The early saint Augustine (354–430) defined Joy (which I always capitalize to emphasize its spiritual roots, as opposed to mere human happiness) as loving God so much that we don't want to choose anything but God's perfect will.[7] This is sheer grace: that the Trinity gives us such deep delight in God's beauty that no sinful thing even looks like a good choice to us. True freedom, according to Augustine, is to want always to do God's will, to live God's way.

Of course, none of us is perfect, so we still need to make choices, and often these involve great struggles, but when God's Kingdom is perfected in us at the end of time, we will want only to live in the consummate way of Christ. Then Joy will be perfected in us.

Thomas à Kempis went beyond Augustine in delighting that God's Joy was infinitely creative and became an increasing source of bliss to the one who loves God. He wrote in his second book, *Consolations for My Soul,* "And He was so inventive when it came to joy—He never repeated Himself once." Again, "And whatever he cooked up became my delight."[8]

Let me hasten to add that it is not necessary for us to expend effort to gain such an attitude toward grace. The very effort, again, denies grace itself. The attitude of delighting in God's ways is also a gift to be received. It is a working of the Holy Spirit within our own spirit, and therefore it cannot be gained by efforts to create certain feelings or to develop certain thoughts or emotions. We don't try to change our body, soul, or mind. Instead, we ask God to work in us to create the spiritual life. Jesus teaches us in John 16:24, "Until now you have asked for nothing in My name; ask, and you will receive, so that your joy may be made full."

Let us, then, invite grace and learn to wait to receive it so that we might learn the fullness of Joy that God promises, for God Himself is the Author of our spiritual life. Those gifts are actually available now and waiting for us because God is waiting for us. The poet R. S. Thomas suggests that in a subtly beautiful poem about a church building that he occasionally visits. He describes the delicacy with which the light infuses his soul "from the serene presence" which always awaits him.[9]

Grace will be hard for us to learn. We will be tempted to try too hard to get it, but it is simply a gift to be received. Just as I couldn't *work* at things for the first two months after my kidney transplant but needed to learn to receive simply the gifts of people in the congregation who brought meals to help us along, so we all need to develop entirely new habits of reception and new practices for accepting deepening grace. "O taste and see that the LORD is good; happy are those who take refuge in Him," the psalmist enjoins us (Psalm 34:8). Another poet reminds us of this:

> For the LORD God is a sun and shield;
>   He bestows favor and honor.
> No good thing does the LORD withhold
>   from those who walk uprightly.
> O LORD of hosts,
>   happy is everyone who trusts in you.
>   (Psalm 84:11–12)

What are some of the habits that can slow us down to receive grace? By what practices could we learn to be more open to receive God's mysterious gifts? What gets in our way and blocks us so that we miss grace?

WHAT KEEPS US FROM
RECEIVING GRACE?

Besides the fact that we are not accustomed to receiving grace
and turn to our usual efforts to earn it, sometimes we hinder
it ourselves because we seek it for the wrong motives. We
might want it solely so that we can find a selfish personal happiness or success. Sometimes we want only our own ease and
comfort, health and wealth. We don't realize that grace is given
to us so that we will pass it on to others, as George Evans
passed it on to refugees in Slovakian camps. The LORD made
this clear when he called Abraham and told him, "I will make
of you a great nation, and I will bless you, and make your
name great, so that you will be a blessing" (Genesis 12:2).

Sometimes we think God is stingy and mean-spirited.
We don't look at the abundance of the beauties in the world
around us and see how generously God sprinkles the hillsides
with flowers and fills the birds with song. As the psalmist says:

> For the word of the LORD is upright,
>   and all His work is done in faithfulness.
> He loves righteousness and justice;
>   the earth is full of the steadfast love of the LORD.
>   (Psalm 33:5)

Sometimes the beauties and the abundance of God's
gifts are hidden from us by our own poverty—but for many
North Americans that is a poverty of spirit rather than one of
physical means. As the theologian, minister, and writer James
Mulholland reminds us, if we have adequate food, clothes to
wear, and a roof over our heads, we are richer than 75 percent of the people in the world.[10]

We are blinded by our own complaining spirits to how richly graced we are. Sometimes North Americans act as if everything possible in all of life should be handed to us on a silver platter. Everywhere I have been in the world, I have seen that those who possess less are usually more grateful for what they do have and are much more generous in passing their blessings on to others. People in other cultures are not so visionless as to miss the grace that has been given to them; they live with a spirit of thankfulness for all the goodness of God.

HABITS THAT PREPARE US TO RECEIVE GRACE

By what habits, then, could we become more practiced in receiving, and being grateful for, the grace that undergirds the world and our particular lives? Above all, I have learned from people in other cultures (including the cultures of the early saints) the importance of constant worship and adoration.

What has kept me from discerning the abundance of God's goodness has often been that I simply don't love God enough. For that reason, when I took some sabbatical time a few years ago, it was crucial for me to begin with lots of sleep and lots of worship services. Without pressing obligations for work, there was freedom to enjoy midweek Eucharist services on Tuesday mornings and Advent services on Wednesday evenings, as well as Sunday morning worship (sometimes in two places) and Advent devotions every evening at home, along with my usual morning quiet time habits. These extra opportunities for worship together with grateful communities filled my life with a much deeper sense of the presence of a gracious God and brought greatly needed healing for my heedless and unappreciative spirit.

Several weeks ago, these wonderfully adoring and grateful words from the monk and archbishop of Canterbury St. Anselm (1033–1109) were the closing prayer in the readings from my daily devotion book:

> We love Thee, O our God; and we desire to love Thee more and more. Grant to us that we may love Thee as much as we desire and as much as we ought. O dearest Friend, who hast so loved and saved us, the thought of whom is so sweet and always growing sweeter, come with Christ and dwell in our hearts; then Thou wilt keep a watch over our lips, our steps, our deeds, and we shall not need to be anxious either for our souls or our bodies. Give us love, sweetest of all gifts, which knows no enemy. Give us in our hearts pure love, born of Thy love to us, that we may love others as Thou lovest us. O most loving Father of Jesus Christ, from whom flowest all love, let our hearts, frozen in sin, cold to Thee and cold to others, be warmed by this divine fire. So help and bless us in Thy Son. Amen.[11]

The saints are excellent models to us for how adoration and worship open our lives to receive grace more thoroughly. A few weeks later, this Eucharistic hymn (a song to be sung in connection with celebration of the Lord's Supper) by the philosopher and theologian Thomas Aquinas (1225–1274) and translated by the famous poet Gerard Manley Hopkins was the fourth reading for my day:

> Godhead, I adore thee fast in hiding; thou
> God in these bare shapes, poor shadows, darkling now:

See, Lord, at thy service low lies here a heart
Lost, all lost in wonder at the God thou art.

Seeing, touching, tasting are in thee deceived;
How says trusty hearing? that shall be believed:
What God's Son has told me, take for truth I do;
Truth himself speaks truly or there's nothing true.

On the cross thy godhead made no sign to men;
Here thy very manhood steals from human ken:
Both are my confession, both are my belief,
And I pray the prayer of the dying thief.

I am not like Thomas, wounds I cannot see,
But can plainly call thee Lord and God as he:
This faith each day deeper be my holding of,
Daily make me harder hope and dearer love.

O thou our reminder of Christ crucified,
Living Bread the life of us for whom he died,
Lend this life to me then: feed and feast my mind,
There be thou the sweetness man was meant to find.

Like what tender tales tell of the Pelican;
Bathe me, Jesu Lord, in what thy bosom ran—
Blood that but one drop of has the worth to win
All the world forgiveness of this world of sin.

Jesu whom I look at veiled here below,
I beseech thee send me what I thirst for so,
Some day to gaze on thee face to face in light
And be blest for ever with thy glory's sight.[12]

One of the most important virtues that grows from a
life of worship and thanksgiving is that of humility. When we
realize the greatness of God and the goodness of all that flows
from triune grace, we learn not to take ourselves too seriously. This God will forgive our mistakes, will guide our steps,

will give us wisdom "generously and ungrudgingly." (See, for example, Psalm 103:2–14, Proverbs 16:9, James 1:5–7, and Proverbs 2:6–11.)

Humility enables us to believe that even our wrong choices will be overruled in the end by a gracious and good God, Who knows all wisdom and cares for us with comprehensive Providence. Equally, in humility we know that all our good choices are made possible by that same graciously gifting God. Thus, this virtue of modesty makes us teachable. We look to God more fervently in prayer when we are seeking God's wisdom, and we turn with greater gratitude to the saints from before and around us to learn God's guidance from them (see Chapter Five). Most of all, we look to Jesus Christ as the perfect model of spiritual direction, for He sought only His Father's will by the guidance of the same Holy Spirit Who is available to us.

God gives us wisdom even while we are sleeping. When our conscious minds surrender control, then God's perfect Mind can work in us. You have probably experienced this, so that the notion of "sleeping on it" becomes for us a lovely illustration of the gifts of grace and the value of humble submission to God's greater wisdom. As we learn from Psalm 37:3–7, we can "Rest in the LORD and wait patiently for Him" (NASB) because "He will give [us] the desires of [our] heart," which will be God's best way to live.[13]

Just to write these things has increased my confidence in discernment, for God certainly wants us to know the best way to live and will guide us to discover it with generosity and graciousness. Will I be humble enough, not depending on my own abilities, but steadfastly trusting to receive the Trinity's gifts?

What other habits or practices could increase humility and generate a deeper spirit of reception to grace?

PRACTICES FROM THE MONKS

Somehow in our day the habits and customs of the ancient and medieval monks and nuns have gotten a bad press—that their efforts were excessive, that their acts of penance were extreme. What is rarely understood is that what these religious figures were doing was not an attempt to escape this world to attain to some sort of holiness. Rather, they already perceived God's holiness filling the world, and their acts of obedience were intended to *bring out* that holiness for the rest of us to see it. Thus, they were cooperating with God in all God's gracious work of creation.[14]

Writer and professor Daniel Taylor, in a beautiful record of his visits to ancient Celtic holy sites, has taught me about the essential shyness of sacredness. He observes that whatever is sacred does not assert itself but waits patiently, without demanding anything of us. We might search for it, give it proper honor, orient ourselves toward it, or ignore it completely because we are too engrossed in our own concerns.[15]

That makes us realize that the huge question for all of our lives is whether or not we have developed habits of noticing. Grace is always present, but it will not insist that we notice its holiness. Will we "turn aside" to see the burning bush, as Moses did (Exodus 3:1–14), or will we continue to walk on by?

Taylor lists many habits that he learned from his explorations of ancient Celtic traditions. He writes that he still hears their "still, small voices," which

> whisper to me of increased possibilities for living. They whisper to me certain verbs—simplify, focus, release, risk, commit, pray, bless, believe. They whisper certain nouns—peace, gratitude, contentment, solitude, discipline, friendship,

reverence. Most of all, they whisper that word which is both verb and noun, action and state of being—they whisper the word *love*. Love of creation, love of kindred spirits and of strangers, love of learning and wisdom and the imagination, love of home and of journey, love of peace and justice, love of prayer and worship. Love of all these things, but greatest love for the one who made them because of love for us.[16]

I must confess that all the verbs and the nouns which Taylor lists I find much more readily in less strenuous cultures, in cultures not so driven by money and power, by busy-ness and an aggressive desperation for security. Those who have less don't have to simplify; those who have fewer commitments attend to them more willingly. Those who do not possess much seem to have more gratitude for, and contentment in, what they do have. Those who are not driven to succeed have more time for friendship and more reverence for all of life.

HABITS THAT SLOW US DOWN TO DISCERN AND RECEIVE GRACE

Those of us who live in a culture of acquisitiveness and power have much to learn from our global neighbors and from those in the midst of our own culture who do not share in the wealth and position that we might have. Can we take the time to learn more richly to love and enjoy the gifts of creation and of the neighbors around us? Can we let the saints of the Christian community teach us to rest deeply in the grace of the moment and the place, in the fullness of God's love throughout time and space?

The tendency in U.S. culture is to think in terms of scarcity—what we don't have and "need" to get. It is much better to think in terms of the abundance of God's gifts—all the wisdom and truth and grace available to us. Then we could respond with more gratitude and more reverent wonder and more discipline toward cherishing this profusion of treasures.

CHINESE HABITS: CALLIGRAPHY, CONTEMPLATIVE GARDENS

In a public lecture in Hong Kong, I mentioned that I wanted to learn what Chinese cultural habits help Christians there with godly decision making. Having forgotten that I'd raised the issue in this lecture setting (because usually it arose in private or small group conversations), I was thoroughly surprised when a man walked up to me afterward and simply said, "Calligraphy." To what was he referring? He explained that ancient habits of calligraphy slowed his people down to be more thoughtful.

When I brought the subject up in future conversations, Paul Chan, an artistic classmate of mine and now director of Lutheran Social Services in Hong Kong, added that calligraphy teaches a person to take things step by step, a process I appreciated when someone taught me the stages to write my Chinese name, Mu Hua, which Paul and three other Chinese friends had given me in college. A third person whom I met briefly, Chen Wei Hong, told of one calligrapher who worked with his left hand in order to slow himself down even more. This habit allows one to practice deliberation. These comments led me to think of Russian icon "writers" who consider the many-stepped discipline their way to pray.[17] Another insight Paul taught me about calligraphy is its emphasis on making writing appealing, which teaches us to look for the beautiful, the good, the gracious, in more of life.

Through all these practices which calligraphy brings, we realize that other arts traditions might offer the same. Reading poetry, drawing or sketching, or simply celebrating people more carefully could teach us to be more observant of all the grace that surrounds us in the world.

Calligraphy is not the only Chinese gift to slow us down to dwell in grace. The gardens of that culture (as well as of Japanese culture) teach us to slacken our pace, savor fragrances, observe changes, pay attention to details, become immersed in beauty.

The Chinese garden in Portland, Oregon, is a favorite place for my husband and me. We visited it yesterday as part of our celebration of the Sabbath day and were immediately enthralled by the reflection pool (a double entendre) with its lotus plants exhibiting the entire range of stages from buds, through flowers, to mammoth seeds.

The lotus is for the Chinese a symbol for the principle of attaining a high moral standard even if one is in a difficult situation; it also symbolizes gaining pure wisdom or enlightenment. I have a cross from China that flows into a lotus blossom to signify that only through forgiveness and the freedom gained for us by Christ's atonement are we able to live wisely with a high moral standard according to the way of the cross. Slowing down to study the flowers at the garden, I thought about this connection and was brought into a deeper sense of the goodness of God's love and will for our lives.

Other features of the garden cleared my mind, settled my soul, and immersed me in grace. The white-edged pink water lilies seen against the softly purpling leaves of a plant on the shore made their bright beauty all the more stunning to lighten our darknesses. What looks like crape myrtle flinging its bouquets of rose clusters, the "Buddha's hand citron" displaying its oddly octopus-like fruit, the strong fragrances of gardenias and jasmine all increased my sense of the magnificence of God's diverse creativity. Everywhere one turns in a Chinese garden there are new perfumes, new shapes and colors, new miniature marvels, new treasures to be discovered in tiny places.

Could we learn to live every day with ardent attentiveness, yearning eagerness to encounter new mysteries, passionate openness to the fullness of grace that undergirds our lives and **frees** us to make the best decisions because we are immersed **in** God's goodness?

MUSIC—THE GIFT OF ALL CULTURES

Singing is a wonderful practice to immerse us in grace—provided the texts that we sing are words of goodness and truth and beauty. But we don't even need to sing texts, for the very practice engages our entire body and floods it with melody and perhaps, if we are singing with others, harmonies. Many mystics associate God with music and insist that God worked by means of music's melodies and harmonies to create the unified, mysteriously interlocking yet diverse cosmos. Everything is music, for the difference between iron and wood is the rate of their respective molecular vibrations, though our ears can't hear those particular ranges of tones.

John Michael Talbot, the Franciscan singer especially of worship music, once taught in a workshop that sometimes as we converse with deep friends or in the midst of music we might break through beyond our mind and emotions into eternity, to taste more richly of grace. During meditative music, he insisted, we can let go of the false self we've settled for, and instead hear not only the notes, but the silent spaces around them, to enter by means of our spirits into the infinity that goes beyond what we think and feel. He used the great phrase that we thereby move from "contortion to proportion" as we slow ourselves down to live our lives obediently, with the authority of truthfulness, with Joy.

SILENCE

Similarly, the habit of silence (oftentimes absent in North American culture because of the multitudes of ubiquitous entertainment devices) is one of the best ways to slow ourselves down, to divest ourselves of physical sensations (body), emotions (soul), and thoughts (mind) in order to enter into our spirit with an openness to, and then in unity with, the Holy Spirit. Perhaps to North Americans this is most accessible in monasteries. Two years ago after a week of worship in a Benedictine community, in which long pauses for reflection began and ended each worship time and were interspersed between the readings and before the doxology of psalms, I came home ready to practice the same discipline here. My husband and I began the habit (though we find it hard to persist in it when the schedule gets full), and he, too, cherishes the thoughtfulness the custom can produce.

Silence slows us down so that we are more open to all that God might say to us during our prayers together. Once, for example, in such a moment of silence I finally understood that my husband really didn't want us to get season tickets to the ballet. Though I love ballet and had been looking forward to attending five performances, I had to acknowledge that we really shouldn't add other engagements to our schedule of several symphony concerts and theater productions. Most of all, I realized that it was more important to channel the money toward alleviating some needs in the world. We allow ourselves a small amount to spend for performances that always bring me closer to God with their delights, but concerns for the hungry and the homeless far outweighed any other desires at that point. Without a time of silence, I wouldn't have discerned either my husband's heart or my own.

Native Americans often begin their rituals with a time of silent waiting. Even the children are not fidgety but know that as they stand in quiet repose, they are preparing for something extraordinary, so their hush is expectantly undesigning and capaciously open.

Perhaps we could encourage our congregations and their leaders to include more times of anticipating silence in the church's worship services. We can more intentionally spend periods in quietness when we have our daily devotional periods. Another good habit is to pause for moments of silent gratitude for the gifts that surround us in the midst of the busy-ness of our days. In those occasions of tranquility, could we learn to relax more in grace, to notice its workings more thoroughly, to learn to trust its goodness and guidance?

LABYRINTHS

One tradition from older times that combines silence and meditation and observation is the walking of a labyrinth. This mysterious practice is made more lovely by the fact that there is no necessarily "right" way to walk one, but that the very practice reveals to us aspects of our approach to life that are made more obvious by the way in which we walk in one. How do we enter it? Do we hurry (or even cheat) to "get to the goal" and not enjoy the process? Do we learn from it and face ourselves as we walk through it? Imagine what we can learn about ourselves, about grace, about life as we contemplate the turns and pathways that we take.

Author, photographer, and biology teacher Gernot Candolini, who lives in Austria, has visited and designed numerous labyrinths. In a book summarizing various insights he has gained from them, he describes a modern flagstone labyrinth near the castle of Grey's Court, England. Candolini loved the soft and sweeping curves of this particular labyrinth, built outside the garden walls by Adrian Fisher in 1981. In its center he found a stone block with this inscription:

> Credo, says the heart,
> Upheld in cradling hands.
> The heart has reasons
> No reason understands.
> Mind's flashing messages
> Fork and fall apart.
> At the center stillness.
> Credo, says the heart.[18]

I love that poem because it gives us important gifts for both walking labyrinths and trying to discern when choices have to be made. The key is to believe (*credo* means "I believe") that we are upheld by God's loving, gracious hands, that our decisions do not depend on us nor does the well-being of our lives. We don't have to get all tied up in worry and second guessing of ourselves.

The next lines, "The heart has reasons / No reason understands," remind us of one of Blaise Pascal's *Pensées*. This brilliant mathematician knew that underneath logic our love knows more, and when we are loved we don't have to get all tangled in the confused and confusing "flashing messages" of our intellects. Grace can teach us such trust.

Grace enables us truly to believe, in the lines of Robert Browning's famous poem "Pippa Passes," that "God's in His heaven—all's right with the world!"

A BETTER WAY

We can believe that all is right more readily if we give up on ourselves and our own abilities and trust that there is a compassionately sovereign Providence larger than we can imagine, and that this majestic foresight is gracious and good. The great thinker of the Middle Ages Desiderius Erasmus (1466–1536) helps us realize with this poem the importance of giving up on ourselves so that we might receive grace more profoundly:

> Sever me from myself that I may be grateful to you;
> may I perish to myself that I may be safe in you;
> may I die to myself that I may live in you;
> may I wither to myself that I may blossom in you;
> may I be emptied of myself that I may abound in you;
> may I be nothing to myself that I may be all in you.
> Amen.[19]

But this is exactly the problem: many of us do not want to give up on ourselves. We still think we can figure out everything on our own. But we don't have a very good batting average, do we? Our world seems more violent, more unjust, more angry and cynical and mean than ever before. There must be a better way to live.

I've become convinced that following God is a much better way. We discover that we really aren't capable of solving all the world's problems by ourselves, but we also realize ever afresh that God's grace is all that we need, and therein we find a true hope that cannot disappoint us (see Romans 5:5). Furthermore, the more we trust in God's goodness, the more we discover the great Joy that God is all that we want.

Surrender to God's grace is not a matter of willpower and grim determination. Rather, we realize the immensity of God's love for us, and then, increasingly, we are ready to give ourselves over to it. As we grow spiritually, we learn how amazingly trustworthy God is, and then, gradually, we become more and more able to commit our lives into God's hands.

FRANCIS OF ASSISI, THE JOYFUL MODEL

One of the best examples in history of such ecstatic surrender to God's grace was Francis of Assisi (1182–1226). All the books and stories about Francis emphasize his great, exuberant Joy in serving God, living in poverty, and ministering to lepers. These accounts also usually mention his wonderful canticles and other hymns of praise, his love for music, his delight in the beauties of creation, his affinity with animals. What a supreme combination he was of the deepest service and the highest bliss![20]

This seems to have come because Francis felt no need for the goods of this world but gladly gave them up to follow Jesus in His simplicity and poverty and suffering. Surrendering everything to God, he seems to have gained a love for everything and everyone. He is known to have tried to bring reconciliation between Muslims and Christians, to have attempted to become friends with enemies, to have endeavored to draw many people into his own glad surrender to God.

Only in the deepest humility is such self-abandonment possible, but it is important to note that this didn't leave Francis in despair or gloom. Instead, it gave him exhilaration and rapture. Even when he was afflicted with the stigmata, the same wounds as the crucified Christ, this seems only to have increased his Joy that he was following Jesus ever more closely.

Many cultures in the world have stressed such humility. A professor whom I met at the Lutheran seminary in Hong Kong, Håkan Granberg, told me of his background in the Pietist tradition of Finnish culture, which stresses what is called *Alatié,* or humility. Håkan himself demonstrated this in taking time to talk with me. Though he is a Swedish-speaking Finn, he also speaks English and Cantonese and is learning Mandarin in order better to serve his students. He lauded the advantages of *Alatié,* the "down road," for making decisions because it certainly helps us deflect the self-importance that often clouds our discernment. Humility opens us up to our need for grace and the fullness of its presence because the cosmos is immersed in the presence of God.

Grace surrounds us, though we often seem unaware of it. We can learn to receive it, if we get rid of the need to be the Messiah ourselves. Just as I wrote that, I received a telephone call from a friend belonging to the church in which we participate, to remind me that she has made a dinner for us tonight and will bring it over in a few minutes. I'm usually embarrassed that I need this help. Instead, worn out from having spent the entire morning in two medical appointments, couldn't I learn simply to receive with gratitude God's gifts through this woman's kindness and, bowing before the wonder, delight in the grace which undergirds our lives because God Himself enfolds them?

The Foundational Word

S t. Augustine (354–430), who had become intellectually convinced of Christianity's truth, was not willing to give up his sensual life. He is famous for having written in his *Confessions* his previous plea, "Make me chaste and continent, but not yet."

One day in the garden, torn between his desire for Christian faith and his unwillingness to give up his present life of what he called "uncleanness," he heard a child's voice say, "Take it and read it." Because he couldn't remember any children's songs or games that used those phrases, he took that chant as a command, returned to the place where he had left his Bible, and read this text on which his eyes first fell: "Not in reveling and drunkenness, not in debauchery and licentiousness, not in quarreling and jealousy. Instead, put on the Lord Jesus Christ, and make no provision for the flesh, to gratify its desires" (Romans 13:13–14). According to Augustine, his heart was immediately filled with a light of confidence in Christ, and all his shadows of doubts were swept away.[1]

A quite different set of texts radically called and formed the whole life and ministry of Francis of Assisi. Gazing at a cross in the church of San Damiano, he heard a voice that seemed to come from the image of the Crucified Jesus which told him three times to "go and repair my house which, as you see, is falling completely into ruin." Later, as brothers began to join him in his attempts to live in poverty and to preach the Gospel to rebuild the Church in more than physical ways, he and his friend Bernard opened the Bible three times in the church of Saint Nicholas and read these three injunctions: "If you will be perfect, go, sell all that you have, and give to the poor" (Matthew 19:21); "Take nothing on your journey" (Luke 9:3); and "If anyone wishes to come after me, let him deny himself and take up his cross and follow me" (Matthew 16:24). On these precepts Francis established his famous rule and inspired what became the Franciscans.

Both of these stories illustrate the importance of a foundational word, a text, or a set of passages from the Scriptures that turns a person's life around or that establishes one's priorities. Though on a much lesser scale, I appreciate the power of such a life-guiding foundational word from God. Having seen in Eastern Asia and India the tragedies of deaths from poverty when I was on the college choir tour mentioned in this book's introduction, I was especially struck when I first translated these verses from the Hebrew (Isaiah 58:6–8a, my rendering):

> Is not this the fast that I choose:
>> to loose the bonds of injustice,
>> to undo the thongs on the bars of the yoke,
> to let the oppressed go free,
>> and to break every yoke?
> Is it not to share your own bread with the hungry,
>> and bring the homeless poor into your own home;
> when you see the naked, to cover them,
>> and never to turn away from any person [in need]?
> Then your light shall break forth like the dawn . . .

That passage led me to choose *Dawn* for my pen name (because my maiden name was not easily pronounced) so that my own working last name would always remind me of this foundational challenge: our wealth is to be divided with others, our call is to care for every needy person we encounter, our lives are to be dedicated to the process of getting to the roots of injustice so that we don't merely lift off the surface problems but undo the ropes that connect the bars of the yokes that keep people oppressed. That is why the publisher will send the royalties of this book directly to Global Health Ministries, which distributes medical equipment and expertise throughout the world, drills wells and provides mosquito netting, recruits medical personnel and helps to train them for clinics in areas of poverty.[2]

One of the greatest gifts of grace is that of language. Because we have language, we can communicate with others. Moreover, because we can discuss things with others verbally, we can be more sure of the meaning of other sorts of communication, too. All together the communications that we receive are primary foundation stones for building our character. What we hear and speak helps us to grow into the kind of person we become. We are what we say far more than we are what we eat.

By what words are you primarily formed? If you are gripped, like Augustine or Francis or other saints in our community, by some sort of foundational word, your life will become conformed to it or you will not be living with integrity. That is not a burdensome duty, but simply the way things are. It reminds me of the time when I heard Russian conductor Valery Gergiev say in an interview that he could play Russian music over and over and not get tired of it "because it is in us; we belong to it." Similarly, we live our language because we belong to it.

The question is, by what words—or Word in the case of Christians who believe that all such words come from Christ, Who is the Word of God made flesh (John 1:1–14)—is your life formed? Many of our daily decisions are made much easier if we have such guiding principles. Discernment becomes a matter of making sure that our actions and choices and attitudes and patterns of thinking correlate with the foundational words (and Word) on which we base our lives.

In many other cultures, common life is formed by some sort of foundational word. For example, Chinese culture is very much influenced by proverbs, primarily from Confucius. The Chinese saying "Memorize three hundred poems and you will be a poet" highlights the Asian (and the biblical) perspective that life is shaped by the primary language we speak.

Usually, there is not just one word. As the Chinese have thousands of proverbs that give them wisdom, so those who read the Bible are formed every time they read it.

BARRIERS TO FORMATION BY MEANS OF FOUNDATIONAL WORDS

One problem, however, is that if Chinese people cite a proverb, they expect that everyone else will know what they are talking about—and everyone will, for almost all of the people have grown up knowing the same sayings. But in the United States there is no longer a culture where everyone knows biblical texts. That is to be expected in a pluralistic culture such as our own, of course, but it is more a matter of grief to me that within explicitly Christian circles not everyone knows the Scriptures well enough to find common ground on foundational words. For example, how much it would change the world if every Christian knew the Isaiah 58 text cited previously so well that he or she believed that care for the poor is not an add-on job but a foundational dimension of what it means to be part of the Kingdom of God![3]

However, this is not the deepest problem. We might know the foundational words and the life of Christ as revealed in the Scriptures, but other factors seem to prevent us from being truly formed by them to live them.

Perhaps the strongest barrier is that North Americans are formed by too many corruptions, degradations, exaggerations, manipulations, defamations, and cooptations of our common language. In these days of what sociologist and ethicist Jacques Ellul called "the humiliation of the word," when advertisements and politicians especially overstate or otherwise inflate their vocabulary with the result that words lose their proper weight, language forfeits its power and meaning. As the great twentieth-century Jewish rabbi Abraham Joshua Heschel notes, in our time words no longer commit their speakers to live them. We will consider this more in Chapter Three as we look carefully at how we are kept from godly discernment because our expressions are inaccurate when we think about our decisions. Here I am especially interested in what forms our language in the first place.

North Americans often find their language formed by television or music or the hyperlinkages of the Web or by the quick abbreviations of common e-mail communications. What we often fail to realize is that our language, in turn, forms who we are and how we relate and what we choose and why we act as we do.

Some children are formed by the distorted language of alcoholic parents; some are formed by the silence of absent ones. Adults, too, continue to be formed by various languages of hate and greed or consumerism and injustice.

That is why I believe it is an enormous gift that God gave us the Scriptures to form our lives to be loving and generous, merciful and compassionate—in other words, to be like Christ, our primary Word. However, some people wonder whether Christianity is a good way to live, or they think that the Scriptures are simply outdated. Perhaps they doubt that scriptural texts can be trusted or be positively formative. Let's consider each of those suspicions briefly.

Christianity has not had a uniformly positive effect on the world. Skeptics quickly bring up the Crusades or the Inquisition or the Holocaust or the recent Iraq war as proof that Christianity is basically violent and abusive, greedy and corrupt. Others point to the continuing damage caused by those who view the Scriptures literalistically, without any concern for understanding them contextually or without interpreting them with grace in human interactions. I certainly agree that there have been (and continue to be) dark periods in our history, but those actions of brutality and destructiveness cannot be called Christian.

If we look at Jesus carefully, we see a man (I believe He was also God, which is why I capitalize the pronouns) Who took suffering into Himself rather than inflict it on others. I see a person Who sought to heal, to comfort, to feed rather than to hurt. I see a God willing to go to the uttermost lengths to win us back to Himself. In short, I see the perfect Lover.

And Jesus calls us to *His* way of life. The fact that so few have truly followed in Jesus' way is proof of why the most important message of Christianity has to be forgiveness and the possibility of a different kind of life through the power of the Holy Spirit. If we look at those who tried most to imitate Christ—people like Francis of Assisi or Bernard of Clairvaux or other great saints—we see people who cared profoundly for the poor, people who were willing to undergo any kind of suffering for the sake of others. The world would be a much better place if all those who claim to follow Jesus actually listened in life to His words about caring for the needy, about being peacemakers wherever we go, about loving God with all our hearts, souls, minds, and strengths, and, thereby, loving our neighbors as ourselves.

And that relates to the objection that the Scriptures are simply outdated. We have to realize that the Bible should be studied in its entirety and its context. Certain aspects of it (as is true for all literature) were timely only in their original settings, but still they show us, through their faithful testimonies to the believing life, how God's instructions formed a godly kind of character and community. The more we study the Scriptures, the more we learn to read its different genres of literature appropriately so that, for example, the Psalms teach us to pray, the Prophets guide us in our battles against injustice and tyranny, the Gospels teach us how to follow Jesus, and the Epistles give us models for dealing with failures and the future as we witness the mistakes that the early Christians made and the good choices that led them to become more like Christ.

One of the reasons that we can trust the Scriptures is the very fact that they include the failures. They give us good examples of bad examples so that we can learn from the mistakes made by previous believers. And the Bible makes it clear that such errors should call us to repentance, reparation, and reform.

The Scriptures are also trustworthy because they are so multivoiced. Sometimes verses from Proverbs are useful to guide our lives, but at other times we need the questioning of Job and Ecclesiastes. Sometimes the leaders of Israel were good kings, but often they needed the prophets to rebuke them. Even in the early Church sometimes Paul had to rebuke Peter (just as did Jesus), and yet Peter's testimony was one of the clearest to the divinity of Christ. Still today some people pay attention to a few select texts and ignore others that keep those texts in tension; this false selectivity needs to be admonished lovingly and carefully corrected.

Indeed, the Scriptures are a superb picture of what the Church must be today—always attentive to the rest of the community so that we are constantly brought back by the language of the faith into a more obedient following of Jesus, Whose way we believe is the best way to live.

The Scriptures, then, can be positively formative if we keep reading them, if we read them in their entirety so that we don't settle on some isolated points that exclude larger patterns of faithfulness. The Bible gives us a language that produces the fruit of the Spirit, the Christ life, which is manifested in such traits as "love, joy, peace, patience, kindness, generosity, faithfulness, gentleness, and self-control" (Galatians 5:22–23). If our lives are not formed into these characteristics, then we are not reading the Bible thoroughly enough.

None of us, of course, is able to judge rightly whether other persons in history or today are truly Christian, but we can assess whether certain behaviors are or are not in keeping with the Christian Scriptures. We must confess that we, too, have not always acted in ways that follow Jesus, for we are still human and make many mistakes. The extraordinary gift of Christianity, however, is that grace frees us to admit those sins and faults, to repent of them, to be forgiven for them, and to be formed so that we become less likely to commit them.

Primarily we realize, then, that if the Hebrew and Christian Scriptures are not positively formative, we must not know their language well enough to live it. Perhaps we do not know enough of the Bible to weigh passages appropriately and, consequently, give too much gravity to a text that is not of principal importance. Maybe we have not immersed ourselves thoroughly enough in the Scriptures to recognize the texts that set forth priorities for the Christian life. Possibly we have not committed ourselves to the biblical texts as foundational words for our attitudes and actions.

Another objection frequently raised is that Christianity is "too heavenly minded to be much earthly good," but, as the great Jewish rabbi Abraham Joshua Heschel points out, the Bible is about commonplace, ordinary daily conduct. The biblical call is not to spend much of one's time contemplating eternity, but instead the Scriptures lay a good foundation to provide much practical wisdom for loving one's neighbors in the here and now.

Some people want absolute assurance that their foundational word can be trusted, but in postmodern times we have learned that there is no such assurance. How do we know what we know? There is no outside-of-time-and-space objectivity (other than in God, which we can't know with our finite brains) by which we could ever prove conclusively that any foundational words are right.

Ultimately, we need to realize, all foundational words are accepted by a community, and we have to see whether we trust that community. When it comes to churches, sometimes I wonder if I can trust my local parish, but when I see how the particular congregation in which I participate responds to my own health concerns and to crises in the world, I realize that this is a group of people to whom I can entrust my life. And this is a community that builds on the faith of our forebears—we sing the psalms of our Jewish forebears; we affirm the creeds of our Christian forebears. In other words, we participate in a timeless community of believers that goes back about four thousand years to Abraham and Sarah, our first parents in the faith, and has been shared by millions throughout time and space since then.

I believe the Scriptures are a superb foundational word, furthermore, because throughout my life and experience I haven't found any better. The Scriptures, above all, point to Christ, the Centering Word, and He is the best hope for humankind that I could find. In the story of Jesus I learn of a God Who loves us all so much that Christ would invest Himself for us, would live among us to teach us how human beings can truly live, would suffer and die on our behalf, and would be raised to life again to teach us what to expect for our own futures with Him. That is an account that gives me hope for humanity, a better way to live than the grasping and greedy self-orientation that predominates in our society.

Moreover, I don't know any other way to live that copes with the tragedies of life. This week, as I write, Hurricane Katrina has devastated the southern coastlands of the United States, especially the entire city of New Orleans. A thousand have died; hundreds of thousands are homeless or without power and water if they are still in their homes. What better word is there to cope with such a tragedy than, paraphrasing Isaiah, a call to all the rest of us to "divide our bread with the hungry, to welcome the homeless into our own homes"? What greater comfort is there than God's assurance that we are enfolded in the Trinity's grace throughout our sufferings?

Furthermore, the Scriptures make it clear what is *not* God's will, and that also makes me realize what a superb foundational word they provide. God does not want that any of His human children should be lost or hungry, homeless or ignored. God is clearly weeping that so many in New Orleans and other cities and hamlets along the coast are suffering this week, and I believe the compassion of God is pouring out of countless citizens as North Americans respond with massive care to the needs of people devastated by the hurricane.

Similarly, I don't know any other way to live than that proposed by the Hebrew-Christian Scriptures that copes with personal loss and desolation. Sometimes, as a side effect from all the medicines I have to take so that my body does not reject my new transplanted kidney, I experience periods of great discouragement and feelings that God has deserted me. At those times, the assurances that I have found in the Scriptures that God does not want to desert me (because of His infinite love for strugglers such as I) and cannot desert me (because of His faithfulness to His own character of grace) have been the key to unlock this darkness and enable me to cast away the gloomy moodiness that the medicines keep perpetrating. Regularly, in my daily Bible readings, I find laments from biblical people who felt the same way I do for various reasons (including illness) and also words of consolation that break through the clouds that seem to hover over me and send shafts of bright comfort and encouragement and solace. Both (the knowledge that I am not alone and the respite that comes from outside myself) are gifts of sheer grace.

I think that the life Jesus calls us to is impossible—because many times we'd rather serve ourselves and please ourselves than minister to others—yet miraculously the Holy Spirit enables us to live it. We discover ourselves loving our enemies, doing good to those who hate us, being willing to bear one another's burdens.

Finally, I believe the Scriptures provide an outstanding foundational word because they respond to my deepest needs and desires. That is not a reason to conclude that their account of the Triune God is mere wish fulfillment, but I realize at root that my most profound longings are for something more than human. What I desire most of all is a relationship with God, and that is what the Scriptures lead me into. And the more I read them, the more thoroughly that relationship unfolds—even in the times when God seems absent, in those times that great saints call the "dark nights of the soul." Even in those bleak times, I keep learning new things about God and from God.

If you find this unbelievable still, stick with me for awhile, and see how you feel about the trustworthiness of the Scriptures by the time we get to the end of our discussion. If you choose a different foundational word, the important key is that it be a word by which your life can be formed and in terms of which your best discernments can be made.

START WITH THE CHARACTER OF GOD

The more we read the Bible, the more we will realize that it shows us a God of surpassing love, a God Who can be trusted because the Trinity keeps promises. The entire First Testament emphasizes that God will make a way for people to be delivered from their self-destructive habits, and then the New Testament reveals how Jesus made such a way through Himself and His work to rescue us.

God has also promised that His Word, namely Jesus, is the truth and that we can stake our lives on Him. The God to Whom we belong wants us to know His voice and His will. That is why we can base all our discernment on the foundations of what God has revealed in the Bible about His desires for the human race. Consider these promises concerning God's desire for us to be in tune with what is best for humanity and for us to know the grace of triune guidance for our discernment:

I bless the LORD who gives me counsel;
  in the night also my heart instructs me.
I keep the LORD always before me;
  because he is at my right hand, I shall not be
  moved. (Psalm 16:7–8)

[The LORD says:] I will instruct you and teach you
  the way you should go;
  I will counsel you with my eye upon you.
  (Psalm 32:8)

Nevertheless I am continually with you;
  you hold my right hand.
You guide me with your counsel,
  and afterward you will receive me with honor.
Whom have I in heaven but you?
  And there is nothing on earth that I desire other
  than you.
My flesh and my heart may fail,
  but God is the strength of my heart and my portion
  forever. (Psalm 73:23–26)

Trust in the LORD with all your heart,
  and do not rely on your own insight.
In all your ways acknowledge him,
  and he will make straight your paths.
  (Proverbs 3:5–6)

All that we have done, you have done for us.
  (Isaiah 26:12)

And when you turn to the right or when you turn to
the left, your ears shall hear a word behind you, saying,
"This is the way; walk in it." (Isaiah 30:21)

When the Spirit of truth comes, he will guide you into all the truth; for he will not speak on his own, but will speak whatever he hears, and he will declare to you the things that are to come. (John 16:13)

Do not be conformed to this world, but be transformed by the renewing of your minds, so that you may discern what is the will of God—what is good and acceptable and perfect. (Romans 12:2)

He has made known to us the mystery of his will, according to his good pleasure that he set forth in Christ, as a plan for the fullness of time, to gather up all things in him, things in heaven and things on earth. (Ephesians 1:9–10)

[Epaphras] has made known to us your love in the Spirit. For this reason, since the day we heard it, we have not ceased praying for you and asking that you may be filled with the knowledge of God's will in all spiritual wisdom and understanding, so that you may lead lives worthy of the Lord, fully pleasing to him, as you bear fruit in every good work and as you grow in the knowledge of God. (Colossians 1:8b–10)

These and other verses like them, scattered throughout the Scriptures, help us see that God wants us to know the best for us when we have to make choices, and the best for us will be what the LORD wants, for the Trinity's all-perfect wisdom and love want the best for us and the entire cosmos. I keep thinking of the African American spiritual "He Never Failed Me Yet." God will guide us if we are open to receive the Triune One's wisdom.

But if God and God's Word are to be trusted, then how can we learn the Scriptures better and let them form us more thoroughly? This is where the habits of other cultures can be extremely helpful.

HABITS FOR LEARNING THE SCRIPTURES

Throughout the world Christians take the Scriptures much more seriously than do their North American or European counterparts. In contrast to Western societies in which decisions are adversely affected by lives shaped to be hyperactive about work and productivity in a technological, consumerist milieu, Two-Thirds World Christians' lives especially seem to be more fashioned by a milieu of humble receptivity and submission to biblical knowledge. Other cultures seem to pay closer attention to the scriptural injunction to "let the word of Christ dwell in you richly" (Colossians 3:16). Like the biblical Timothy, many believers have "from childhood . . . known the sacred writings that are able to instruct [them] for salvation through faith in Christ Jesus." They believe that "All scripture is inspired by God and is useful for teaching, for reproof, for correction, and for training in righteousness, so that everyone who belongs to God may be proficient, equipped for every good work" (2 Timothy 3:15–17).

In more remote places, this immersion in, and practice of, the Scriptures might be attributed by cynics to the fact that all the entertainment distractions of wealthier nations aren't available, but even in advanced places such as Singapore and Hong Kong, Christians seem to make the choice to spend much more time in Bible reading, study, and discussion so that their lives can become more grounded in God's foundational Word.

My goal here is simply to raise the question: if we want to discern well when we make decisions about our daily lives, are we willing to spend the time necessary to know the Scriptures so thoroughly that our lives are truly formed in accordance with them? The early saint Augustine said, "O Lord, Thou didst strike my heart with Thy Word, and I loved Thee." His comment invites us to give God the opportunity to strike our hearts each day so that our love for the Trinity is always growing, so that each day we are more eager to live in accordance with the Lord's best will.

We can learn much from Christians in the British Isles between the fourth and ninth centuries. Michael Mitton, an author and the director of Anglican Renewal Ministries in England, urges us to follow the model of the Celtic church "with its humble love for the Bible, its placing of scripture above reason and tradition, its willingness to learn large parts of it by heart, and its determination to live according to its guidance."[4]

Early saints often chose to enter into a religious life in order to be able to alternate periods of labor with periods of reading Scripture and worshipping, but most of us don't have that option, often because of family obligations. How can ordinary people, working in ordinary daily jobs, find the time to immerse themselves in the Scriptures?

In the early 1700s, Count Nicholas von Zinzendorf asked that question, too. He had invited the Moravians, a persecuted religious group, to live on his estate, Herrnhut in Saxony, and he wanted to support their character formation. On May 3, 1728, he began the practice of offering each day a Word for the Day, a text for the people on the estate to ponder as they went about their regular chores. Soon this custom developed into the practice of providing a Watchword for the week and two texts for each day—one verse from the First Testament and a related, more doctrinal verse from the New

Testament. Then the texts were matched with appropriate hymn verse responses and a closing prayer, and by 1731 the Moravian *Daily Texts* was printed. The book was distributed worldwide by 1739; the first U.S. edition appeared in 1767.

Today the *Daily Texts* is published in forty-one languages and dialects, and the yearly book provides an invisible bond between Christians on all continents. The volume is truly ecumenical, transcending all sorts of barriers of denominations, races, languages, and politics. Since 1788 the initial texts have been chosen by lot from a collection of around two thousand suitable First Testament passages, and then members of the Moravian Church select matching New Testament texts and hymn verses and write the prayers.[5]

Similarly, since early Christian times, the global Church has prepared lectionaries, or lists of texts, to be pondered on a daily basis. These are available in many forms that either match the seasons of the Church year (so that, for example, in Lent the reader ponders the events of Christ's suffering and death) or that simply set out a reading plan for a person to become more thoroughly acquainted with, and immersed in, the Scriptures. Various suggestions for lectionaries are printed in Catholic breviaries, denominational prayer books and hymnals, and many other books printed by Christian publishers.[6]

MEMORIZATION: CHINESE AND INDIAN EXAMPLES

Many of the correspondents who taught me about other cultural habits and practices have impressed me with how thoroughly the people with whom they live and serve immerse themselves in the biblical Word, especially by memorizing large portions of it. Missionaries and medical personnel in as diverse places as Guatemala, Guinea, Tanzania, Madagascar, and India have reported deep habits of biblical study and memorization.

The habit is, of course, deeply rooted in the practices of Christianity's forebears, the Jews. Noted twentieth-century rabbi Abraham Joshua Heschel, who was born in Warsaw, talked about how Eastern European Jews understood that their mission was to fulfill Torah so that what was impaired in the cosmos could be repaired. This understanding made them diligent in learning and memorizing the Hebrew Scriptures and, at the same time, made their every act an artistic work.

I will focus on Chinese Christians as an example of immersion in the Bible because of extensive conversations I had with the faculty at the Lutheran Theological Seminary of Hong Kong, a rather large divinity school (approximately 250 full-time students) that attracts Christ's followers from sixteen nations, including Laos, Vietnam, Burma (Myanmar), Malaysia, and Korea, plus exchange students from Germany, Norway, and the United States, and even some university students from China who are not from churches. The faculty, under the presidency of Lam Tak Ho, includes professors from Denmark, Finland, Sweden, Germany, Canada, the United States, and, of course, Hong Kong.

The professors reported, from their diverse backgrounds, that contemporary Chinese Christians understand unquestionably that memorizing the Scriptures is an important foundation for living well. Several conversation partners mentioned that the cultural habit (reinforced by the Chinese education system) of extensive reading and rote learning helps Christians in China make more biblical decisions. Chinese pastor Dr. Chung Ming Kai suggested that this supports the Lutheran Seminary's emphasis on spiritual formation because the students come from strong family backgrounds in Bible reading.

The Chinese were more ready to adapt to memorizing biblical passages because of their cultural orientation to memorizing proverbs (which we will discuss more thoroughly in the following chapter in connection with symbolic reframing). Chaplain Reverend Chan Kwok Kuen (a.k.a. Patrick) expanded this by pointing specifically to the Buddhist custom of approaching a holy text by memorizing, instead of analyzing, as is more common in the West. Chinese people, consequently, are more apt to know a truth more deeply and therefore to live it.

Furthermore, Patrick said, the character of Chinese people is to obey, so their proclivity, more so than in North America, is both to read the Bible more extensively and then more simply to obey it. This is comparable to what I notice whenever I spend time at a Benedictine monastery: the sisters there have meditated on and lived the Scriptures in a profound practice for hundreds of years, and the whole place exudes this biblical way of life. For example, each sister who encounters a visitor is immediately attentive to the guest's needs; all of the sisters seem observantly gracious whenever they speak to me.

At the Hong Kong seminary Professor Jim Bergquist, from his own additional experience as a pastor and a teacher in India, added that Christians there also live more fully within the biblical tradition. The early missionaries to India, Africa, and Asia were quite sure about the importance of reading the Bible, were very pious, and truly accompanied the people they served. Being a minority in the culture helped because the missionaries did not impose Western values in a paternalistic way (as many present stereotypes suggest), but they placed the Gospel within the cultural patterns and habits of the people. For example, out of seven hundred hymns in a 1790 hymnal published in India, only ten were Western. The missionaries simply invited new Christians to imitate their habits of deep immersion in the Scriptures, and the cultural patterns contributed to the development of that practice in the Indian churches.

One of my Indian friends later underscored the importance of this avid biblical reading and obedience when he commented that Christian women in his home region did not wear gold wedding bands because of Peter's command in 1 Peter 3:3 that women should not adorn themselves with gold ornaments. Though my friend said that earlier he had wondered whether it was too simplistic for his native friends to obey that injunction, he had come to realize that it was important in his culture, too, for the women to refrain from wearing such ornaments, in order to show the contrast between the Christian community and Hindu women who customarily wear lots of gold jewelry.

In Hong Kong, Professor Ted Zimmermann commented that biblical literacy is far higher with, and has a good shaping effect on, both Indian and Chinese Christians. In fact, the seminary where most of this extended conversation took place has 150 students in its lay school of evening classes by which, in four years, these full-time workers in other fields earn the Master of Christian Studies degree. How might it increase the effects of genuine Christianity on North American decisions if more lay people were so invested in scholarly biblical study and their lives were shaped by this rich milieu of biblical knowledge?

THE VALUE OF MEMORIZATION AND REPETITION OF SCRIPTURE

North Americans, whose educational system now stresses discovery and self-motivation, might scoff at an emphasis on repetition and memorization, but we must ask deeper questions about its value. The abuses of rote learning are certainly evident when the subject matter seems nonessential to the students or when the methods of learning are painful or dull. But the Bible is absolutely essential as a foundation for Christian growth, and its texts are so interesting that, without doubt, means for learning the Bible can be appropriately matched to the content.

In her chapter "Abraham Lincoln and the Last Best Hope," the author Jean Bethke Elshtain, a noted professor of social and political ethics at the University of Chicago, makes this positive defense of habits of repetition in learning:

> Today, of course, memorization is routinely dismissed as
> "rote learning," and priority is given to "self-expression"
> in the service of "authenticity" and other presumed goods.
> Reflecting on the experience of Lincoln (and innumerable
> others subjected to "rote learning") may lead one to suspect
> that there is much to be said for having one's mind formed
> by the best that others have thought and said before giving it
> unbridled expression. All those hours spent reading by dim
> firelight the same book over and over (they say little children
> still like to be read to) were to contribute to Lincoln's being
> the foremost master of prose among our presidents. Indeed,
> he has few peers in our entire history.[7]

Abraham Lincoln is a good example of one who was formed by his rote learning into a godly character capable of making crucial decisions for the well-being of an entire nation at great cost to himself.

I am immensely grateful for my own background with all its rote learning. Because of the privilege of attending a Christian elementary school (my father was the principal, and both my parents taught in the school), for eight years I was given daily assignments to study and memorize the Scriptures. This was my favorite subject, and I never thought it was boring because I was always learning new things about God from His Word. To this day, that background has been immensely helpful as my memory places biblical texts into my conscious mind when I am pondering decisions about courses of action to take. Of course, knowledge of texts is insufficient by itself. The question is whether contemplation of those texts leads to faithfulness in following Jesus by the power of the Holy Spirit to the glory of the Father.

Memorization is especially important in childhood, when it is easy, so I always urge parents to do all they can to place the Scriptures into their children's minds. Furthermore, all the research about Alzheimer's disease shows that the last things to be forgotten by people who have this illness are the first things they learned, so what better gift could we give to future sufferers than texts about God to nurture their final days? I see the immense value of this in patients I have visited in nursing homes, whose minds seem to be completely gone until I start reciting well-known texts like the Good Shepherd Psalm (23) or the Lord's Prayer, and then they can join in word for word. As my own father begins to struggle in the middle stages of Alzheimer's, I am supremely grateful for the strong foundation he has from his own childhood memorization of the Scriptures and of many hymns.

Furthermore, memorization gives us materials so that we can ponder biblical texts throughout the day and so that they can, in turn, more deeply form our lives. The First Testament prophet Ezekiel was told by God to eat God's words (see Ezekiel 1 and 2) so that he could speak them clearly to the people of Israel. By investigating God's words as deeply as we can, by ruminating on them, by questioning them and studying them, we, too, can become more profoundly like

God so that we live and speak in God's name (which means, in God's own character). The more we know the Trinity's language, the more we live like the Three in One because we live in closer union with the Godhead.

SCRIPTURE SURPRISES

One of the aspects of daily Bible reading that ceaselessly surprises me is that so often a text assigned for the day seems to match precisely my needs or moods. Some of the passages included in this book arose in my morning's readings and came to my mind later in the day while I was writing. God's grace always is present in every day's texts, but these little visions of God's special care for our daily lives are an amazing gift.

As one particular case, on the morning that I began the sabbatical month which initiated this project, I happened to open an ancient, undated book of inspirational Bible verses. Sometimes such books are trite; often they are wisely edited to stimulate thoughtful responses. This one seemed to hit the nail on the head with these first listings for the beginning of my sabbatical time:

> *Prayer:* Cause me to know the way wherein I should walk.
>   Ps. 143:8
> *Promise:* I will direct all his ways. Isa. 45:13
> *Precept:* In all thy ways acknowledge him. Prov. 3:6[8]

I had applied for the sabbatical grant because I wasn't sure how to choose which speaking engagements to accept to live most fully within God's best will so that God would be glorified in what I do. I realized that I didn't have very good skills for discernment. As I looked at these texts, I realized that the first one indeed stated my prayer, for I longed intensely for God to "cause me to know the way" for walking and how to discern it. I also had to admit that I lacked the necessary skills for listening to God and prayed that this project would increase my training.

The second verse made me wonder, Can I believe God's promise that He will direct all my ways? My failure to trust arises when I don't follow the third text and acknowledge God in all my ways. In three short verses I saw both my failures and the immensity of God's grace to overcome them.

That same day I glanced at English literature professor, author, and theologian C. S. Lewis' anthology of writings by George MacDonald. His collection listed this for its first entry:

> That man is perfect in faith who can come to God in the utter dearth of his feelings and desires, without a glow or an inspiration, with the weight of low thoughts, failures, neglects, and wandering forgetfulness, and say to Him, "Thou art my refuge."[9]

What a relief that the Scriptures keep inviting us back to grace! In fact, for the second day of readings the old book of inspirational verses listed these:

> *Prayer:* Save me for thy mercies' sake. Ps. 6:4
> *Promise:* I am with thee, saith the LORD, to save thee. Jer. 30:11
> *Precept:* Look unto me, and be ye saved. Isa. 45:22

God keeps rescuing us from our selves, from our fears, our inabilities, our stupidities, our weaknesses and insecurities. This is grace.

It is grace when Scripture texts seem to match our days. But it is grace also when they don't seem to, for in reading them, studying them, memorizing them we lay a strong

foundation for character formation. Out of a character biblically formed we can discern more clearly how best to live
to the glory of the Triune God.

In this chapter we have learned from other saints in
the larger Christian community the Joy of knowing the
Scriptures well so that our character is formed in the image
of the God to Whom we belong. We will continue to listen
to the saints and the Scriptures as we discover other skills
for discernment in the following chapters.

3

"Rectifying the Names"

I magine the expressions on people's faces in this comic strip: two children enter an ice cream shop with their father. After the clerk asks the little girl what she wants, she debates within herself, Do I want a sundae or a banana split or a milkshake or a . . . ? Her father interrupts her thoughts, "Just tell him if you want a chocolate or a vanilla cone." Turning to her brother, she says, "Decisions are much easier when you have a cheap dad."

Having laid a foundation in Chapters One and Two in the grace of the Triune God and in God's Word so that our discernment flows out of a sense of being loved and from our desire to live according to God's will, we now turn to more particular aspects of our decision processes. If we think carefully about the obstacles that keep us from discerning well, we might first recognize that often our understanding of our choices is murky or ill defined. Decisions are more difficult if we don't know specifically and rightly what our options are.

Sometimes we don't acknowledge how much our pet assumptions (which are usually unquestioned) are giving us false perspectives. At times we don't realize how much our own health or sense of well-being (or lack of it) is adversely affecting our perceptions of our choices. Perhaps negative (or even positive) experiences in our background are harmfully influencing our quest for clarity. Possibly, we haven't gathered the facts accurately. Maybe we have pre-prejudiced ourselves toward one choice or another so that we haven't given each option a fair assessment. Predictably, with its inimical prioritizing of power and money, prestige and control, the society around us is antagonistic toward godly decision making.

There are numerous reasons for our failing to examine properly all the issues connected with a decision so that we can evaluate everything appropriately. Asian cultures will help us first with this aspect of the discernment process.

CONFUCIAN THOUGHT

When teaching in Japan for a short time, I first encountered Confucian principles prevalent there that give insight into the problem of our lack of clarity in discernment processes. Confucius, or K'ung Fu-Tzu, lived in the Chinese province of Lu (presently Shandong) in the last half of the 500s B.C.E. and well into the first quarter of the 400s. Though he grew up in poverty (and even after his marriage had to spend several years doing menial labor before he became known as a teacher), he had received an excellent education. He was, above all, a teacher of moral reform and emphasized the value of ancient morality according to the venerable classics, which he worked hard to transmit. Although he did have the opportunity to put his suggestions into practice as an administrator in the provincial government, a neighboring province's jealousy over the power exerted by the province he served so well led to his dismissal. We will see in the following chapter that his emphasis on moral virtues is still highly valued in

Asian contexts, but for this chapter another of his principles is our primary concern.

Perhaps the most helpful of all of his insights for me has been the priority Confucius placed on the discipline of "rectifying the names." One of the most popular of stories to illustrate this discipline in the Analects (the collected teachings of Confucius) concerns his discussion with Tzu-lu, an obtuse disciple who kept asking him for a plain explanation of all his teachings.

Tzu-lu wondered, for example, how Confucius would handle the government if asked to do so by the Duke of Wei, who had usurped the throne violently. Confucius answered that the first thing he would certainly do would be "to rectify the names"[1] or, in our idiom, "to call a spade a spade." Confucius reiterated that government cannot function honestly if the names are dishonest.

In our society, we frequently encounter instances of dishonest names: "Tax Reform" measures that do nothing to reform; reasons for going to war that turn out not to be true; numerous accusations against political candidates' opponents that are discovered to be unfounded; local or state governments that act deceitfully. Visualize how much better life would be for the whole nation if everyone involved in government sought "rectification of the names."

Imagine how much it would help in family or church discussions if both sides in arguments would rectify the names. Envision how much it could help in personal decisions if we would rectify the names of our desires, of our goals, of the issues involved.

The importance of Confucius' principle in Chinese thought is illustrated by the novel *Safely Home* by Randy Alcorn, which is about the persecution of Christians. In the novel Ben Fielding, a foreign businessman, thinks the Great Wall of China is a magnificent achievement (as do most Chinese), but his friend Li Quan sees it as a tombstone for tens of thousands of Chinese peasants who died under forced labor. Li Quan explains that its greatness ought to be measured by "the standards of a peasant woman who sacrificed her husband and sons to stones and mortar. We have a saying for this, too. 'The beginning of wisdom is to call things by their right names.' That is why I no longer call this the Great Wall. I call it the Wall of Suffering."[2]

Earlier in this novel, Li Quan subtly rectifies the names and adds another Chinese proverb to make his point. Ben wonders why Li Quan couldn't be more secretive about his Christianity and asks, "Couldn't you have gotten a job teaching if you'd exercised a little more . . . discretion about your faith?" But Li Quan answers, "Discretion? Do you mean denial? There is an old proverb, 'He who sacrifices his conscience to ambition burns a picture to obtain the ashes.'"[3]

We will discuss the Chinese use of proverbs for the sake of clarifying terms further on, but here the important point is that we must question our word choices or perhaps our criteria or even our assumptions. We must call them by the right—and true—names.

On a much smaller scale, since learning this discipline in Japan, I have been asking those who invite me to participate in speaking engagements to "rectify the names" by clarifying exactly why they want me, rather than any other lecturer, to speak for their assembly. At some events one can easily feel like merely the next entertainment on a list of people who have been the group's guests. Those are the occasions I now feel more free to refuse. Unless there is a specific aspect of my work that the events' participants would find particularly helpful for their ministries, then any speaker would do, and my schedule needn't be filled with such episodes.

THE BIBLICAL EMPHASIS ON TRUTH

Of course, this emphasis on rectifying the names is stressed throughout the Bible, which includes many passages that call for truth—and for truth spoken in love (see Ephesians 4:15). That dialectic is the best way I know for rectifying the names, for truth can become violent if it is not always grounded in love, and love becomes mushy sentimentalism if it is not truthful. To practice speaking the truth in love is to take careful precautions always to choose words that clearly enunciate the state of matters as clearly as one can understand them and to focus that clarifying toward the well-being of others.

The same dialectic is evident early in the Bible when Moses' father-in-law, Jethro, gives him this wise advice for lessening his workload:

> "You should also look for able men among all the people, men who fear God, are trustworthy, and hate dishonest gain; set such men over them as officers over thousands, hundreds, fifties and tens. Let them sit as judges for the people at all times; let them bring every important case to you, but decide every minor case themselves. So it will be easier for you, and they will bear the burden with you. If you do this, and God so commands you, then you will be able to endure, and all these people will go to their home in peace." (Exodus 18:21–23)

We notice in Jethro's advice that the judges Moses should appoint ought to be both trustworthy and God fearing, so that they recognize humbly that their truthfulness is watched over by the LORD. They are to care for the peace or *shalom,* the well-being, of the people they serve, to seek no dishonest gain, and to share Moses' burden. Thus they will speak the truth in love for the people. (We will consider Jethro's advisory emphasis on communal sharing of burdens in Chapter Five.)

Joshua, who took over the leadership of Israel after Moses died, asked all the people for the same combination of love and truthfulness. In his final speech he urged this:

> "Now therefore revere the LORD, and serve Him in sincerity and in faithfulness; put away the gods that your ancestors served beyond the River and in Egypt, and serve the LORD. Now if you are unwilling to serve the LORD, choose this day whom you will serve, whether the gods your ancestors served in the region beyond the River or the gods of the Amorites in whose land you are living; but as for me and my household, we will serve the LORD." (Joshua 24:14)

That final clause is often printed on decorative plaques that people place in their homes, but I wonder if they have thought clearly about the context of the verse. Joshua is actually rebuking the people for their idolatries and calling them to renewed devotion to their God, Whose name is the LORD or "I AM."[4]

When we are trying to discern well in order to live well, we, too, must pay attention to our idolatries. What are the real gods that we love? Perhaps our decisions are adversely affected by our longing for power or our craving to be important. In connection with lecture invitations, for example, I realized that the temptation to be on the lists of "famous" people who speak for various events is very strong. That is why it is necessary to ask whether I'm accepting an engagement just to be added to such a list or because there is a particular contribution that God could make through me for the well-being of the people I would be serving.

God will always work through us with this combination of love and truth if we remain in relationship with Him. The psalmist reminds us of this:

> Good and upright is the LORD;
>   therefore he instructs sinners in the way.
> He leads the humble in what is right,
>   and teaches the humble his way.
> All the paths of the LORD are steadfast love
>   and faithfulness,
>   for those who keep his covenant and his decrees.
>   (Psalm 25:8–10)

Notice again that love and truthfulness characterize *YHWH,* the LORD. Are we listening to this God or to our various idols as we try to rectify the names? Notice that a necessary virtue is a humble willingness to listen as God guides us. God's decrees, found in the Scriptures, will guide us to keep the names of our choices and behaviors, our attitudes and goals honest and compassionate, loving and true.

Because we want to think clearly in our processes of discernment, we pray to the LORD with the psalmist:

> You desire truth in the inward being;
>   therefore teach me wisdom in my secret heart.
>   (Psalm 51:6)

In the New Testament, the apostle Paul insists on the same standard of faithfulness when he writes to the Corinthians, "For we cannot do anything against the truth, but only for the truth" (2 Corinthians 14:8). Again, he asks the Galatians,

"Have I now become your enemy by telling you the truth?" (Galatians 4:16).

Sometimes people will be offended when we rectify the names and require complete honesty, but if we are living for the Trinity, then we won't want anything but the total truth, according to God's truth. That honesty must always be spoken in love, however, so that we seek with our utmost efforts to enable others to receive that truth and accept it.

We can be helped in this process by a practice of re-framing, of gaining a new perspective by entering into a symbolic world that changes our orientation. Other cultures not so driven by facts and technological data are more likely to be skilled in learning from symbols.

SYMBOLIC WORLDS— CHANGING OUR IMAGES

When I was visiting with the faculty of the Lutheran Theological Seminary of Hong Kong, several of my conversation partners commented on various aspects of the symbolic world in which the Chinese live. For example, their paintings are composed of symbolic figures, such as the shape of the tree and the position of the rock in the painting I have, from an artist in Kunming, of Jesus and the celebrative crowds gathered around Him. Chinese writing characters often contain whole stories. (A person needs to know three thousand characters to read the newspaper and seventy-five hundred for a university education.)

As an example of the helpfulness of this symbolic world, a pastor of a local church, Dr. Chung Ming Kai, remarked that Chinese characters can be used to explain the Gospel. For example, bats are a symbol of blessing and bamboo stands for peace, so these symbols are used on Christian banners, and everybody who sees them instinctively associates the story of Jesus with blessing and peace.

Perhaps most significant for discernment are symbols provided by the picturesque proverbs in the Chinese "books of sayings." For example, in the story of Li Quan cited earlier, he quoted the proverb, "He who sacrifices his conscience to ambition burns a picture to obtain the ashes." The graphic illustration of the stupidity of destroying a photograph or a painting for soot makes it very clear that ambition must be tightly guarded lest it tempt us to renounce our own conscience.

In such a way "Cheng yu," or Chinese proverbs, often provide guidelines for discernment. In Asian contexts people cite them as evidence for their decisions, and they expect, as did Li Quan in the novel, that others will understand what the proverbs mean. In the same way, Christians in China understand that the Bible can be cited as an explanation for one's decisions, yet they cite it not in a literalistic and legalistic way (though that could be a danger), but as part of the habit of symbolic reframing. In other words, the Chinese proverbs or the Bible texts invite a person to enter into a different frame of reference to look at the questions or issues of life.

Daniel Chan, who has translated several of my books into Chinese for publication in Hong Kong, sent me some examples of proverbs that urge the Chinese to let history guide them in reframing their perspectives on present situations. For example, one proverb translated literally for us by Daniel means, "a warning taken from the overturned cart in the front." In other words, we can rectify our names by means of "a lesson learned from the failure of one's predecessor."

Daniel told me how in the olden days certain government officials were responsible for writing the history of former dynasties. Once a daring historian dedicated his book to the emperor and said that he hoped that by reading the book the emperor could learn better how to rule the country. The situations of the past enable us to reframe our perspective, to rectify the names from what is faddish and "up-to-date," so that we can discern more appropriately what is really happening and how to respond.

Even as Chinese proverbs urge the people to pay attention to history, so does the Bible, especially in its frequent use of the verb *remember*. People in the First Testament are frequently exhorted to remember the sins of their forebears so that they don't make the same mistakes and to remember the LORD's faithfulness so that they place their lives under God's control. Similarly, Christians in the New Testament are urged to recall the way God has fulfilled all His promises in Christ so that the Trinity is trusted for the future.

The biblical book of Proverbs offers scores of pictures for the sake of reframing. Some proverbs are just one graphic verse to paint an unforgettable picture, such as "The rich is wise in self-esteem, but an intelligent poor person sees through the pose" (Proverbs 28:11). Others are extended pictures to teach us the character of wisdom (Prov. 8) or the gifts of a valiant woman (Prov. 31:10–31) or the consequences of being a fool (Prov. 26).

Both the biblical and the Chinese proverbs contain immense wisdom. One day in chapel at the Hong Kong seminary, Chaplain Patrick used a Chinese aphorism that correlated with his sermon on Jesus' declaration "Truly I tell you, just as you did it to one of the least of these who are members of my family, you did it to me" (Matthew 25:40). He told me later that because the Chinese proverbs are held in common by all the people there, they provide an added spur for obedience to the biblical text. The Chinese are accustomed to dwelling in the symbolic world the proverbs paint and that helps them more easily to dwell in the biblical world and to develop a biblically founded character.

A different type of symbolic reframing to influence decision making arose in a conversation scheduled with international clergy in Hong Kong. Coy, a woman from the Philippines whom I had met previously at an international conference in Japan, serves Filipino maids in Hong Kong through her ministry at a Methodist church. She presented to the group the problem that she never could develop leadership in the parish because the members constantly moved on to work in new locations.

A pastor named Scott suggested that she reframe her picture of what her ministry is, and he offered the model of places of hospitality in the Middle East. He was thinking particularly of some places he knew in regions just outside of Damascus in Syria which acknowledge that their gift is hospitality. These places perceive that their ministry is only transient, but they still do it as well as they can. Similarly, her church might be equipping people for their future lives elsewhere and not necessarily for how they will contribute to the church's life there in Hong Kong. With a vision for hospitality, Scott encouraged, the church's ministry could be extremely important in the lives of the Filipino women they served.

The same sort of symbolic reframing is actually what preachers here in North America do regularly if their sermons invite listeners to step into the experiences of people in the biblical narratives. As an example, in Advent one year, a preacher let the First Testament Lesson for the day, Isaiah 64:1–9, invite us listeners into the experience of a captive people. If that experience seems distant to us, Father Bob Rhodes clarified, that is only because we don't know how captive we are to the consumer culture that surrounds us.

In Isaiah 64, the Israelites cried out that God would "tear open the heavens and come down" into their captivity and make Himself known again. The text uses images from elsewhere in the First Testament (see, for example, 1 Kings 19) of God's epiphany or coming—fire, earthquake, the mountains quaking. But because the people had chosen to ignore the LORD, Isaiah asserts that "our righteous deeds are like a filthy cloth" (v. 6). God's absence, we must realize, is due to their (and our) sinfulness. They (and we?) had stopped listening so God retreats.

Isaiah's language might seem quaint in a society flooded with images disguised or designed to sell us products. But we Christians are given the Advent season, the four weeks set aside to prepare for Christ's coming at Christmas, as a time to face ourselves. We are invited to join Isaiah in this claim:

> O LORD, you are our Father;
>> we are the clay, and you are our potter;
>> we are all the work of your hand. (v. 8)

Texts challenge us to hear them truly as a converting word, the treasure of the Word of God. Will we let that converting word orient us into a right perspective on our own sinfulness and our need for God? Will we also hear in it God's grace so that we delight in being clay in our Father's hand? Then the text can inspire us to trust the Triune God to mold us to be people who live well, not according to the consumerism of our culture which tends to hold us captive, but according to His will and to His glory. Will we let the reframing of the Scriptures guide us as we try to discern by God's grace how to live in this society?

My good friend Marguerite, who is a highly skilled spiritual director, once helped me several years ago with a necessary reframing because I was worried as I faced delicate oral surgery that had the possibility of breaking my jaw. I kept thinking about how difficult it would be to get nutrients because my protein- and phosphorus-restricted kidney diet prevented me from drinking the milk shakes that are usually used, and my potassium limitations negated the use of mashed bananas or other fruits.

"I don't have a very good batting average for avoiding complications," I complained to Marguerite.

"Yes," she consoled, "but you have a great batting average for getting through them."

Her wise response empowered me to redefine my trust on the basis of history. She gently forced me to acknowledge that I'd been asking God for an easier life, rather than for a sense of the Triune Presence in the midst of whatever difficulties I might encounter. Whom did I trust—myself or God? God had always sustained me to deal with handicaps in the past. Could I not believe God would empower me to deal with whatever complications might arise in the future?

That oral surgery went perfectly well, and my jaw did not break. What a waste of time it had been to worry and imagine all kinds of troubles! Of course, this is usually the case: most of what we worry about never takes place. We could instead practice the kind of reframing, of rectifying the names that Marguerite demonstrated. Could we not learn from biblical history and our own that God can always be trusted?

THE DANGER
OF CATEGORIZATION

One of the problems that can arise with practices of reframing in order to rectify the names is that sometimes we establish principles (through proverbs or verses of the Scriptures or

faddish methods) that put people or even situations into cat-
egories that too tightly confine who they really are. I think
of some of the methods by which people decide that they
are of a certain personality type and cannot change. Once at
a youth event for which I was one of the leaders, another
speaker divided people into those who were Organized Or-
anges, Ready-to-Go-Reds, Ingenious Greens, or True
Blues—each with a particular list of defining characteristics
that would cause us to place ourselves in that category. It
seemed to me that the daily lives of most of us present could
have put us in all the groups at one time or another.

I am wary of all personality tests that are used to guide
us. Because the Scriptures hint (by the creation account of
Genesis 2) that God takes an intimate interest in our individual creation, and because we are each uniquely made in the
image of God (Genesis 1), why should we reduce the delightful mystery of singular selves into one of sixteen or so
personality types? It is true that these tools can be useful in
helping us to understand a bit more of our dominant traits or
of our relationships with other people, but we are always full
of surprises, even to ourselves, and ought not to restrict our
own development of character by confining ourselves to a
tightly defined image of ourselves.

The same thing can happen when people decide that
they have certain spiritual gifts and no others, according to the
lists of gifts in Romans 12, 1 Corinthians 12, Ephesians 4, and
1 Peter 4. Instead, the biblical texts invite us to view the specified gifts they contain as samples of the myriads upon myriads of gifts the Holy Spirit bestows.

A literal translation of Romans 12:6a shows this by the
emphasis of its last word: "But having grace-gifts according to
the grace which has been given us—*different* . . ." That means

that our spiritual gifts might change over time. At different points in our lives God uses us in different ways, but any time the Trinity's grace flows through us, we are manifesting spiritual gifts—whether that be by teaching or serving, administrating or doing-the-dishes-in-the-kitchen-after-a-church-potluck-with-so-much-exuberance-that-everyone-wants-to-be-in-there-helping. I put that last phrase all in hyphens because one of my childhood friends really had that as a spiritual gift, a Holy Spirit–empowered charisma for bringing God's grace to the clean-up crew at community events.[5]

When we want to rectify the name of whatever spiritual gift we might have, let's not confine ourselves to terms already used. God is always doing new things, always working through each of us in creative and unique ways. We might have to make up a new name or keep searching for a more accurate rectification of the names for skills and spiritual gifts with which God endows us so that we don't miscategorize ourselves and thereby fail to discern well.

SORTING PRIORITIES

The cultural habits described throughout this book provide a sampling of the great wisdom given to me by my conversation partners in other cultural settings. One added delight for me in my travels and correspondence was that I could offer to my friends in exchange the concept of "focal concerns," which has been for the last few years a means for me to rectify the names by sorting out our priorities in decision making. The concept was originally a gift to me from the book *Technology and the Character of Contemporary Life* by Albert Borgmann, a professor of philosophy at the University of Montana.[6] I have described this notion thoroughly in my book *Unfettered Hope,* so I won't elaborate it extensively here.[7]

Simply put, focal concerns are those preeminent dimensions of life to which we are most committed and around which our choices for attitude and action will center if we live with integrity. I believe that for Christians our primary focal concern is the double-sided Great Commandment: to love God and to love our neighbor. I assert this because it is consistently emphasized throughout both testaments of the Scriptures and because when a lawyer asked Jesus which was the greatest commandment, this was His response:

> "'You shall love the Lord your God with all your heart,
> and with all your soul, and with all your mind.' This is
> the greatest and first commandment. And a second is like
> it: 'You shall love your neighbor as yourself.' On these
> two commandments hang all the law and the prophets."
> (Matthew 22:37–40)

What would happen if all our discernment hung on this focal concern, this double love mandate?

It helps immensely, when confronted with various decisions, if we ask how each choice contributes to our focal concerns. Then we often are able to discern among all the options one preference that fits most closely with the top priorities of our lives. When we choose our closest friends, for example, we could ask ourselves how a person deepens our engagement in our focal concerns. We could ask whether this person will help us to love God and our neighbor more thoroughly.

When I was engaged in conversation with the pastors who serve Chinese and Filipino people in Hong Kong, we found a way to take the helpfulness of focal concerns to another level. Through one situation, for example, we realized that we sometimes have to deal with subsidiary concerns that are temporary until certain problems are solved that will then enable us to focus more on our primary goals.

We were discussing the situation of a pastor whose foremost desire was to equip his people to take leadership roles. As we discussed this focus, he began to realize that it would probably be necessary to spend time first in the mundane task of helping the candle bearers get organized (because that was an important ministry for the people he served, who were usually disenfranchised Filipinos). Later someone could be equipped to be in charge of that ministry (and find even more importance by taking a leadership role), and then the clergyman would become more free to concentrate on his pastoral priorities.

I have discovered this notion of focal concerns to be remarkably helpful for discernment when there are too many ministry choices and when I'm having trouble rectifying the names. If I can keep in mind that the most important criteria are that by engaging in a certain action I might love God and my neighbor more, I find some decisions easier to make.

Seminary president and author Donald McCullough reports that a friend of his therapist was doing research in South Africa and discovered a remarkable instance of rectifying the names by means of concentrating on focal concerns. The researcher discovered that the Bambemba tribe in South Africa places a person who has acted wrongfully

> in the center of the village, alone and unfettered. All work
> ceases, and all the men, women, and children gather in a
> larger circle around the accused. Then each person, one by
> one, speaks to him about all the good things he has done in
> his lifetime. Yes, the *good* things. Every incident and every
> experience that can be recalled is recounted as accurately
> as possible. All positive attributes, generous deeds, strengths,
> and kindnesses are recited carefully and at length. No one is

permitted to fabricate or exaggerate or be facetious. This
ceremony often lasts several days and does not cease until
everyone is drained of every positive comment that can be
made about the person in question. Then the circle is broken,
a joyous celebration takes place, and the person is welcomed
back into the tribe.[8]

What an extraordinary way to restore an erring member
of the community! What a unique method for rectifying the
name of a person's character! What a godly way to love the
transgressor and change that individual's name to "friend"!
Think of how our society deals with people whose actions
have been irresponsible or wrongful. Would we deal with them
in the same way if we remembered that our focal concern is to
help them change their behavior and to restore them to the
community? How might it transform our attitudes and actions
if we tried to rectify the names of what exactly we are trying
to do with them and for them in response to their wrongdoing? Oh, if only all of us could live according to our focal concerns and love God and our neighbors so well!

Coupled with other practices of silence, taking more
time, seeking communal counsel, symbolic reframing, and
praying, accentuating my focal concerns is a habit I want to
deepen for the sake of thinking more clearly at times of discernment. Because loving God and loving the neighbor are
two sides of the same coin, this dual focal concern actually is
another way to say a proverb that has been important to me
ever since I read Søren Kierkegaard's book of the same title,
"Purity of heart is to will one thing." Kierkegaard's axiom is
inspired by these verses from the New Testament:

> If any of you is lacking in wisdom, ask God, who gives to
> all generously and ungrudgingly, and it will be given you.

> But ask in faith, never doubting, for the one who doubts
> is like a wave of the sea, driven and tossed by the wind; for
> the doubter, being double-minded and unstable in every
> way, must not expect to receive anything from the Lord.
> (James 1:5–8)

When we ask God for wisdom, James urges us, let us have a single focus—a desire to do God's will, which would be primarily to love God and our neighbor. If we have other gods—such as a deep desire to serve our own self or to attain success or prestige, or if we harbor jealousy or want to exact vengeance against an offender (contrary to the earlier account of the Bambemba tribe)—we are double-minded. Purity of heart is to want only what God wants, to make the Trinity and the triune will of love our focal concern.

We can't even begin to grasp what kind of multiplying results God will accomplish if we choose the less influential route in order to stay in the center of God's will. Imagine what wonders God can work through us if we give up our need to be approved, our undue pride, our doubts and fears, and other double-mindednesses in order to focus solely on loving God and loving our neighbors.

In the beatitudes, the series of benedictions that Jesus bestows on people of various virtues at the beginning of the Sermon on the Mount, He says that the "pure in heart" are "Blessed" because "they will see God" (Matthew 5:8). If we want to see God, to comprehend the Trinity's guidance when we are making a decision, there must be only one goal—to be right in the center of God's will, whatever that might be.

May God be glorified and more clearly seen by us as we conduct our decision making with singleness of heart and mind!

PRAYER AND THE SPIRITUAL EXERCISES OF ST. IGNATIUS

I have not written much in this book about prayer because that would require an entire volume in itself—and the works of several stellar mentors on prayer are listed in the bibliography. However, as is probably obvious, the practices of rectifying names and discerning our focal concerns of which this chapter speaks are best accomplished by means of prayer, listening conversation with God that takes place more thoroughly when we rest in God's grace and the Trinity's enfolding friendship.

One very helpful guide to prayer for rectifying names and discerning focal concerns is the pattern laid out in *The Spiritual Exercises of Saint Ignatius.*[9] Saint Ignatius (1491–1556) was a highly experienced spiritual director who founded the Society of Jesus (the Order of Jesuits). Over the course of a thirty-day retreat (or stretched over a much longer period of time if one is not able to make such an extended retreat), those who follow these spiritual exercises grow to depend more thoroughly on God's grace instead of on themselves.

We are trained by the exercises to turn to God in repentance for our sin and failures and with a firmly established resolve to remain nonattached to anything in creation that we might trust instead of the Trinity. Then we are taught to become more deeply rooted in the Scriptures so that we comprehend the world through biblical lenses. Various exercises instruct us in contemplation of Christ and His incarnation, life and ministry, passion, and resurrection so that our lives become more conformed to His, to the glory of the Father by the power of the Holy Spirit. We are also given guidance in the practice of prayer, as well as rules to assist us in perceiving and understanding our own interior experiences of intellect, will, or feelings that come either from ourselves or from bad or good influences.

Such rooting in the Scriptures, in prayer, and in an awareness of the origins of our own experiences helps us to sort through facts, to notice more astutely their sources in cultural effects or in our own burdens so that we separate what is true from what might be assumption or bias. Ignatius also strongly encourages consultation with others, a topic we will address in Chapter Five.

One special tool he advocates that is particularly related to rectifying the names is his advice to us to imagine ourselves acting on the least-favored of our options and then for the same amount of time to live with our most preferred alternative so that we can note how we react to those two ways of choosing. By means of such exercises we can often clarify for ourselves what really fits with our primary focal concerns, what really matters to us, and what seems to be in most accord with God's best will.

All the practices I have listed in this chapter are ongoing disciplines for clarifying the issues in periods of discernment. Until we are perfectly transformed into the image of Christ at the end of time, we will never be able totally to rectify the names or to live with purity of heart in accordance with our focal concerns. But meanwhile, we know the Joy of continually directing our lives to our highest commitment: to love God and our neighbor. And the Bible, the early saints, the Indians and the Chinese, and others will continually invite us into deeper symbolic worlds so that we can constantly reframe our perspectives, especially concerning Who God is, and move ever more closely to the truth about ourselves, our lives, and our choices.

Prioritizing
Virtues and Morals

A few years ago, during some weeks when I was giving a series of lectures for Chinese Christians in Hong Kong, I asked my conversation partners and audiences to name for me any habits or customs from their native culture that helped them better to discern. The most frequent response I received from young people was a strong lament that they and their peers have lost the Chinese people's traditions (largely those of Confucian thought) that helped previous generations make better decisions. One young man named Paul insisted that in the past "virtue and morality took first place" and people thought about other people first. He said, with sorrowful regret, that now the younger generation seems to be more concerned with being efficient and effective.

This is a cry that echoes throughout the world. It seems that almost everywhere individuals, especially young adults, realize that our speed and push for success inhibit the kind of virtues, such as goodness and patience, that lead to godly decisions which consider the well-being of others. Yet everywhere the pace of life continues to escalate without much communal effort to restrain it. Persons have to be hardy souls to resist the tide, to establish boundaries. One boundary that can be very helpful is setting aside an entire celebrative and restful Sabbath day in which one does not work or even worry about one's work.[1]

Sabbath is a helpful boundary, for it is a day set aside to focus on God and others. Concentrating on God, Who is the source of all good attributes and moral values, gives us a clearer picture of the kind of people we want to be—characterized by love, kindness, perseverance, integrity, trustworthiness, humility, gentleness, and other such virtues exemplified in Jesus. Concentrating on others enables us to practice such morals as honesty, consideration, modesty, and respect.

Our concern in this chapter is with an important spiral, to which we will add a second in the following chapter. Here we realize that the more deliberately we seek to be formed with biblical virtues and moral priorities, the more easily we will discern choices that reflect Christian values. Furthermore, the more intentionally we make such choices, the more our character will be formed with godly virtues and morals. This ongoing spiral is seen much more readily in other cultures where the societal customs and habits are not so inimical to Christian practices.

EXTERNAL OBSTACLES TO VIRTUES AND MORAL PRIORITIES

External obstacles to the types of virtues and moral thinking necessary for good discernment seem almost to be universally escalating. When young people throughout the world lament the loss of various traditions from their heritage, they feel helpless to counteract the forces that seem to cause that loss. Sometimes they blame wealth (though, as we shall see, great poverty is equally destructive). In many countries where I have taught, people grieve that societal speed, power, the need for success, and the resultant narcissism in the culture have squelched the sorts of values that guide good decision making.

Societal structures that prevent training in critical moral thinking are also prominent obstacles to wise decision making. These structures vary from the stifling effects of communism on people's trust in their capacities to gain wisdom (as I discovered in conversations in eastern Germany, Poland, the Czech Republic, Hungary, and Slovakia) to the effects of peer pressure in the United States (as is evident in many persons' conversations about the 2004 elections in light of subsequent developments and indictments in 2005–2006).

In one of my conversations with Chinese Christians in Hong Kong, one man admitted that his work as executive head of an immense corporation is so hurried that he can't take time to contemplate issues in order to discern well. When I asked, "How then can you make the most godly decisions?" he confessed that he simply couldn't worry about it. "I just decide," he responded, though he admitted that this was not the Chinese way to do things and that he would like to be more careful and care-full. This man is known as a deeply poetic, thoughtful, and considerate person, who formerly took time for such things as engaging in reflective conversation. Probably because he mirrored my own encumbered and pressured self, I found it painful to see him so hasty and harried by the crush of his work.

The experience stands as a warning to me: do others perceive my presence as rush and rudeness? It is crucial that we all make the necessary decisions so that our lives are slowed down enough to pay genuine attention to the people we are with in each circumstance—and so that we can make better decisions in turn. What other virtues besides kindness and gentleness are lost in the time crunch? What moral priorities are set aside in the push to get ahead?

It is a temptation to blame our decline in virtues and morals only on the speed and wealth of North America. But that is to escape our internal decline by indicting external circumstances. With enough purity of heart, we could choose to step away from the pace and make better choices to live more sanely. Our wealth could be put at the service of good decisions, especially when we have too many choices in opportunities for service, but it would require a strong undergirding in appropriate values and character attributes.

Carol Barrera, with whom I have corresponded for years though we've never met, works as a Bible translator with the Achí people in Guatemala. She helped me realize that the external circumstances of those without wealth can be equally problematic. She wrote:

> I think the Achí culture and particularly Achí Christians do
> have insights that could help well-off (materially) Americans.
> However, I'm not sure they do any better on the issue of
> discerning God's will, given many choices of service. For
> one thing, their circumstances and poverty limit where they
> can go, what they can do. I see a lot of burn-out—people who
> are dedicated, but over-committed, to the detriment of their
> health, families, and ultimately, their own spiritual welfare.

This is an important comment, lest we think that wealth (and its related burnout) is the primary inhibitor of virtues; perhaps poverty is equally so. Each side presents its own pitfalls to character.

Burnout, whether caused by too much pressure for success or by deprivation, can be extraordinarily destructive to the moral fiber necessary for discernment. But does it have to be?

Perhaps burnout could be avoided in the first place with better decisions. Jesus carefully chose to pull away from people into private conversation with His Father so that He could continue to serve people better.

I'm not minimizing at all the incredible power of our North American society to control us. In *The Winner-Take-All Society,* Robert H. Frank and Philip J. Cook make very clear how the wasteful competitions and income discrepancies, the violent media and polluting activities of our culture shape our tastes and abilities and adversely affect the well-being of ourselves and others.[2]

Nor do I believe that we can overcome the influence of our society with merely a mental decision to resist it. As Robert Kegan shows in *In Over Our Heads: The Mental Demands of Modern Life,* we need a "qualitative change in the complexity of our minds" to handle all the demands of postmodern society on them. Without giving the spiritual answers that we are finding, he asks the same basic question as does this book—by what principles do we weigh and sort everything in our lives?[3]

Let me accentuate those spiritual answers, rooted in God's grace, because I do not believe we can resist the onslaughts of external forces to our moral character and virtues merely by acquiring Kegan's "fifth order of consciousness," a complexity of mind matching the demands of postmodernism. Instead, what we need is a new will, enfolded in the triune will, and a new character transformed into the likeness of Christ by the power of the Holy Spirit to the glory of the Father. We will turn to that after we consider briefly the internal forces that prevent such a development of moral will and virtuous character.

WHAT INTERNAL WEAKNESSES KEEP US FROM DISCERNING WELL?

Besides the externally related (but not necessarily *controlling*) hindrances to thoughtful, wise, and genuinely Christian decision making—the speed of life, the push for success, others' expectations, overcommitments, the oppressions of former and present tyrannies of governments and cultures—there are, of course, inner and more powerful hindrances.

David Tomlins, the abbot of the Australian Cistercian monastery at Tarrawarra, writes, "The most deafening voice is our own. Desires, fears, anxieties and obsessive worries, a treadmill of thoughts, issuing from a constantly chattering mind."[4] Related to Tomlins' list we might specify particular internal obstacles, such as one's personal lack of single-mindedness (or willing one thing), one's need for approval or success, one's wrong private expectations, or one's lack of love for, and trust in, God.

We have already considered single-mindedness in connection with our discussion of Christian focal concerns in Chapter Three. When we look more deeply, we might discover that what keeps us from purity of heart and thereby from good discernment is simply that we don't love God enough. Assess the state of your own worship life—both in public, corporate worship services and in private devotional habits. Do we serve God because we ought to or because we delight in it? Throughout this book we continually recognize by biblical means that the best way to grow in our love for the Triune God is to pay attention to how much God loves us first.

Earlier, Tomlins mentioned our desires as a major element in our "chattering minds" that keeps us from hearing God's voice for discernment. Oftentimes, we are helped to draw closer to God's wisdom if we rectify the names of what we really desire. Do we really want what God wants (and, therefore, what is best for us), or do we hang on to our own petty cravings and mundane yearnings?

In *Encounters with Silence,* Catholic theologian Karl Rahner likens our souls in the presence of God and God's unerring truthfulness to a clamorous bazaar in which all sorts of wheeler-dealers gather to hawk the tattered treasures of the world. He pictures the soul as a mammoth warehouse piled anywhere and everywhere with no method or manner and jammed to the brim with what is banal and irrelevant to what really matters in life. He realizes that only by the mercy and illumination of God can there be any moments of grace and genuine worth in the midst of our lives.[5]

Another tenacious obstacle to good discernment is fear. By the grace of God, a very wise spiritual director, Benedictine Sister Ruth Stanley, once cogently exposed the deep fears that get in the way of my decision making. She helped me see that my outer work will continue to suffer if I don't deal with the inner work of learning to trust God in the face especially of the escalating physical handicaps that cause me the most anxiety. What apprehensions and worries detrimentally distort your character and hamper the development in you of godly virtues?

Our fears, of course, are aggravated by a society that continually makes us feel that we should *accomplish* a lot, that we should have great *influence* on others. Against those forces, let us return to what God tells us about His love for us and to the fullness of triune grace. Whatever might be accomplished, whatever influence might be exerted is due solely to that grace in the first place; furthermore, God accepts whatever gifts we offer and does not judge us for the level of our achievements or prestige. The question is simply whether in glad response to the fullness of triune grace we live and serve with faithfulness. These truths could do much to combat whatever fears inhibit our godly discernment of paths to ministry and choices in life.

What other false expectations or obsessive stresses issue from our "treadmill of thoughts," our "constantly chattering mind[s]" (to use Tomlins' phrases)? What virtues in our character and what aspects of moral will could help us overcome these wrong desires and anxious habits so that we could more tightly cling to God and discern God's best purposes?

BIBLICAL VIRTUES

When I first began working on this cross-cultural study project, I was greatly encouraged by a wonderful book written by a member of the faculty of the Hong Kong Alliance Bible Seminary, for which I once taught. Herrick Ping-tong Liu's *Towards an Evangelical Spirituality* primarily studies the great seventeenth-century saint Richard Baxter's work through the lens of his own Chinese cultural context to gain insight into the practice of spiritual disciplines. Both Baxter (1615–1691), an English Puritan author and a church leader, and his Chinese interpreter share our question about discernment—recognizing that "the commonest difficulties among cases of conscience [are] to know which duty is the greater, and to be preferred."[6]

The most important accents from this Chinese study for our purposes here are, first, that the spiritual life is not something we achieve by our own strenuous efforts, and second, that a strong focus on our eternal hope is crucial for the vitality of this spiritual life.[7] The first point emphasizes that we receive from the Trinity the character that we desire—for this chapter, the virtues and the moral will to resist the influences of our culture and our own failings in order to discern well. Our Christian character is God the Father's gift, created in us by our union with Christ, and ceaselessly nourished by the Holy Spirit.

For the second insight, theologians use the word *eschatological* (from *eschaton,* which means "the end") to describe our hope. Truly biblical Christian eschatology is not all about end-time tortures and gruesome battles, raptures and calendars. Rather, the Bible emphasizes that in Christ's death and resurrection, our eternal hope was made sure and even begun. Through faith in Christ by the gift of the Spirit, we now are being changed into the likeness of Christ, and we actually participate now to some extent in the gifts of heaven. I like to stress that heaven is not just "pie in the sky in the bye and bye when we die," but a genuine reality in the present and a sure promise for the future, both of which enable us to live by God's grace in His reign in the midst of a world in which many other forces claim to be god.

We especially live in God's reign now because the resurrection of Christ delivers us from our fear of death, which, according to psychologist Carl Jung, causes most people's problems these days. In contrast, in Christ we know that death is simply the removal of the last barrier that keeps us from knowing God face-to-face. We are also delivered from our guilt and self-absorption because Jesus has given us both forgiveness and an entirely new purpose for living. Furthermore, by the Spirit's power we are presently being transformed into Christ's likeness. Thus, our eschatological hope

gives us an eternal Joy in this life that can't be found anywhere else.

I can't stress enough how important it is to realize that
our spirituality and the character of our Christian lives are
gifts of God's grace. Otherwise, too many of us try to crank
out being virtuous, instead of receiving Christ's life through
us. (I know: I keep trying to make myself better, instead of
trusting grace and, as a result, being more what God would
have me be through the Spirit's power.) When we strain to
create our own spiritual life, we actually separate ourselves
further from God because we are failing to let God be our rescuing and renewing God.

Even the Ten Commandments in the Bible do not
merely say, "You better shape up and keep these rules or else."
Instead, the commandments begin with God's declaration of
Who He is so that we can trust Him: "I am the LORD your
God, who brought you out of the land of Egypt, out of the
house of slavery" (Exodus 20:2a). As a result, we *want* to obey
this precept: "You shall have no other gods before me" (2b).
Why would we want any god beside the one true LORD Who
effectively delivered us out of slavery to this world's gods and
to the gods of our own misguided passions?

Similarly, when the New Testament writers urge us to
"put on" certain attributes of character, their invitations
begin with statements of the fullness of the triune grace that
enables us to put them on. I'm thinking especially of my favorite list of virtues in Colossians 3, which emphasizes that
we are "God's chosen ones, holy and beloved" (v. 12a). We
didn't choose ourselves; we did not make ourselves holy; we
aren't beloved because we are great. God chose us in Christ;
the Holy Spirit works our sanctification; the Father names us
"beloved."

Of course, then, we will rejoice that the Trinity will "clothe" us with the virtues of "compassion, kindness, humility, meekness and patience" (12b). We will gladly receive the gifts of moral will described in the rest of this list, as rendered in Eugene Peterson's *The Message:*

> Be even-tempered, content with second place, quick to forgive an offense. Forgive as quickly and completely as the Master forgave you [notice the additional reminder of grace]. And regardless of what else you put on, wear love. It's your basic, all-purpose garment. Never be without it.
> Let the peace of Christ keep you in tune with each other, in step with each other. None of this going off and doing your own thing. And cultivate thankfulness. Let the Word of Christ—the Message—have the run of the house. Give it plenty of room in your lives. Instruct and direct one another using good common sense. And sing, sing your hearts out to God! Let every detail in your lives—words, actions, whatever—be done in the name of the Master, Jesus, thanking God the Father every step of the way.
> (Colossians 3:13–17, *The Message*)

Imagine how much easier our discernment would be if these virtues and aspects of moral will were developed in us because we have learned to rest in God's choice of us, God's work to make us holy, God's treatment of us as the Trinity's beloved!

I chose Peterson's *Message* for that text from Colossians because most other English renderings use words like *should* or *must* for verse 13's injunction for us to forgive—an emphasis that is not in the original Greek, which instead simply says, "Just as the Lord forgave you, so also you." I note that because too many Christians live by "should, have to, ought to, and must," instead of by "chosen, holy, beloved." Think of the huge difference it makes in our being characterized by biblical virtues and in our ability to live by God's commandments whether we live by what we *ought to be and do,* or by what we *are privileged to be and do by the grace of God at work in and through us!*

Let me also highlight a few biblical texts that accentuate our eschatological hope, the second point emphasized here from Liu's book. The apostle Paul, for example, writes that "If anyone is in Christ, there is a new creation; everything old has passed away; [behold!], everything has become new!" (2 Corinthians 5:17). I put the word *behold!* in brackets because the New Revised Standard Version (NRSV) uses instead the translation *see,* which doesn't seem to me to be strong or lively enough. I see lots of things that I don't really comprehend. Instead, this text shouts, Pay attention! The new creation in Christ is truly something to behold!

Once we have entered into the new life made possible by Christ's incarnation, earthly life and ministry, passion, death, resurrection, and ascension, *everything* is new. We look with a new perspective at everything, even those external hindrances to the development of a virtuous character that will help us to discern better—we will understand that those forces need no longer control us. Heaven has come to earth in Christ; God's Kingdom reign has started, and we are being transformed. In this we find confident hope for our own growth in virtues and moral will.

When Jesus first began "proclaiming the good news of God," according to the Gospel of Mark, He was saying, "The time has become fulfilled (and will remain so), and the Kingdom of God has come near (and will continue to prevail); be repenting and be believing the Gospel (or Good News)" (Mark 1:15; my translation of the original Greek to accentuate some key verb tenses in the verse).

In the coming of Jesus into the world (and specifically now that He has begun preaching), the time everyone was waiting for became fulfilled, never to be ended. The Kingdom of God has actually come to earth in the person of Jesus. As a result, we will never want to stop repenting for all the times we forget that, and we will continue to believe this eschatological hope. As we abide in belief, God's Kingdom will continue to reign in our lives and positively affect our discernments for the sake of others around us, for the sake of the world. As we dwell in faith and hope, in the truth of God's Kingdom, we will find ourselves being formed into ever deeper, eternal Joy. And, as we frequently experience, we make better decisions when they are made out of God's Joy.

MONASTIC VIRTUES

That God's reign in our lives forms and frees us with its grace and Joy is what the great monastic founders—the Celtic saints, Benedict, Francis of Assisi, Dominic, Ignatius of Loyola—discovered and taught. Contemporary Benedictine Sister Joan Chittister ends her book *Wisdom Distilled from the Daily* with a lovely story that accentuates this biblical point. The story involves people who came from the city to the local monastic teacher because they wanted to know how one searches for union with God. The Wise One responded:

> "The harder you seek, the more distance you create between God and you."
>
> "So what does one do about the distance?" the seekers said.
>
> And the elder said simply, "Just understand that it isn't there."

"Does that mean that God and I are one?" the disciples said.

And the monastic said, "Not one. Not two."

"But how is that possible?" the seekers insisted.

And the monastic answered, "Just like the sun and its light, the ocean and the wave, the singer and the song. Not one. But not two."[8]

Chittister underscores the motif of this tale by beginning her book on living St. Benedict's rule today with chapters on "Listening" as "The Key to Spiritual Growth" and on "Prayer and *Lectio*" (referring to a monastic practice called *lectio divina* or "divine reading") as "The Center and Centrifuge of Life." Only when we listen to God and grow in triune grace and only as we converse with God and attentively read the Scriptures are we formed into the character of other Benedictine virtues, such as humility, mindfulness, hospitality, peace, obedience, stability, and *conversatio morum* (or a way of life that enables us to react readily with helpfulness to situations that arise at the moment). Benedictines understand even work as not really our own, but as "Participation in Creation."

This rooting in the grace of the God to Whom we belong is emphasized by the Benedictine rhythm of prayer and work, by which work is dignified and undergirded with the praise of God. On a card listing Core Values given to me at St. Benedict's Monastery in St. Joseph, Minnesota, where I go for retreats and spiritual direction, the first value listed is "*Awareness of God:* We acknowledge the primacy of God and seek to follow Christ in the ordinary events of every day."

Wil Derkse, a Benedictine oblate and a professor with a technical university in the Netherlands, underscores this orientation for life when he poses this daily question: "Was I rooted today in streaming, living water?"[9] From that fountain of God's grace, the deepest life of virtue and moral will is grown and flows out for the benefit of others.

For the rest of this chapter we will look at examples of various virtues and aspects of moral character as these are seen in contemporary cultures elsewhere in the world—in Asia, Africa, and Madagascar (which lies between and combines elements of those two continents).

VIRTUES AND MORALITY IN ASIAN CULTURES

Over the last few years it has been my privilege to teach for a few weeks at a time and learn from my students and hosts in Japan, China, and Singapore. During that same time, news reports and other literature have highlighted what is easily observable—that certain moral foundations and cultural habits lead to noticeable differences between Asian communities and North American cities. For example, my various hosts in Tokyo all commented on how safe they feel on that massive city's streets.

Many of the differences, and the resultant social stability, can be traced to Asian peoples' grounding in Confucian thought. Remember from Chapter Three that Confucius especially espoused ancient principles of morality. In *Confucius Lives Next Door,* the journalist T. R. Reid highlights these aspects of Asian countries' social stability that can be attributed to the people's grounding in Confucian morals:

> the world's lowest rates of violent crime, theft, and drug
> use; strong, stable families with low rates of divorce, and
> virtually no single parents; public education that tests out
> as the best in the world; a broad sense of equality that
> gives almost everybody a stake in the society and thus

helps assure, for the most part, safe and peaceful living conditions.[10]

Notice how well these characteristics would also be achieved if Western societies were still grounded in Judeo-Christian principles of Hebrew law, especially the Ten Commandments.

Reid quotes Ogura Kazuo, a senior diplomat in Japan's Foreign Service, who names these Confucian attributes that lie behind this relative social stability:

> "The Asian spirit involves discipline, loyalty, hard work rather than inheritance as the key to entitlement, long-term investment, a focus on education, esteem for the family, concern for the collective harmony of the group, and control over one's desires."[11]

These very values could also have been named as Christian virtues, but they are still quite deeply rooted in Asian societies, whereas the Judeo-Christian heritage of North America has declined in the face of the onslaught of technological advancement, the growing gap between the wealthy and the poor, extreme narcissism and independence, escalating self-indulgence, and mindless entertainment.

As Reid reports, many Asian leaders are convinced that Western societies have slid into a bog, but that their own cultures have escaped that swamp because of their moral character. Japanese scholar Katsuta Kichitaroo insists, "'By following the insights of Confucianism, . . . we can avoid the social catastrophe befalling the West, the result of centuries of individualism and egotism.'"[12]

In a chapter on Confucian and biblical thought, journalist Reid points to their mutual emphasis on leading by character. Those of us who desire as Christians to make better decisions would be better formed in moral virtues if we constantly remembered that the most important use of our time is focusing on our spiritual practices in the Christian community of prayer, worship, Scripture study, and so forth, by which God works in us to develop our character and thereby to nurture our skills of discernment.

Reid discloses that Asian public schools devote substantial "time, energy, and ingenuity to the teaching of moral lessons: community virtues, proper social conduct, appropriate behavior as a member of a group."[13] Reid's list obviously contrasts with Western education, which teaches morals both rarely and as individual virtues, not as attributes embedded in communal life.

Christianity, in contrast, has always underscored the importance of the new life possible in union with Christ and through the Holy Spirit's power and has understood the virtues and the moral will as developed through *shared,* communal disciplines of character growth. Moreover, Confucian teaching places moral virtues within holistic education composed of intellectual, athletic, social, and artistic components; in relation to this Christianity espouses a larger framework, embedding all those aspects within the spiritual and recognizing that spiritual wholeness is best formed within a community of faith.

AFRICAN LESSONS IN VIRTUES

Best-selling author Alexander McCall Smith, a professor of medical law at Edinburgh University in Scotland, has written a series of witty and profound stories from his background in Africa. Born in the area now known as Zimbabwe, he formerly taught at the University of Botswana. Throughout these stories, Mma Ramotswe, the first female detective in Botswana, keeps reflecting on, and displaying, the old African morality and the magnificent virtues that cause her to discern well what she should do and how she will behave in various aspects of both her work and her life.

In the second novel, *Tears of the Giraffe,* for example, she notices gladly that an American woman receives a gift from her with the appropriate Botswana custom of taking it politely with both hands. It is considered rude if a person takes a present with a single hand; that action makes it seem as if the recipient is disrespectfully snatching the gift from its giver.[14] I read that with great shame because I realized how often I seem to snatch God's gifts with one hand—not responding with immense gratitude for the glorious deluge of blessings God so superabundantly provides.

Our culture has taught us the dangerous notion of entitlement. We think we deserve to be healthy and wealthy, to live without struggle and to be continually happy. As a result, we take our countless blessings for granted. Persons from less prosperous cultures today seem to have a much deeper sense of gratitude, as we saw in the story of George Evans in Chapter One and as I keep noticing as I encounter international students at the various colleges and seminaries where I speak. Gratefulness is a much stronger basis for good discernment than is complaint or thanklessness.

Another moral value essential for good discernment and demonstrated in *Tears of the Giraffe* is honesty. Mma Ramotswe and her assistant Mma Makutsi discuss together the importance of not lying to their clients. Mma Makutsi raises the question of what to do if a murderer comes to you and wants information as to the whereabouts of someone whose precise location at that time you know. She wonders if it is wrong in such an instance to tell a lie.

Mma Ramotswe responds that such a lie is permissible because it is not our responsibility to tell the truth to murderers. But she insists that it is our moral duty to speak only the truth to clients, spouses, or the police. She differentiates between those incidents on the basis, we might say, of rectifying the names of our obligations. She is also thinking of the end result, the focal concern we call it, of taking care of our neighbors.

Mma Makutsi objects and insists that if at any time a lie is a misdeed, then lying should always be considered a wrong. Then she realizes further that the real issue is every person deciding for him- or herself what is right or wrong. She recognizes, but does not articulate, the dire consequences of people all making up their own rules. Mma Ramotswe replies that this is exactly the trouble when old communitarian understandings of morality are forgotten.[15]

Beginning with the moral presuppositions of honesty and abiding by a culture's moral values frees Mma Ramotswe for easier and more positive discernment in daily situations. In contrast, in Western cultures in which those basic presuppositions have been lost, people often decide under difficult circumstances to turn from honesty into such destructive habits as false flattery, little white lies, "fudging the truth," and misleading irony.

This is the pitfall of a type of ethics called "situation ethics" that has been and continues to be lauded at various times and by different theologians. The idea is that each person should decide the rules of morality according to each specific situation. The weaknesses of such a system are augmented by a person's lack of accountability to the larger community. Virtues and moral character are formed by patterns of responsibility set down by a community over time—and, in Christianity's case, by that community's faithful interaction with the Triune God throughout history since Abraham and Sarah.

At one point in another story Mma Ramotswe ponders this necessity for communal development of moral character. She reflects, "Moral codes were not designed to be selective, nor indeed . . . to be questioned." A person could not simply decide which prohibitions to observe and which to ignore.

> Morality, Mma Ramotswe thinks, concerns doing what is right because it had been identified as such by a long process of acceptance and observance. You simply could not create your own morality because your experience would never be enough to do so. What gives you the right to say that you know better than your ancestors? Morality is for everybody, and this means that the views of more than one person are needed to create it. [This is what makes] modern morality, with its emphasis on individuals and the working out of an individual position, so weak. If you gave people the chance to work out their morality, then they would worm out the version which was easiest for them and which allowed them to do what suited them for as much of the time as possible.

To do so would be "simple selfishness," regardless of the names one might use to deny it.[16]

Mma Ramotswe had been led to these thoughts about the communal basis for morality because of a situation she observed of a friend who behaved badly toward her maid, who seemed to be hardworking and pleasant. Mma Ramotswe realized that such behavior was the result of ignorance concerning the other's goals and desires. The consequence was a lack of consideration for the other's feelings.

To understand those feelings was, she thought, the "beginning of all morality." Understanding how someone felt would lead to imagining oneself in the same state, and then one wouldn't wish to cause any more suffering because to do so would be as if one harmed oneself.[17]

Alexander McCall Smith's books frequently emphasize the basic virtues of consideration for others, kindness, and civility. In contrast, recently many commentators in the United States—in news journals, academic books, and literature—have noted the lack of civility in our culture, so noticing the supreme regard in Smith's novels has been refreshing.

For example, in the fourth tale of this series about the "No. 1 Ladies' Detective Agency," Smith shows how the moral consideration of the people is obvious even when someone takes a photograph. Mma Ramotswe notices that "everybody was looking at the camera with *courtesy,* with an attitude of moral attention. That was the old Botswana way—to deal with others in this way."

Her companion, Mrs. Moffat, observes how her friend's eyes are filled with tears as she grieves over the people in the photograph and the values they held that might also be passing away, and she gently reaches out to touch Mma Ramotswe. Together they think about Botswana, "that country that had been—and still was—a beacon of light in Africa, a country of integrity and generosity in both the simple and the big things."[18]

If the fictional Mma Ramotswe and Mrs. Moffat grieve that some old values are passing away in Botswana, how much more must people in the United States grieve the ruination of courtesy by cultural forces here. Christians must mourn that loss even more so because kindness, goodness, and consideration are virtues strongly urged by the Scriptures. They contribute powerfully to the spiral of godly discernment and subsequent moral behavior.

The virtues and moral disposition of Smith's literary characters stand out and invite us also to manifest them. What a great witness it would be if Christians were known in the world as bearers of civility and sustainers of kindness! Imagine how much it would affect our decisions if they arose from such a sensitivity to how we treat others. Envision how it would influence our discernment if everything we chose emanated from "compassion, kindness, humility, meekness, and patience," from "bear[ing] with one another" and "forgiv[ing] each other, just as the Lord has forgiven [us]" (Colossians 3:12–13).

LESSONS FROM MALAGASY (AND CHINESE) LIFE

This virtue of courtesy is related to, and extended by, an important moral characteristic demonstrated by the people of Madagascar. A former long-term missionary in Madagascar, Arlene (Renie) Lellelid, introduced me in correspondence to her Malagasy friends, Dr. Andry Ranaivoson and his wife, Bako Ramihaminarivo. This couple wrote to me that a central virtue transcending the decision-making process in their home culture is that of respect for the elders. They described two customs which are essential to the decision-making process that stem from this central concept—namely, asking for advice or counseling and asking for blessings.

Young people will always refer to the elders for advice or a blessing for any project because they are taught that elders are the source of wisdom and knowledge. These leaders need not be members of one's immediate family, though they may be uncles, aunts, or grandparents. The general belief is that a project will inevitably fail if it has not received the blessings of the elders.

The same emphasis on asking the elders for a blessing was mentioned to me by How Chuang Chua, a man of Chinese origin from Singapore who serves as a missionary in Japan. How Chuang told me that his father had to flee to Singapore because of conflict with the Japanese when he was sixteen and never could go back to his area of China until the 1980s, so he never had the opportunity to see his parents again.

How Chuang explained that it is a strong Chinese tradition to stay united as a family. Thus, when he wanted to ask Kaori, a Japanese woman, to marry him, it was essential that he seek a blessing from his parents, because the Japanese had created the original division of his family between China and Singapore. Without their blessing, How Chuang also could not have become a missionary to Japan. He said that he would not have done so if they had totally objected.

This essential habit of obedience to the parents' will is also important to the Malagasy, in correlation with and reinforcing the custom of asking for a blessing. Bako and Andry wrote that good manners are taught and impressed on children from a very early age. As a result, children should never talk back to their parents or disrespect anyone, particularly anyone older than themselves.[19] Attentive listening is considered a very special virtue and is always appreciated.

Andry and Bako emphasized that these attitudes cause Malagasy believers to find strong affinities between the Bible and their native culture. They are more immediately comfortable with trust, faith, obedience, and listening to the Scriptures than their counterparts from other cultures might be. This led the first Malagasy Christians into a period (1831–1861) of extreme persecution and martyrdom. Their obedience to the Word of God was, in Andry and Bako's words, "complete and total, which brought them to a certain death."

People in North American culture might immediately object that such a morality of obedience to, and respect for, one's elders is no longer possible today or that it leads to cruel tyranny. However, there are numerous exceptional examples of families in which these values still pertain, and they persist without any hint of oppression.

My point in citing the Malagasy and the Singaporean illustrations here is to suggest that other cultures present to us various virtues and moral stances that can positively affect our processes of discernment. As we look at them, we realize that we need to belong to an entire community of support if we want such attributes as listening trust and faithful obedience to characterize our lives and decisions. That is why we turn in the next chapter to the crucial issue of community and its contributions to the discernment process.

5

Communities
of Discernment

———

H ow do you introduce yourself? When we are at
meetings and are told to say our names and a little
bit about ourselves, the North American custom is
to tell about our jobs or where we went to school or what
we do. In New Zealand, I learned, the Maori people (the first
people of New Zealand, who came largely from Polynesian
islands and now compose almost 16 percent of New Zealand's population) have very different introductory customs.
My correspondent told me that when she and other Maori
people in her unit at the university in Auckland want to visit
people in an area to do research, they demonstrate respect by
discovering first what the customs are in the place to which
they want to go. They do this because when they visit, the
mana or prestige and competence (and much more) of the
whole group, each individual person, and all of their families
and tribes are represented in them.

When they introduce themselves, they name the river,
the mountain, and other geographical details of their homeland and the *waka* or canoe on which their tribal ancestors
traveled to get to Aotearoa (the Maori name for New Zealand), as well as their parents' names, before mentioning their
own names. This symbolizes their place in the world. Because

their listeners will make connections (as my correspondent says, for better or worse), the visitors are mindful that they carry responsibility for any future relations of their people—their tribe, their family, and so forth—with the people they visit. The Maori people are divided into tribes (called *iwi*), which are composed of clans (*hapu*), made up of family groups (*whanau*), so all these are represented in any individual.

Maori people are thus always aware of the long-term consequences (to future generations) of their actions here and now. Of course, this has definite effects on all decision-making processes. How much more carefully all of us might tread if we were more consciously attentive to everything that is at stake in all of our interactions with other people and in other places.

Because of this emphasis on one's behavior reflecting on the whole family and tribe, my friend would want me to stress for you that she does not consider herself to be speaking for all the Maori people. She emphasizes that this is merely one person's perspective and should not be taken as representative of the whole. (We will return to the necessity for that disclaimer further on.)

Nonetheless, her comments are crucially important for us because they point out to North Americans and others in the world who might need the caution, how individualistic we are in our thinking and acting, how alone we often are in our behaviors and decision making. What are we missing because we do not conceive of ourselves as belonging to a community and do not realize that our actions and attitudes reflect on our people as a whole? I often thought of one person's influence on a people's reputation when I was on the college concert choir tour and observed North Americans' behaviors in other countries. In many places tourists from the United States earned a bad reputation for the

country as a whole because of their inconsiderate or conde-
scending manners.

At the beginning of this book, we noted that one of our
problems is that we make our decisions in terms of "who I
am," instead of with regard to "whose I am." This chapter at
the center of the book is pivotal, then, in more ways than one
and more extensive than the others because it deals with a
major element missing in North American culture.

In Chapter Four, we noted the continuing spiral of
character formation and practicing virtues and moral behavior. In this chapter, we will focus on another spiral—that of
the effect of communal practices on the forming of an individual's character, which, in turn, upbuilds the whole community. This underscores one of my major theses for the past
several years—that Christians' faith and life in the United
States are not as strongly shaped according to Christian truths
and values because we do not live in deeply connected
Christian communities.[1]

These two interlocking spirals are crucially important.
The more Christians make very deliberate choices to engage
in distinctively Christian practices, the more their character is
formed with Christian virtues and morals, which will lead, in
turn, to more thoroughly Christian discernments. Furthermore, the greater the number of Christians making such
alternative choices, the more Christian communities will develop a biblical culture, which will, successively, help people to
make those intentional choices and thereby form people more
deeply with Christian character.

In this chapter, we especially pay attention to the importance of community participation in processes of decision
making, which was stressed in conversations throughout the
world. For example, in all the countries I've visited that were
formerly under communist rule, people told me about the

significance of the family (especially because loved ones were the only people who could be trusted in a culture of spying and reporting). A Slovakian couple (who are both clergy-persons) stressed how influential their own parents were in their decision making.

North Americans might turn to their parents or to other people in certain crisis situations or when faced with a major decision, but do we understand the importance of recognizing the community to which we belong in all our minor decisions, in the interactions of our everyday lives, in all our exchanges with other people? Especially if we are Christians, we have the added benefit of living in light of the whole community of faith over time and space—especially as we try to live out of our immersion in the Scriptures, which record the wisdom of that community, and in a lively present faith community of saints. Do we realize that our moral character and godly virtues are formed best through the context of the entire Christian community?

Howard Baker, a spiritual director whose book *Soul Keeping* is subtitled *Ancient Paths of Spiritual Direction*, emphasizes that we need the mentorship of the complete Christian community because of the deceitfulness of our hearts. He writes, "The voice of ancient guidance delivers us from a culturally determined spirituality. The voice of contemporary guidance rescues us from a do-it-yourself spirituality. And the voice of personalized guidance saves us from a one-size-fits-all spirituality."[2] In other words, we need the wisdom of those who have gone before us and the good sense of a community that is with us and knows us so that we can best discern what to do and how to be to become more truly ourselves.

Instead, in North America we are taught to "be ourselves" without that rooting in a community or are told to "march to the beat of our own drummer." We are thereby urged to make up our own stories, but as professor Charles Pinches of the University of Scranton says in his book *A Gathering of Memories,* "The advice has the effect of making us think that we really must find ourselves separate from the communities that sustain us by their memory."[3]

As we will see from the stories in this chapter, to participate in a fellowship of memory—especially the family, the local community, and the Church or faith tradition—enables us to know ourselves more deeply and to discern more truly what is best for the sake of others and also for ourselves. When we know to whom we belong, we find more profound meaning for our lives because we are part of such a people and because we have such a God.

HONOR AND SHAME

In earlier chapters, we have rarely mentioned negative aspects of the gifts that we have been pondering, primarily because we would not normally find difficulties, for example, in people displaying caring virtues and a character deeply formed in moral will (Chapter Four). Nor is it a hindrance if we rectify the names (Chapter Three), though, of course, it is problematic if we think we are clarifying the issues when instead we are arriving at prejudiced perceptions. But in this chapter, we will observe that the great gift of community also has several possibilities for complications.

Though community counsel for decision making is an aspect lamentably missing in North America, the effects of community values can indeed be both positive and negative. In one Chinese city which my husband and I visited, teachers working with local students said that the Chinese culture's emphasis on honor and shame for the family caused some difficulties. (Unfortunately, because I can speak only a few words in Mandarin, I could hear only one side of this story.)

In one case, the school had problems with a young boy's misbehavior. It seemed that his parents wouldn't deal with the actual wrongdoing, but instead they worried only about the shame to be brought to the family name if he was expelled. The result of that choice on their part caused destructive effects not only on the school, but even more on the primary family.

I began to wonder, and then discussed it with Chinese friends, whether this high emphasis on not causing the family shame makes repentance difficult because that would bring dishonor to one's relatives. It would also adversely affect one's decisions about truthfulness. My conversation partners agreed and insisted that churches must be careful to teach a deeper understanding of both confession and forgiveness so that people have more true freedom to repent.

Also, many Chinese acquaintances told me that it had sometimes been difficult for them and their friends to become Christians because it was thought to bring their families shame. I wonder if Christians in North America would take their faith more seriously if their decision to engage in Christian practices forced them to pay the price of family ostracism.

As could be expected, all these issues are further complicated by the difficulties of being Christians in China under the communist government. The schools are required to teach all religions; teachers asked me how then it could be possible for them truly to train children in habits of the Christian faith. In our conversations they realized that their own character in the midst of the more full Christian character of the entire community in general was preeminently significant. If students became interested in the character of the Christian community and asked a school's teachers for a

Bible, faculty members were permitted to give them one, though they were not allowed to make a widespread distribution.

On the issue of honor and shame, then, what we see is a clash of two communities' values. The Chinese culture emphasizes that children should not have anything done to them (such as expulsion) that would bring shame on the family, whereas the Christian community is more concerned that the boy's character be formed for him to realize the extensive trouble that his severe misbehavior was causing the teachers and other students. Or perhaps this is a case of not rectifying the names. Perhaps the parents are misunderstanding their own culture's emphasis on what is truly shameful to the family.

A man named Edward from Korea commented further on the benefits and detriments of the Asian emphasis on honor. He said that it was more helpful to make persons mindful of the community than was the Western accent on the personal. But he said that it could sometimes take precedence over consideration of right and wrong (as we saw in the earlier school case), it could become an intolerable burden, or both. Another conversation partner, Christina, agreed that the mentality that one's decisions affect the whole family could put enormous pressure on a person. For example, some of my students from Singapore at Regent College in Vancouver, B.C., took classes under the monumental strain of having to get all A's to "preserve their family's [or their nation's] honor." One was told that people from Singapore should always be the best students in any class in North America. This was an unreasonable hardship not only for the students, but also for the professors, who sometimes had to give a poorer grade because a student's work was not up to par.

This shows us the necessity for the virtues and moral will. One would hope that a family or a people would enfold the individual with such care that the responsibility to be accountable to the whole community would not become an intolerable burden but would be seen as encouragement and support, as a privilege and an assistance. That is the goal in the Christian community—to embrace one another in the unity of love and the bond of peace, so that the counsel of the larger body is truly for the best of the individual and the well-being of the whole.

Asian churches, in general, have the added problem that they are composed of a majority of young people (partly as a reflection of the demographics of the larger culture). As a result, many churches that we encountered do not have enough people to assist the pastor in leadership (usually as elders) because not many persons are old enough or wise enough.

Because the culture calls for listening to the counsel of community members with authority, one seminary professor told me, this puts tremendous pressure on the pastors. As a result, a large percentage of them burn out and leave the ministry. Similarly, the notion of shame can be hard on pastors because people judge them adversely if their families have any problems.

In another conversation, Peter from Singapore pointed out another problem of communal guidance—namely, that a person's obedience to the authority of elders, parents, or pastors might become mere outward compliance. Moses from Hong Kong agreed, but he emphasized that Christians in general knew that their higher authority was in God, so they took very seriously those who were in leadership over them and under God.

Moses' remark makes apparent one gift of the Christian community to counterbalance the enormous responsibility pastors and elders bear in their leadership roles. Because they are shepherding the community under the authority of God and the Church of which Christ is the Head, they can place themselves in turn under the leadership of the whole Church throughout time and space in order to gain more wisdom. They can also more readily confess to the congregation their failures and burdens because they are truly trying to serve under God and not attempting to take the place of God.

In a completely different direction, my friend Carol Barrera, the translator who works with the Achí people in Guatemala, pointed out a problem that missionaries can have when they live in a communal culture. She disclosed this difficulty that she encountered:

> There is also a strong sense that it is inappropriate to single out someone for special attention. For instance, if you can't afford to build a nice house for everyone, don't do it for *anyone.* After the earthquake of '76 the majority of people needed to rebuild. It was acceptable to give a little to everyone, but not a lot to a few.
>
> We found this out the hard way. Friends in the States gave us some funds to administer. Our idea was to choose three or four "worthy" families and build them simple, decent houses. People hated us *and* them. (Jealousy?) The next gift we got, we consulted with a leader. He suggested giving everyone a pittance. We did. Everyone was happy (except us, because we felt we had helped *no one,* really).

Carol's observations enable us to perceive how different is the outcome when people think of themselves as part of a whole. Then everyone is responsible for the well-being of everyone else. That is hard for us to understand if we have been formed by the individualism and the sense of who is "deserving" that prevail in North America. After thirty years of serving with the Achí, Carol realizes that the word *worthy* had to be put in quotation marks and that more is going on than simple jealousy when a few people are singled out for help; perhaps the issue also includes the problem of help from outsiders who are considered to be very rich and who, therefore, should help everyone. But we must also realize that the entire communal way of life of that culture challenges our ideas of how best to help and makes us acknowledge that perhaps encouragement of everyone might be a better goal.

In the same way, it is difficult for people formed by individualism to understand why the Maori person cited at the beginning of this chapter would not want her remarks to be interpreted as representative of the Maori people as a whole. People from that culture would not wish to be quoted and do not want in the slightest to be perceived as speaking "on behalf" of the Maori. There are two very important explanations for this. First, there is the issue of "authority" or *mana,* a more comprehensive word of the Maoris, who always ask which person has the *mana* to speak for the rest on a particular issue. Typically, the proper person would be a very senior person raised in the traditions of the culture. The notion of *mana,* I am told, is somewhat similar to the English concept of "prestige," although it additionally encompasses an amalgam of one's spiritual authority, lineage and people, age, competence, and learning.

I experienced the "catch-22" of *mana* when I was hoping to talk with a group of Maori people while I was in New Zealand. Those who were senior and would have had the authority to speak were not able to meet with me because of their own business and my conflicting speaking engagements, and those who would be more junior might not have really known enough about Maori cultural matters to recognize that they didn't have the *mana* to speak with me about them. In that case, their information would more likely be unreliable.

The other explanation for Maoris' reluctance to be quoted is one that gives me pause as I try to be appropriately sensitive in including pieces about their culture in this book. The Maori people have a rightful dread that comments could or would be construed as giving away their cultural treasures. North Americans can understand this if we regret that more and more cultural and intellectual property winds up on the Web regardless of copyright covenants.

Also, from historical experience the Maoris know that such betrayal of cultural gifts can come back and "bite" them in various ways. Again, North Americans might be able to understand that concern (though we cannot comprehend the pain of the Maoris' experiences) as we think about how Native Americans have been treated in the past and are still treated today. Or we witness betrayals of the Amish people and their way of life when the media continually invade their homelands and exploit audiences' curiosity about their "strangenesses." The most extreme case of this might be the inclusion of Amish youths in a television reality show attempting to disclose how they might adapt to "the rest of the world" and yet displaying no genuine consideration for their faith life and cultural treasures.

As I share cultural gifts in this book for the sake of our learning better skills of discernment, please receive and handle those treasures with respect. They are introduced in these chapters for the sake of our mutual growth in wisdom, faith, and life and therefore should never be taken lightly or in a way that does not honor those from whom we receive them. It is especially important to say these things in this chapter, which concentrates on the gifts of the community for our discernment processes. This entire book is intended to be a sampling of treasures from the global community so that people whose methods of discernment are primarily individualistic and characterized by values taken from the technological consumerist milieu in which we live can receive better tools and make better decisions for the well-being of the whole world.

BIBLICAL EMPHASIS ON COMMUNAL DISCERNMENT

In Chapter Three we met Jethro, Moses' father-in-law, who exhorted Moses to appoint trustworthy, God-fearing people who could care for the *shalom* of the people they served, who would not seek dishonest gain, and who would share Moses' burden. This was one of the first examples in this book of the importance of communal help for the sake of making better decisions. We have encountered other examples from the Scriptures and from other cultures in the earlier chapters.

One of the most important reasons for seeking communal instruction for discernment is apparent in the very writing of the Bible. Almost all of its verbs outside narratives of Jesus are plural. With the exception of the books Timothy, Titus, and Philemon, which were written to those individuals, most of the rest of the Bible's instructions to discern, choose, make wise decisions, and so forth are primarily in the plural. We are more likely to discern and decide wisely if we do it in the midst of the community.

For example, in the book of Proverbs, fools are so named because they "despise wisdom and instruction" from others (1:7b). The wise are urged ever to continue to "hear and gain in learning" (1:5a). We can never know enough to act on our own. We always need the greater wisdom of the whole community.

One special note in the Scriptures helps us particularly realize the immense value of gaining communal wisdom for discernment. The apostle Paul's list of spiritual gifts in 1 Corinthians 12:7–11 specifically cites "discernment of spirits" as one of those gifts (v. 10). This means that in the Christian community there are persons who have a remarkable gift to ascertain whether a certain mode of action is from God or from other spirits—such as those of the society which envelops us.

I have had the wonderful experience more than once of a group of members in the Christian community helping me to see whether a choice I was making fit in with God's purposes or seemed to come instead more from my own inner longings or from pressures on me from the outside. Such gifts of others' discernment were invaluable in steering me away from selfishness and the values of society into more godly choices, choices that reflect the God and people to whom I belong.

Furthermore, Paul's enumeration of spiritual gifts (charisms) lists various other endowments from the Holy Spirit that contribute to better discernment. Charisms such as wisdom, knowledge, prophecy, and healing can all be beneficial to enlighten us, prod us, console us in our decision processes. Sometimes we need to be built up in order to choose well. Other times we need to be spurred. And often we need healing of past wounds before we can make better choices for the future. All together, members of the Christian community provide many gifts that bring about greater wholeness in ourselves and the entire body so that the best decisions possible can be made by all of us. Only within such a framework of community can we really discover our spiritual calling and true selves.

Throughout, the Scriptures call God's people—both Jews in the Hebrew Bible/First Testament and Christians in the Second/New Testament—to become a community characterized by faithfulness to God and love for God and the neighbor. In addition, many attributes of the people of God are named or described. These include such traits as that they should be a community of hospitality, generosity, reconciliation, suffering, and celebration—traits that we will ponder in the last chapters of this book as especially helpful for godly discernment and still exemplified in cultures throughout the world.

The New Testament book of the Acts of the Apostles demonstrates all these traits. We notice the hospitality of such people as Lydia, who welcomes Paul and Luke (the writer of Acts uses the word *we*) and perhaps Silas and others (Acts 16:13–15) and the church (v. 40) to her home. We observe the generosity of Barnabas, who sold a field that belonged to him and gave all the money for the use of the apostles and the church (Acts 4:36–37). We see many of the apostles suffering at various times, but we also glimpse as many examples of great celebration throughout the book.

One especially wonderful example of reconciliation that offers supreme guidance for communal discernment takes place in Acts 15. Certain people in the fledgling church were stirring up a disturbance because they didn't want new believers to be welcomed without their undergoing circumcision according to the Jewish law. Consequently, the apostle Paul and his companion Barnabas, Peter and the other disciples of Jesus, and the elders in the community assemble together to consider the matter.

After Paul and Barnabas give a complete report (15:12), James suggests a way to proceed that negates the necessity for circumcision (vv. 13–21), and then the apostles and the elders make a decision on how to move forward—with the consent of the whole church (v. 22). When they compose a letter, they write to the believers who were confused because of the troublemakers, "For it has seemed good to the Holy Spirit and to us to impose on you no further burden than these essentials" (v. 28).

This sentence signals two indispensable ingredients in communal discernment: a corporate seeking of the mind of God and a consensus of the whole group that God's will has been discovered by the power of the Holy Spirit—in this case, that new Christians need not first obey Jewish law. Two examples of these intentions to seek God's mind by consensus in contemporary communal discernment will be given at the end of this chapter, after we turn to see the corporate life of various fellowships in other cultures of the world.

CELTIC AND MONASTIC COMMUNITIES

The ancient Celtic traditions make clear what the Bible only subtly suggests—namely, that God's people belong in a community as a response to, and in imitation of, the Trinity, which is a perfect community. The Bible only hints at this in the Genesis 1 creation account (as we saw in our discussion of the Trinity in Chapter One) when God, Who is not yet revealed as three named Persons, says, "Let us make humankind in our image" (Genesis 1:26). If we grasp that to be in the image of God involves relationship, then we are violating the very substance of our creation when we try to live and act, discern and choose on our own.

The Celts loved the Trinity profoundly. Many of the prayers of the Celts are deeply trinitarian; they usually name the Father, the Son, and the Holy Spirit, often in choruses with a common refrain after each Person is named and described. Then, many of these prayers and songs widen out to emphasize the community of believers. Thus the faithful, influenced by Celtic traditions, are formed to think in terms of communal life.

In his book on Celtic spirituality from Wales, Patrick Thoms quotes a wonderful saying, *"Cadw ty mewn cwmwl tystion,"* which means "keeping house in a cloud of witnesses."[4] The phrase *cloud of witnesses* refers to this exhortation in Hebrews 12:1–2:

> Therefore, because we are surrounded by so great a cloud
> of witnesses, let us also lay aside every weight and the sin
> that clings so closely, and let us run with perseverance the
> race that is set before us, looking to Jesus the pioneer and
> perfecter of our faith, who for the sake of the joy that was
> set before Him endured the cross, disregarding its shame, and
> has taken His seat at the right hand of the throne of God.

This exhortation follows right after a long list of faithful saints in the First Testament, who died while still looking forward to the fulfillment of all of God's promises. If we "keep house" in the midst of this cloud of witnesses, of course, we will be encouraged by their faith and trust to persevere in the challenges of our own lives.

Thus, the Celtic saying invites us to live in the company of all the saints—both those alive and sharing with us in the same community and also those who are already living fully in the presence of God. How much better we would discern if we were conscious that we dwelt in the midst of such a wise company as we together keep looking to Jesus, the pioneer and perfecter of our faith.

Besides being conscious in their discernment of the whole cloud of witnesses, monastic communities specialize in communal counsel. This has been true from the beginnings of Christianity, for it arose from Jewish roots, which are communal. Jesus Himself called twelve to be "with Him" as His closest community (Mark 3:13–19), sent out the seventy not alone but in pairs (Luke 10:1), and promised to be among them where two or three are gathered together in His name (Matthew 18:20).

At the beginnings of monasticism when Christianity needed reform, the Desert Fathers and Mothers, the first monastics in the fourth and fifth centuries in the Middle East, soon began gathering into communities that reached out with the Gospel to the people around them. The Good News of the Trinity would be more convincing to the society around us today if Christian communities were stronger in their sense of belonging to one another, in their care for each other, and in the vitality of their witness made possible by deeper discernment of who they are and how they might serve the world.

Francis of Assisi knew that his crucial decision concerning whether to remain in solitude or to preach required the counsel of the community. He sent brother Masseo to ask his two deeply spiritual friends Clare and Sylvester for their discernment—and they both said, "Preach!" He obeyed, believing that their wisdom was the word of the Lord.

Monastics, in general, model deep belonging together so well! At the Benedictine community in Minnesota where I go for retreats, I can hear lavish spiritual unity especially when the sisters sing psalms together, for the blend of their voices is deepened because of the profound fellowship of their life together—just as the unity of a touring concert choir becomes more sumptuous the longer the members live together and grow in their knowledge of each other and their affection for one another.

In Chapter Four, I mentioned a card the sisters gave me which lists the Core Benedictine Values. One of the first specified is "*Community:* We are committed to respecting each individual, forming stable relationships, receiving counsel from the community and affirming the common good." Notice that a major aspect of communal life is that an individual's discernment involves the counsel of one's sisters or brothers or both.

For this to happen outside the monastery and in local Christian communities, two essentials must be in place. There must be a community skilled in, and willing to, give counsel. And the individual must be open to the wisdom of the larger body and ready to receive it. Does the first exist in your church home?[5] Does the second exist in you?

People in North America hunger for community but don't know how to find it or build it. In addition, many societal forces keep folks from being together for more than mere acquaintanceship. Perhaps we would find more motivation to work at building community if we could sample some cases from other cultures of communal care and if we could see how communal discernment might be conducted.

COMMUNAL DISCERNMENT— LATIN AMERICA

One day in Guatemala an Achí choir, made up entirely of volunteers, traveled for many hours in overloaded boats and then hiked many more hours across mountains to a remote village to teach people Christian songs in their own language. When they finally got there late in the day, they saw that the congregation needed to plaster their church building, so the Achí choir decided to carry sand from the river and get to work. The local people didn't think it could be done, but the choir corporately took the lead and the project was finished. That dramatic incident sent by my friend Carol Barrera displays graphically the positive side of communally dependent decision making.

It is hard to believe that the choir did all this after such an arduous journey. Such an immense gift seems to me to be possible only in cultures formed in habits of communal care and profound faith-put-into-action. The choir members decided together ("It seemed good to the Holy Spirit and to us") that they could be the ones to help the congregation with its much-needed construction work.

COMMUNAL DISCERNMENT— AFRICAN COMMUNITIES

Barbara Robertson, who was introduced in Chapter One, wrote from Haydom Lutheran Hospital in Tanzania that the people with whom she worked employ several gifts of the community when making decisions. From the cloud of witnesses, they use a lot of African proverbs and seek direction through the Scriptures. Also, besides spending much time in prayer until their hearts feel settled and at peace, they discuss the issue with trusted and respected people.

Another missionary, whom I met at a conference and who served in Asia and also in Tanzania for many years, reports that when he was first in Tanzania, the head evangelist in an area (someone who had been to Bible school and was responsible for supervising several local evangelists) told him that after the worship service in a village congregation they would be going to the home of a young couple who needed some counseling.

He was surprised that the entire church council of the congregation went to that couple's home. When they arrived, the elders simply told the young man what he was doing wrong and what he needed to do right. When they had finished telling him what they had discerned together, they went home.

The missionary pastor (who hadn't needed to say a word) was quite surprised at the elders' forthrightness and the young man's openness, respect for, and obedience to, the elders. In fact, a year later, when the pastor visited that village again, the young man came to him after the worship service and thanked him for saving his marriage!

Another story that this pastor told me gives us insight into the source of that young man's receptivity and respect. In the small Tanzanian town where the pastor and his wife lived, there was no electricity, and the economy was bad so many people could not afford to buy kerosene for their lamps to obtain light after dark. Because the people did not go out after dark, the missionaries wondered what folks did in their dark houses without radios or televisions or lights.

The pastor asked a small neighbor boy one day what he and his family did at home after dark. He wrote that the small boy "gave me an incredulous look that said, 'Where are you coming from?' His answer was simple, 'We talk.' My immediate reaction to that was, 'You lucky kid!' Every evening he sat with his extended family and talked."

How much it might change our respect for one another and our receptivity to one another's counsel if we spent evenings together talking and learning to listen! How much more accurately we might discern our right place in the world if we learned better from others who we truly are!

My husband's fifth-grade students always rebelled initially when national "Turn Off the TV" week came around, but usually by the end of the week they were discovering all sorts of wonderful things about their families and themselves. Maybe some of our gadgets are destructive to our communal life and ought to be viewed with greater caution.[6]

In Alexander McCall Smith's novel *Tears of the Giraffe,* Mma Ramotswe can't imagine what it would be like if a person were not closely connected to a community of any kind. She realizes that for unfathomable reasons, some "white people" seemed to be content without relationships, but she envisions that they must be terribly lonely—"like spacemen deep in space, floating in the darkness, but without even that silver, unfurling cord that linked the astronauts to their little metal womb of oxygen and warmth."[7]

How dreadful that image makes the lives of many of us seem. I went back to a family reunion in Wisconsin a few years ago and was deeply moved to reconnect with my mother's first cousins and their children and grandchildren, cousins twice and three times removed from me, but immediately close as kin. One of Mom's cousins gave me pictures of my mother as a child. I am overjoyed now to display in my dining area a portrait of my mother together with her mother, grandmother, and great-grandmother. That connects me to four older generations of my people and a way of life on the farm from which I am too much detached.

How grateful I am, therefore, that in the church community I have another web of relationships—new brothers and sisters, aunts and uncles in Christ—from whom I can receive counsel and guidance. But it will take a great deal of work to build most churches into the kind of community that makes genuine relational discernment possible.

We loved it that for several years my husband and I were able to belong to an African-American congregation in which we were uncle and auntie to all the children of the community. I miss that communal intimacy, which is more naturally a part of Africans' understanding of themselves. Only such a culture in which all the people perceive themselves more communally than personally could make possible such an entity as South Africa's Truth and Reconciliation Commission.[8]

ASIAN PATTERNS OF COMMUNITY

That the Chinese people value "collective wisdom" is illustrated by some proverbs sent to me by Daniel Chan, the translator from Hong Kong introduced in Chapter Three. The first is "Three mediocrities with their wits combined is better than Zhuge Liang, the mastermind." Daniel explains that Zhuge Liang, a very famous historical figure in China, was the prime minister of a kingdom in the era of the "Three Kingdoms" (A.D. 220–280). The story of his famous talents in the military and elsewhere has become popular among the Chinese through a historical novel called *The Romance of the Three Kingdoms.*

Two other proverbs accentuate the importance of the elderly being part of that collective wisdom. "If one does not take heed to the advice of the aged, one will soon suffer losses" and "An old person is like a treasure to the family." Would that the input of senior citizens were more widely valued in North America and the elderly themselves more passionately cherished as active members of the community!

In addition to the Chinese tradition of asking for blessings from the elders, as mentioned in Chapter Four, the missionaries who were introduced there, Kaori Chua (Japanese) and her Chinese (Singaporean) husband, How Chuang Chua, described for me the supreme valuing in Japan of relational harmony and consideration for others. They said that these moral values lead to a strong sense of community. Many Japanese argue that individuals should not act outside of the group, as is emphasized by the Japanese proverb "The nail that sticks up will be hammered down."

We might say that such communal care is essential in such a supremely crowded land as Japan, where the world's seventh-largest population of 125 million people dwells in a small area in which only 10 percent of the land is livable. But such dense conditions would not necessarily lead to the wonderful Japanese process called *nemawashi* (pronounced "nay-mah-wah-she"), which means that one talks to everybody.

Kaori explained that *nemawashi* literally emphasizes "circling around." She gave the example of the process of transplanting a big tree. About one or two years before the transplant, the person desiring it will dig up the surrounding soil and leave a big main root, but cut off all the little roots. In the same way, a leader will deal with little problems by settling them so that there is less controversy in making a major decision.

Kaori said that Japanese culture can overuse or abuse the word *nemawashi* if one avoids talking to those people who might object to a certain course of action. However, when the process is positively employed, it really keeps harmony. Then the group can modify a decision according to the needs of those who disagree. Kaori's husband, How Chuang, confessed that at first he thought this process took too much time, but gradually he realized that at the end there are better decisions made and more harmony achieved.

Imagine what might happen in North American culture if participants in a group decision-making process did not try to resolve the issues hastily by means of majority vote but instead "circled around" and heard all the concerns of everyone present so that whatever was causing apprehension could be addressed.

THE AUSTRALIAN EMPHASIS ON COMMUNITY

The positive side of a sense of community equality was pointed out to me by a native of Australia, whom I met when she was serving as the chaplain at St. Deiniol's Library in Hawarden, Wales (where I was studying monastic founders for this project). Kathy said that her Aussie compatriots have one advantage over North Americans and Europeans in their cultural habits because the first immigrants were originally convicts who resented what they called the "tall poppies," people of influence and power. To this day, she reported (and my teaching experiences in Australia confirm it), the whole nation has an ethos of equality. Kathy and I both long for that equity to be fully extended to the Aboriginal people, and we have seen evidence that now that goal is increasingly becoming the case. The phrase "We wouldn't want to be a 'tall poppy'" is quite common and underscores the ethos that no one in Australia wants to be elevated above one's peers.

Of course, there can be disadvantages to this ethos if it causes people to cease striving for excellence or if it leads to a dearth of leaders. Every good habit or practice sketched in this book can become negative if taken to an extreme.

In a conversation with me and more thoroughly in a paper he wrote, Chris Gilbert, also a native Aussie, highlighted the idea of "mateship" as a chief social value of Australia. People will go to great lengths—even dying—for their mates because this is such a strong community ideal. One important hero for the Aussies is a Private Simpson who used a donkey to carry wounded men out from Gallipoli and died in the process.

Gallipoli was the site of a disastrous offensive in which, alongside British and French troops, a large number of volunteers from the Australian and New Zealand Army Corps (ANZAC) tried vainly (largely because of bungled leadership) to launch a campaign against the forces of the Ottoman Empire in the Dardanelles, the area of a Turkish peninsula on the Mediterranean, southwest of Istanbul. April 25, 1915, the date of the invasion in which both sides suffered severe losses, is remembered and celebrated each year by New Zealand and Australia as Anzac Day for its contribution to the national identity of both.

All wars have heroes and significant legends of folks who went to great lengths for their comrades. However, the fact that for Australia a primary story of national identity is not one of a famous leader or a mighty person but of a private who sacrificed to care for his mates illustrates the greater emphasis in that country on equality and community.

MENNONITE DISCERNMENT OF THE SPIRIT

The religious denomination in which I have experienced the deepest sense of equality and community and the most skilled culture of discernment is the Mennonites. Two different processes which they customarily use—one for community decisions and one for private, individualized ones (with communal guidance)—offer tremendous potential for all of us to make better choices because we are given the counsel of a caring fellowship.

Recall that in Acts 15 the early Christians made a decision about new Gentile members because "it seemed good to the Holy Spirit and to us" (v. 28). This biblical precedent underlies the Mennonite practice of finding consensus when a congregation needs to make a decision.

I experienced this process of consensus gathering first when I wanted to join a Mennonite congregation (for reasons to be explained in the next chapter) during the time that I lived in South Bend, Indiana, to do graduate studies at the University of Notre Dame. Because I had been baptized as an infant in the Lutheran church of my family heritage, the leaders determined that the question of my membership in their community should be a matter of congregational consensus. (I was always welcome to visit, but membership is taken much more seriously in Mennonite churches because both the congregation and the new member make serious commitments to each other to care for one another and to participate in the mission of the community together.)

On the morning of the discernment process, I was asked to make a brief presentation of the importance to me of my infant baptism and of the nature of my faith in God as a result, because Mennonites actually first arose in protest to the requirement (often without faith) of infant baptism in countries where the state churches demanded it. In response to my faith statement, all the congregation members, who were seated at tables of eight, wrote down what they believed was the best procedure to follow concerning my request for membership.

I, who had never experienced such an event before, found the process exceedingly interesting. At their tables, the individuals wrote down and passed their comments to the person on the left so that everyone's remarks were read aloud objectively by another person. Then each table came to a consensus about whether or not my membership appeal should be accepted. Then the consensus of each table was brought to the entire group, and a final consensus was reached to invite me into membership.

In connection with that decision I learned that the process of consensus building does not necessarily mean that everyone has to concur exactly as an agreement is being formulated. All reservations are included in the final process. One member of the community, a philosophy professor, told me his concern that technically I could not be an "Anabaptist" (or one who denies the validity of infant baptism and chooses instead to be "baptized again"—the literal meaning of the word—as an adult). Nonetheless, he thought it was a good idea for me to be a member of the community (and, in fact, he and his wife were the ones who gave me a ride to worship and Bible class each week). Because of how valuable my baptism as an infant has been to me throughout my life, I totally agreed with his reservation and was and am delighted to participate with him and the other members in the community's mission in the world for my years in South Bend and still today by prayer from a distance.

The ritual in which the community and I made our membership promises to each other was equally moving to me, and I still consider myself deeply connected to that community even though I moved far away many years ago. Last year it was my privilege to preach for a Sunday morning worship service there, and I felt equally welcomed and at home with those dear friends.

Many of the reasons for my close connections with that Mennonite community will be mentioned in the next chapter, but here it is important to present another example of group decision making that powerfully affected my life and that offers to us all the possibilities of a great resource for better discernment.

There came a time when I wasn't sure I should continue in my graduate studies at Notre Dame, so one Sunday morning I asked the Mennonite pastor to pray for me as I tried to make a decision. He said, "I'll do better than that— I'll call a meeting to discern the Spirit." I had never heard that language before so I was eager to learn what a "meeting to discern the Spirit" was.

One evening soon thereafter ten or so good friends in the congregation gathered with me in someone's home. The leader explained that those community members would pray with me and ask me questions, that there might be long periods of silence in which people would ponder what they heard and would listen for the Holy Spirit's voice. After the process began with prayer for the Holy Spirit's guidance and for harmony in our mutual interaction, the group asked me to explain the decision before me and some of the reasons for my confusion. Then the questions began.

Some of the people asked me to clarify things I had said. Others wanted to know more about me, my goals and dreams, and needs that I observed in the world. Interspersed with fruitful silences, their inquiries seemed to be like a funnel channeling the issues into more orderly patterns than they had been in my own mind. I was overwhelmed that these friends were willing to give up an evening to help me so carefully to sort through my thoughts and options.

Near the end of the evening, the woman who gave me rides on Sunday mornings asked the question "How do you envision your life?" My reply, "As a bridge," led to the further query, "What kind of a bridge?" I answered that I tried to serve as a bridge between denominations of Christians, between sides in denominational arguments, between the old and the young, between Christians and people of other faiths, between scholars and lay people.

She responded, "A bridge needs to be planted on both sides of the river." When I didn't understand that remark, she continued, "You are planted firmly on the lay people's side with your work in churches and through conferences and such, but what plants you firmly on the scholarly side?"

It was like a lightbulb went on. Suddenly, it was clear that my previous graduate degrees in several fields weren't sufficient, that it really was most desirable to bring my work together into a fusion through the Ph.D. program in which I was involved. When I voiced that insight, the rest of the group commented on their reactions, and, in the end, a consensus was reached, my decision was made, and final prayers of blessing sealed the finding.

What an amazing and Joy-full process! I promised myself after that evening that I would never make a major decision alone again. Ever since, members of the Christian community in scattered places have asked questions, prayed with and for me, and shared insights in various meetings to discern the Spirit on both minor matters and such important life issues as whether or not to accept my husband's proposal of marriage and whether or not to accept offers for faculty positions. Each time someone's question has provided a turning point, and the answers to my choices have become clear.

The Christians Equipped for Ministry (CEM) board, the group of seven people that oversees my work as a freelance theologian and determines the use of all of CEM's funds, makes all of its decisions by consensus. If consensus is not reached on a particular matter, the group spends time in prayer and then discusses the issue again. If consensus is still not reached, the subject is tabled until a later meeting. We have never failed to reach total consensus on any matter for the twenty-seven years of CEM's existence. The practice of communal discernment has become indispensable to us.

Two other elements of the discernment processes—both for corporate, public decisions and for personal choices— should be pointed out for the sake of future possibilities of using these two processes in your own decision making. First, the Mennonite ideal is that no one speaks unless he or she can say, "I believe that the Holy Spirit is giving me this to say for the well-being of the community"—and the well-being of the individual if the subject is a personal matter. That practice prevents anyone from speaking too hastily or too selfishly.

In the other practice, the leader will purposely call on the quiet ones in the group to ask them what the Spirit might be teaching them for the benefit of the rest. That way, everyone is encouraged to participate in the process. The practice prevents anyone from dominating the conversation.

Both of these practices were evident in the two acts of discernment described in this section. When I mention these practices and processes in public lectures or discussions, any Mennonites present usually remind me that I shouldn't praise them too much (Mennonites generally are very humble) because they, too, don't always live up to their ideal practices. However, even as the New Zealanders and the Aussies in general manifest the character of attention to equality and mateship as portrayed in the preceding section, so Mennonites by and large seem to pay more attention to hearing what the Holy Spirit is saying through each and all members of the community, without any one voice dominating, so that communal discernment can flourish for the sake of reaching consensus together.

It is my prayer that this chapter has whetted your appetite for deeper involvement in community and for the gifts of a community for your own (and perhaps your church's) decision-making processes. When we know more profoundly and listen more attentively to the God and the people to whom we belong, we make better decisions that reflect the character of that community and that God. In the final four chapters of this book we will look at some very helpful elements of communal character that enable the results of our discernment processes to be more beneficial for ourselves, our communities, and the whole world.

6

A Culture of Welcoming

The desolation that Valentine's Day was dreadful. I was afraid of the men who were hanging around the airport terminal in Monterrey, Mexico, and the contact person who had invited me to come for several speaking engagements had not shown up. Equipped only with a two-high-school-textbooks-in-five-weeks understanding of Spanish and almost two thousand miles away from my fiancé of two weeks, I wondered why on earth I had come. After an interminable wait (probably not more than half an hour), spent mostly trying to figure out how to ask in Spanish for a flight back to Houston, I was elated to see my host arrive, waving his arm out the car window, beaming a brilliant welcome, and full of plans for my time in Saltillo and elsewhere.

As I spoke for youth groups and Bible studies, a pastors' conference, and village worship services, it became very clear why I had come: I needed to learn from my new Mexican friends the meaning of hospitality.

People everywhere gave me their best rooms, their warmest blankets (it was unexpectedly cold and rainy), their best food, and their supreme kindness when I was so slow in learning to understand and answer back. Children from the village church shrieked with delight when they saw me taking a walk near their school during recess; they eagerly introduced me to their friends and taught me new words. At the church building they were always calling to me, *"Ven, ven"*—Come, come!—and taking my hand to help me (my leg was newly crippled), for there were exciting things to show me, secrets to share, and places to go where we hadn't yet been.

One evening near the end of my stay when my language was somewhat improved through the people's gracious instructions, one of my new friends met me as I was setting out for a walk. She invited me to come see her home, chatted gaily about her few special treasures so that I could enjoy their beauty and her genial welcome, and then insisted on walking me back again to where I was staying. It was obvious that she was more delighted to welcome me and more eager and generous to share her few possessions than are most people in my homeland who own a vastly greater share of the world's bounties.

This has been my experience wherever I have gone in the world to teach. I'm always astounded by the colossal hospitality and phenomenally sacrificial generosity with which strangers are welcomed in other cultures. To be that way is intrinsic to the character of many peoples in the world, and it affects the way they make their decisions.

I'm not saying that North Americans are not generous. For example, I have experienced numerous kindnesses from many people who have gone out of their way to care for my husband and me since my kidney transplant. It simply seems that if we were more aware of the huge discrepancies between the income and possessions of a high proportion of people who live in the United States compared with the rest of the nations, North Americans could not—especially Christians who intend to follow Jesus could not—tolerate the differences and would endeavor to do all we can to put our own resources more thoroughly into the service of building justice in the world.

You might wonder why this is important in a book on spiritual discernment. In this and the following chapters I am concerned about the character out of which we make our decisions. Is it our propensity to make decisions that might cost us but will benefit instead a great number of others? Is it in our character to let hospitality, welcoming, generosity, and kindness take priority over concern for self and our own comfort? And when we make decisions that lead to congeniality and charity, then our character becomes more formed to discern ways that we can be generously hospitable to those near us and even those far away.

I am ashamed to admit that my character tends toward securing my own welfare first. I can rationalize that really well and say that it is necessary for me to take care of my health first so that I am well enough to start investing in concern for others—but I know that such thinking can easily become merely an excuse for selfishness.

Perhaps you struggle, too, to become more hospitable and charitable and to make decisions that are welcoming and generous toward others. (If not, maybe you could skip this chapter.) I pray that the stories in these pages will inspire us, possibly shake us out of our lethargy, perhaps even begin to transform us more into the likeness of Jesus, Whose welcoming generosity and graciousness went to the most extreme lengths for us. If we would become more like He is, then our discernment would more easily flow toward the upbuilding of others and the establishment of genuine justice in the world. The more we are formed into Christ's likeness, the more deeply we know the eschatological Joy of being ever more generous and hospitable in the image of the Triune God.

To become formed more in God's image is, of course, to become more truly ourselves and to belong more deeply to God and God's people. God created us for love and not selfishness, for hospitality and not isolation, for generosity and not stinginess, for service and sacrifice, goodness and grace. Thus spiritual director David Benner describes our true selves:

> Our vocation is always a response to a Divine call to take our place in the kingdom of God. Our vocation is a call to serve God and our fellow humans in the distinctive way that fits the shape of our being. In one way or another, Christian calling will always involve the care of God's creation and people. This realigns us to the created world and to our neighbor, moving us from self-centered exploitation to self-sacrificing service and stewardship.[1]

It is a wonderful interconnection to think about stewardship in terms of hospitality and generosity. Often, supposed stewardship leads to stinginess, a way of thinking that we must store up enough so that there is plenty for our own future. In this chapter we will explore instead a habit of stewardship that is open-hearted and directed toward spreading graciousness and resources around now for the sake of the well-being of everyone in the present.

WHAT KEEPS US FROM HOSPITALITY AND GENEROSITY?

When I was a child, we never locked our doors. We felt safe to walk the streets in the dark because the whole town was hospitable. We belonged to each other. We sat on the porch swing in the evenings and visited with neighbors and strangers who might be walking by. Anyone who came was welcomed into our homes, and people would simply drop in for a visit if they were in the neighborhood. Everyone seemed ready at any time to bring food to anyone in need.

I'm not romanticizing the past; everyone is aware that these days are different and more precautions are required. My point is simply to ask whether we have to let fear dominate, or if we can be hospitable to strangers and, especially, more hospitable to those in need. One of the great gifts that arose from the tragedies associated with the spate of extensively powerful hurricanes that hit the Americas in the fall of 2005 is that a large number of people opened their homes to strangers. In response to those storms and the disastrous earthquake that struck Pakistan and its neighbors shortly thereafter, many opened their wallets, purses, and resources to help.

According to the United Nations, however, the response of the world to the Pakistani crisis has been inadequate; many are still without shelter as the cold winter comes. Just now I heard a BBC news report that the UN is asking for donations of $4.7 billion in order to help those suffering from war, famine, and natural disasters. UN General Secretary Kofi Annan said that this amount represents only forty-eight hours of global military spending or two cups of coffee per rich person.

What could help those of us who have a home, clothing, and plenty to eat to realize that we are those rich people? How can the wealthy nations of the world learn greater generosity? It would profoundly change the world if such character were formed in us that our immediate reaction to needs would be mercy and our instantaneous impulse toward others would be to be welcoming and receptive. The questions we must face concern both the kind of character it takes to discern better ways to address the crises of the world and also the sort of motivation that would impel us to act on what we discern. How can we learn more profoundly that all of us belong together to humankind?

In a fifty-page series of articles, *Time* magazine presented a feature section on "Saving 1 Life at a Time"—medical crises around the world and people who are doing something about them, including Bill and Melinda Gates, who have given more than $6 billion toward global health through their foundation. Nonetheless, author Nancy Gibbs reminds us, "We Americans like to see ourselves as a generous people, but the rest of the world sees us differently. Among advanced countries, the U. S. ranks last in foreign aid development giving as a percentage of national income."[2]

It is odd that this is so, because the United States is thought to be a Christian country. Nationally, the amount of development giving is low partly because of a disproportionately high military budget. On the individual level, we must each ask what percentage of our income we give for the sake of others and how much we think we "need" for ourselves. How much do we have to possess?

Many religious and social commentators have observed that the main issue is whether we view the world from a feeling of scarcity or from a conviction of abundance. If we approach life from a stance of scarcity, then we will worry that we won't get our *share* and will do all we can to acquire whatever we think is necessary to secure our future. If we believe that there is an abundance, then we will be more ready to *share* and will not be desperate to stockpile goods or love or whatever for ourselves. (Isn't it a funny sign of the times that the word *share* could be used in the last two sentences in connection with both hoarding and philanthropy?)

My goal in this chapter is simply to encourage each of us to ask ourselves whether we discern and live from scarcity or abundance. When a situation of need confronts us, is our character such that we will immediately work to discern how best we can assist? In situations with strangers, is our natural habit to look to discern how best we can welcome them? We are more likely to respond with gracious care if we belong to a community that is generous and hospitable. As Christians we are called together to reflect the embracing goodness of our God. Is our character such that our choices tend toward hospitality, generosity, graciousness? Perhaps the examples of those traits in this chapter could inspire us to develop such habits. Could our attitudes become more formed by the practice of gratitude overflowing in grace toward others?

THE BIBLICAL PRACTICES OF WELCOMING AND GENEROSITY

That last question hints at the primary emphasis in the Bible. The Scriptures overflow with examples of the hospitality and generosity of the God to Whom we belong. In thankful response, then, we are continually invited to be welcoming and unsparing in our giving to others. For example, the letter of James (1:5) underscores that God "gives to all generously and ungrudgingly" when he tells us to ask God for wisdom. In gratitude, people with true wisdom will make choices that imitate God's lavish bestowing of gifts.

In the apostle Paul's pleas to the Corinthians to give bountifully, he offers this as a basis for their own lavishness: "For you know the generous act of our Lord Jesus Christ, that though he was rich, yet for your sakes he became poor, so that by his poverty you might become rich" (2 Cor. 8:9). Many other passages in both testaments testify to the extravagant grace of God (see, for example, Romans 5:18–20 and 1 Timothy 1:14), with the result that we are invited to the

thanksgiving that leads to our own generosity, which produces more gratitude, and so on in a spiral (see 2 Cor. 4:15,
8:1–2 and Rom. 12:1–8, 2 Cor. 9:8–15).

The same is true for hospitality, which is another form
of generosity (and vice versa). We are invited by the Bible to
welcome, accept, receive others because God has previously
done that for us. Paul says to the Romans, "Welcome one another, therefore, just as Christ has welcomed you, for the
glory of God" (15:7; see also 14:1–3). Jesus is, after all, the
One Who welcomed the crowds who followed Him (even
though He had tried to withdraw privately) and Who "welcomes sinners and eats with them" (Luke 9:10–11 and 15:2).
He even washed the feet of Judas and perhaps also offered the
sacrament of His own body and blood to this disciple who
betrayed Him.[3]

Just after those events at the Last Supper and just before
Judas went out to lead Jesus' enemies to Him, Jesus extended
our understanding of hospitality by declaring:

> I tell you most solemnly,
>   whoever welcomes the one I send welcomes me,
>   and whoever welcomes me welcomes the one
>   who sent me. (John 13:20, *Jerusalem Bible*)

This is echoed elsewhere, such as when Jesus asserts that
"Whoever welcomes one such child in my name welcomes
me" (Matthew 18:5; see also 10:40–42).

As a result, the first Christians were extremely hospitable. Paul extended Jesus' assertion and told the slave
owner Philemon that he should welcome back his runaway
slave Onesimus as if he were receiving the apostle himself
(Philemon 17). Many other examples in the New Testament
letters encourage fellow Christians to embrace and support

one another (see Romans 16:2, Philippians 2:29–30, and Colossians 4:10), and the book of Acts is filled with cases of warm hospitality (Acts 15:3–4, 21:17, 28:7, and 28:30–31).

Reading the Bible also makes me think about how we greet people because that is usually our first opportunity to welcome someone. Do we merely say, "Hello," which doesn't mean anything more than the exclamation to attract attention ("Hollo") that gave rise to it? Something like "Good morning" is, at least, more courteous and initiates a wish for that greeting to be the case for the one addressed.

My favorite greeting in the Bible occurs in the book of Ruth, in which Boaz comes from Bethlehem to the harvest field and salutes the reapers, "The LORD be with you," and they answer, "The LORD bless you" (Ruth 2:4). Many churches still use this salutation and a response of "And also with you" in worship services, so that the community remembers that we are the people of God together—pastor or priest and congregation—in the presence of God and that we are committed to each other and responsible to and for each other. What a gracious welcome either phrase from the book of Ruth would provide as we encounter others; thereby we could extend reminders to them of God's presence and countless blessings. We ourselves would remember that we, together with those whom we greet, belong to a benevolent and hospitable God.

Similarly, the apostle Paul almost always reminds readers at the beginning of his letters of God's grace and peace by proffering those gifts to them. Many years ago when I met with a youth group for morning prayer and singing before its members crossed the street from the church building to their high school, some of the students decided to greet their school mates with phrases like "Grace to you" or "Peace be with you." They said it was a great reminder to themselves to recognize God's (hospitable) presence and (generous) gifts throughout their day.

Several years later I met a woman whose habit it was to answer her telephone with a brief moment of silence and then the gentle word "Peace." It always calmed me down to ring her! Her custom made me want to find a way to greet callers with such hospitality, but I knew that I couldn't make my voice as gentle as hers, so I began to answer the telephone with the phrase "I wish you Joy." Somewhat selfishly I must admit that perhaps the greatest benefit of this greeting has been to myself, for it forces me to check my attitude before I pick up the receiver. Do I recognize the presence of God, Who fills me with His Joy?

That is why I have introduced these paragraphs on the ways we greet people. Perhaps the words we choose can be reminders to us and gifts to others, even as we hope that our demeanor and actions are welcoming and hospitable, gracious and of a generous spirit.

EARLY CHRISTIAN SAINTS' PRACTICES OF HOSPITALITY AND GENEROSITY

We saw in the previous chapter that the ancient Celts highly valued community life because of their intense love for the Trinity. In this chapter we extend that notion to underscore that genuine community life in its very nature is characterized by the Trinity's hospitality and generosity. If we belong together, we will make sure that everyone is appropriately cared for, and we will be open to welcoming others to become part of the community also.

Once again for the purposes of this book, note the spiral between godly character and spiritual discernment. If one's character has been formed to imitate the God to Whom we belong in the Trinity's fullness of hospitality and generosity, then Joy-full choices will be made out of that character to welcome others and to treat them with goodness. Furthermore, the more one lives in such a way and the more one intentionally belongs to such a community, the more easily one will discern ways to be congenial and to give liberally. When one is confronted with choices, the person trained in the virtues of hospitality and generosity will prefer options that are gregarious and unselfish.

The most obvious example of this in recent times has been Mother Teresa and the Sisters of Mercy who are formed in the same character. They radiantly welcome the poor and the dying as if these people were Christ. This attitude is based in the parable of Jesus concerning His coming again in His glory to judge humankind. As King, the parable announces, the Son of Man will welcome into His kingdom those who fed and clothed Him, gave Him something to drink, welcomed and visited Him when He was sick or in prison. Those who are invited into the kingdom will ask:

> "When was it that we saw you hungry . . . or thirsty, . . .
> a stranger . . . or naked . . . sick or in prison . . . ?" And
> the king will answer them, "Truly I tell you, just as you
> did it to one of the least of these who are members of
> my family, you did it to me." (Matthew 25:37–40)

The rest of the parable emphasizes that those who have not received and welcomed others have not been gracious to Christ Himself (25:41–46).

This parable was probably also the basis for the following ancient Celtic poem:

> O King of stars!
> Whether my home be dark or bright,
> Never shall it be closed against anyone,
> Lest Christ close His home against me.[4]

What a wonderful culture of welcoming this poem represents—that someone would never close his or her doors against anyone, even if that person's home is filled with sorrow or gladness, poverty or bounty. I know that I find it much easier to be hospitable and generous if everything is going well for me. How could we develop such a character that we make choices for welcoming and goodness toward others no matter what is happening in our own lives?

One striking example of enormous hospitality was the first of Ireland's saints, Ciaran of Saighir, who was born at the beginning of the sixth century. Around 538 and after studying in Rome, he was ordained a bishop and returned to Ireland before Saint Patrick. The tales about Ciaran say that he was so gentle that even wild animals, such as a wild boar and others, gathered around him, as well as all the people who came to the well where he resided and had built a church and became fellow worshipers, monks, and nuns.[5]

Tales of saints, such as Mary of Egypt[6] and Ciaran and Francis of Assisi, who were so hospitable that animals were drawn to them, are common in the literature. Perhaps you have known people whose character was similarly gentle and inviting. Both the tales and the experience of such people caution those of us who live in highly technologized and urbanized cultures to be more aware of how our societal patterns endanger the habitats of wild creatures and put us at odds with our environment, rather than enabling us to be generous with the animals and hospitable to forces of nature (by, for example, reestablishing wetlands, tidal lands, and flood plains).

One manifestation of the type of "culture of hospitality" this chapter is advocating (and which I have more thoroughly experienced in less wealthy societies) is the deep ancient Celtic practice of "blessing" everyone (and perhaps everything) that one encounters. Of course, more deeply, this is part of the biblical command to bless one another, to bless our neighbors and enemies, and, thereby, to bless the name of the Lord. This practice brings an additional instrument to our repertoire of cultural habits for discernment because it would certainly make a great difference in our choices if we were always asking how what we decide will bless others and thereby bless God.

Sadly, the word *bless* is often misused in vague ways, but I mean the word here to connote bringing gladness and well-being to others. More deeply, the word signifies specific prayers and benedictions for God's grace and favor on others. In connection with God, we rejoice to know that our prayers and praises in corporate and private worship and our godly actions in daily life bring pleasure and blessings to God.

I raise this habit of blessing here because some of you reading this book might be afflicted with various handicaps or illnesses or difficulties in life that make it impossible for you to make any decisions at all except to survive (which is, in itself, a good decision and a sign of the presence of the God of life). Perhaps you are reading this book with the hopes of finding some means to discern a way forward in spite of all the obstacles you are encountering.

When all our energy has to be focused on staying alive or getting through an ordeal, those who struggle with chemotherapy or paralysis or imprisonment or any other hardships must delve deeply within themselves and draw on their inmost determination merely to continue existing and then to exist as well as possible. If we keep in mind the habit of blessing others to the glory of God, even situations of deprivation or affliction can lead to opportunities to let God's presence be radiated toward others as we survive.

For example, I had read about the Celtic habit of blessing others shortly before my kidney transplant. While recovering and in the worst phase of trying to get adjusted to the antirejection medications, which took all of my energy and time and left me feeling quite exhausted, the only "work" I could do was to try to compliment all the people who served me—nurses, doctors, hospital aids, floor sweepers, garbage collectors. When my body was struggling with side effects from overmedication, I tried out the habit and attempted to bless others by making some sort of comment about how well someone did her work or how healthful it was to have such a well-cleaned room or what a smooth injection he had just given me.

Some might say such blessings are patronizing, but they were genuine reactions to the gifts I had received first from the people's kind assistance. Those initial attempts sometimes led to new friendships, and—because many of the workers were from other countries—to delightful conversations about their home cultures.

The situations also made me ask myself how to become more hospitable to the service of others. It is hard to be dependent. How can we be generous to those on whose generosity we rely?

We are trained by our culture—and perhaps by our personality types—to be independent and proud, self-reliant and autonomous. What could form in us a humble character that leads us to discern how to be hospitable and generous with the people we need? That is an ability I long to develop.

To almost everyone's life will come times of dependence. What kind of character and what abilities to discern do we want to develop now so that in such periods of inadequacy and necessity we are able to be hospitable and generous? What choices might we want to make in our behaviors now to prepare us for such times?

Think again of the spiral (which will dominate the rest of the chapters in this book) between character and discernment. The more we make choices in godly directions, the more our character is formed to be people who will more easily discern godly options, attitudes, and habits. Furthermore, that spiral is intertwined with another and deepened when we belong to a community seeking to make godly choices, a community of people who long to reflect the character of the God to Whom we belong. Then that God and community become more formative of our character, and we will more often discern choices in keeping with the nature of that community and God who embrace us.

For the topic of this chapter we are greatly helped by the extraordinary sixth-century saint Benedict and his followers. Benedict himself was an enormously generous man. He not only established a monastery and wrote its rule, but also devoted much of his own time to the needs of the larger community by distributing alms and food to the poor.

Furthermore, a core value in his monastery—and thereby in other Catholic orders, because he is often called the father of monasticism—is, still to this day, hospitality. On

the "Core Benedictine Values" card first mentioned in Chapter Four, "Hospitality" is explicated in this way: "We seek to
respect all persons and to welcome them with warmth, acceptance and joy."

The habit of respect for each person and the goal of a
warmhearted and glad reception would surely lead us all to
greater hospitality. It certainly helps us if we see each person
as a representative of Christ. How might our growing gratitude to God for the fullness of the Trinity's blessings in our
lives enable us to discern new ways to be generous?

Sister Joan Chittister's book on living St. Benedict's
Rule today emphasizes that hospitality must be continually
practiced so that it is there for the isolated instance when it
is sorely needed. She writes that it "doesn't exist unless we go
out of ourselves for someone else at least once a day." For that
reason her chapter on the subject is subtitled, "The Un-
boundaried Heart," and she cites the fifty-second chapter of
Benedict's Rule to highlight "honor, courtesy, and love" as
the "hallmarks" required for "hospitality of the heart."[7]

Sister Joan also complains that hospitality seems to be
defined these days as the graciousness of the affluent. She explains that "the biblical value of hospitality has been domes-
ticated and is now seen more as one of the social graces than
as a spiritual act and a holy event."[8]

The hospitality and the generosity I am seeking in this
chapter do not signify mere niceness, proper etiquette in high
places, giving from one's surplus, or kindness to one's supposed "inferiors." I am hoping that more of us can develop
the character of biblical hospitality and generosity, which are
spiritual acts that create holy events, full of the self-donation
of God's own gracious welcoming and charity toward us all.

Let us turn to some examples of habits of hospitality
and generosity in other cultures that might encourage us in

the formation of such a character and offer us possibilities by which we might better discern ways to be welcoming and benevolent.

THE INUKSHUK OF THE INUIT

In my writing study at home are two reminders of a wonderful welcoming practice for the Inuit people of Northern Canada. In Canada's most northern regions and territories, residents make an "Inukshuk" (pronounced "in-ook-shook" and meaning "in the image of man"), a lifelike figure of rock placed as a directional signal for travelers. Because the North's barren landscape makes it difficult for travelers to mark their way, these replicas of people stand as silent messengers showing the path, as guideposts for the journey. The card that came with one of the gifts to me says that the presence of the Inukshuk symbolizes the link we have to our natural surroundings and reminds us we are not alone. They stand as eternal symbols that people everywhere depend on one another and belong to each other. The fact that we need one another when we are on our way underscores how much we need one another throughout life.

The two models of the Inukshuk given to me also remind me of the great hospitality of their givers. One rendering of the Inukshuk, made of two kinds of maple wood and backed by a magnet (so it can show me the way into my filing cabinet!), was given by a very gracious welcomer when I gave a lecture series in Ontario. The other Inukshuk, made of metal and standing at the end of a letter opener, was given by the Salvation Army officers who serve with the Inuit and others in Alberta and the Northwest Territories. Their extraordinary hospitality and the generosity of their sacrificial

way of life in order to be present with the people of the Far
North were great models to my husband and me when we
were with them for their training retreat.

MAORI GREETINGS

Similarly, when I spoke for the commencement of Carey
Baptist College in New Zealand, it was very inspiring to me
that the program began with a *powhiri* (pronounced "po-fear-
ee"), a Maori celebratory chant to welcome strangers or special guests. A Maori professor from the school sang to greet
the principal of the college, the president of the school board,
me as the speaker, and the family and friends of the gradu-
ates. It was lively and inviting music, and the chanter was
enormously gracious—his facial expressions and gestures
helped us to grasp the significance of his Maori words.

The *powhiri* chant felt very ennobling. The singer's greeting lifted me up and encouraged me to do my best in gratitude for that warm reception. His *powhiri* also made me wish
that we white people did things more elegantly, with warmer
rituals of greeting and acknowledgment of our roles in serving each other.

I was hoping to participate also in a smaller gathering
with some Maori elders to learn more about their traditions,
but our schedules prevented that from happening. If it would
have been possible, it would not have been an individual
meeting, for the Maori way is to visit collectively. I'm told
that time would have been allowed for more formalities,
speeches, and singing and then talking would go on until
some sort of consensus would be reached about the matters
of discussion (see Chapter Seven). Such rituals of hospitality

would have enabled me to know the people much more deeply than would the usual Westerners' one-to-one meetings without any ceremonial manners.

After writing the previous paragraphs, I turned away from my study to prepare for noontime guests—two friends, a mother and her son, whom I have known for more than thirty years, though we live a great distance apart. After they left to go on to see other friends who live in the area, I wished that I had spent time before their visit to develop some special rituals of greeting.

We engaged in the typical catching up on happenings since the last visit, mealtime prayers, and signing the guest book, and we spent commemorative time grieving the loss of their husband and father, but that very loss made me want all the more to develop some distinctive traditions for welcoming guests to our home. The Hawaiians present leis and the Maoris offer a *powhiri*—what could become a ritual of hospitality for us?

Also, it will affect our discernment for our behavior if we have developed a character open to welcoming the grieving of others. You probably know people to whom you can confide your sorrows and others who do not know how to receive such confidences. What choices for time and attitude could we make that would enable us to develop deeper habits of openness to those who grieve?

In what other dimensions of life can we learn to discern better patterns for nurturing the well-being of others? For example, because of the lessons people elsewhere have been teaching me about their rituals of greeting and their communal practices of hospitality, I have become very aware of how rude in general are my business letters and international e-mails. I tend to get right down to business without much thought for the well-being of the other person, without any custom of greeting. When we consider the depths of hospitality and generosity that the Bible illuminates, what choices for rituals of welcoming and care might we develop so that our correspondents and guests feel enfolded in God's love and grace and tenderness?

A large proportion of North Americans do not live in very hospitable environs. Many of us do not know our neighbors; people move so frequently that we are hesitant to become well acquainted. Furthermore, our neighborhoods are generally separated from others by class, so that we do not directly and intimately know the needs that call for our charity. As a result, we do not have deep patterns of hospitality and generosity written into our cultural character. Perhaps we might ponder how we could overcome that cultural selfishness before we read on to consider a few inspiring patterns of culturally cultivated generosity.

GENEROSITY IN BOTSWANA AND GUATEMALA

In Alexander McCall Smith's novel *Tears of the Giraffe,* Mma Ramotswe investigates a man who, she notices, did not have a gardener, even though he was well-employed in a white-collar job. Those who have such a position, she ruminates, have a social responsibility to engage domestic help because so many people are always nearby and in dire need of work. Because the communal practice is that everyone who is well-employed hires some household help, then those staff members can also feed their families. Such a system thereby produces jobs.[9] This is one of several examples in Alexander

McCall Smith's novels about Botswana that reveal a culture with specific habits that nurture generosity.

Though it is not as easy in the United States to hire domestic assistance because of Social Security laws and other cumbersome governmental policies, we can support the labor of others by investing in agencies that furnish micro-loans to people in poorer economies or we can support those organizations in our own communities that provide work opportunities for the poor, the handicapped, and the unemployed or underemployed. In our local community we have such agencies as Goodwill Industries, the Arc, and Friends of the Carpenter.

In what other ways could a goal to help those who need jobs influence our discernment of how to spend our own money or how to utilize our time? Our local communities might offer us other opportunities, if we take time to discern them, that would contribute toward building a culture of greater generosity in North America. How could we help to develop a community of more widespread charity?

My friend Carol Barrera, who is a translator in Guatemala, gave me a superb example of profound generosity among the Achí people with whom she works. Her remarks demonstrated both the collective discernment of the people and their entire culture of altruism within which the people serve one another.

She wrote, "Here the choices are more culturally determined than a case of individual decision. There are expectations that most people fulfill." As an example, she said that everyone brings gifts, such as money or food, for a family in mourning, or if there is sudden misfortune (a house burning down or a flood), or in chronic cases (an invalid without family support or a deranged person). In such instances, everyone chips in, no matter how poor or rich they might be, though "the rich person is expected to give more. A poorer person always finds some way to help, even if it is only with a basket of fruit or 5 cents." Because there is no welfare system, every single person in the community "takes turns caring for the down-and-outers."

Furthermore, employers are expected to provide for the "health needs of their workers and their extended families and for the costs of big fiestas for weddings, baptisms. This isn't a written law, but an unwritten one." They also help with the educational costs of workers' children.

I'm sure you are as astonished as I am at the great contrast this is to North America, where companies increasingly employ mostly part-time workers or send their jobs elsewhere in order to cut costs. What does this say about our society as a whole and about our culture's decision making?

Imagine what it would be like if everyone in the community—no matter how poor themselves—chipped in to provide for those who have hit especially tough times! Generally, I have found it to be the case, and statistics on giving show, that those with less are typically much more generous in the proportion of their possessions and their time that they are willing to give to others.

I especially added "time" to the previous sentence because it is easier for me to give away money than time. Perhaps you are the same. We who have such a financial excess, compared with the rest of the world, give from our surplus instead of sacrificially, and we usually think that we don't have a surplus of time.

How would it affect our choices in matters of discernment if we began from a stronger character of generosity, if we participated in a generous community, if we remembered more often that we belong to a generous God? Could we learn a new way to discern time—not from an attitude of scarcity but from a conviction of its abundance?[10]

WELCOMING AND MERCY IN NIGERIA

Hospitality can sometimes be a means to slow us down so that we become more ready and able to discern well. For example, Dr. Bea Haagenson, who served for twelve years as a missionary in Nigeria, wrote that Northern Nigeria's custom for greetings impressed her immediately when she arrived as a young nurse. The people's habit goes far beyond the typical North American "Hi" and "Good-bye" and "How are you?" (without expecting a reply).

Instead the Nigerians hold in-depth conversations, with both parties listening attentively and responding. The greeting includes questions about the other party's wife or husband, children, children's school, health, house, work, farm, and the weather, and for Christians there are additional questions about the church. When Nigerians greet a missionary, there will also be questions about news from home and perhaps a request for world news if the greeter assumes that the missionary listens to the radio or reads a newspaper.

Bea emphasized that the people are genuine in their greetings and inquiries. She realized very early that such greetings gave her time to slow down and listen and share. They are a significant cultural component; people are considered rude if they cut a greeting short. She quickly perceived the importance of such respectfulness and the value of taking the time to slow down—even to sit down—to listen.

The hospitality of the Nigerians' greetings widens into the generosity of their care and concern for family, neighbors, and even strangers. Listen as Bea describes one special case:

> In our village, Numan, there were some women who were former slaves. They didn't have a home and depended on the charity of the people in town and especially the church women, who would give them food and a place to sleep.
>
> Our hospital evangelist, Obida, spent some time in Denmark at the invitation of the Danish Mission. While there he visited a nursing home and was impressed with the care given to people who could not live alone and take care of themselves. Obida made the comment that "in Nigeria we don't really need nursing homes—we take care of our elders in our homes until they die." But returning to Nigeria he decided [to combine what he had seen in Denmark with his own culture's habits and thus] to build a "compound" consisting of a few round huts for the former slaves. They then had a place they could call their own, and the church women could go there and make sure they had food, water, clothes, firewood and other necessities. Obida would also visit and share the Gospel with the women. He had turned the custom of caring and sharing into something that changed the women's lives from being beggars to being part of the community. The smiles on the women's faces clearly told how grateful they were.

Such caring and hospitality of the local people, Bea reports, was also extended to patients in the hospital she served. These patients often came from far away and might need food, clothes, or hygiene supplies. Bea concludes, "Obida and his 'helpers' would make rounds at the hospital, read from the Bible, pray in the person's local language and provide for their needs." Then the Nigerians would invite the missionaries to share in their hospitable generosity, as the latter were often asked "to pitch in with a little money so some necessities could be bought in the market."

What wonderful models these Nigerian friends are for us of the welcoming and gracious care of God! How might it build our character if we intentionally try to discern opportunities in which we could help the "beggars" of our society become part of the community? What new ways to care for our neighbors might we discern if our character is formed to be more like the God to Whom we belong— more open to the needs of others and more openhanded in attending to them?

HOSPITALITY AND GENEROSITY IN MADAGASCAR AND TANZANIA

My new Malagasy acquaintances (introduced in Chapter Five), Dr. Andry Ranaivoson and his wife, Bako Ramihaminarivo, described for me two striking habits from their culture concerning generosity and hospitality. The first is that all the neighbors share in fieldwork.

Because most of the people are small subsistence farmers, they follow a special custom called *valin-tànana* (which literally means "repaying hand"). Andry and Bako said that in the community any one person's field operations are arranged so that all the able bodies in the village can contribute or "give a hand." This may be done through the gift of their actual hands or by the loan of cattle. Neighbors either let the person borrow a few cattle or they come and work alongside their fellow community member during any seasonal work such as seeding, fertilizing, weeding, or harvesting the rice.

The second custom in Malagasy culture concerns funerals, for the expenses of which everyone in the village will contribute financially. Because the funeral wake might last for several days, neighbors contribute so that food and beverages can be provided for those who attend.

A superb example of such neighborly generosity of time and material goods was sent to me by Barbara Robertson, who serves in Tanzania. When her mother became critically ill, Barbara was deeply touched by the way the Tanzanians gathered around her. She wrote, "In a place where death is a frequent and familiar occurrence, I, as outsider, was brought into the community as one who mourns."

As she prepared to come back to the United States to be with her mother and say farewell, five young men who were the instrumentalists for the church choir in which she participated came one evening to her home to comfort and encourage her. This is how she described their visit:

> In a manner that is formally informal (unique to Tanzania,
> I think), these fellows stated their objectives: to pray with
> me, to encourage me, to pray for my mother and family,
> and to pray for the long journey that lay ahead. Each one
> then took a turn reading some Scriptures and giving a short
> explanation as to why he had chosen those lines. Then they
> prayed for my family and me. They closed our time together
> by singing a few tender hymns a cappella in lovely four-part
> harmony. I was not very successful in holding back tears.

After Barbara returned to the village following her mother's funeral, she was overwhelmed by the people's incredible kindness, demonstrated by her experience of *kupewa pole* (which is "to receive condolences") and *rambirambi* ("the receiving of gifts of sympathy").

Barbara underscored that "being with" is very important in Tanzanian culture, so they are a people who surround the bereaved to help them forget their sorrows. Day after day people came to her to pay their respects and to give her encouragement for the difficult days after her mother's death.

The second or third night after her return, her work colleagues came to her house, crowded into her small sitting room, and presented her with gifts such as a crate of soda, twenty pounds of rice, ten pounds of sugar, tea, coffee, vegetables, and money. Barbara wondered how she would use all these things but soon found out that they would be needed to welcome all the guests who would come to her home.

Some of the people who came were her friends. Others were acquaintances from villages near the hospital where she worked. An entire staff from an elementary school came— she had gotten to know them when the Sunday School at her home congregation in the United States had gathered money for the school's students to have chalk, books, pens, notebooks, and school uniforms for the poorest.

One day thirty members from the church choir came, packed into her house, and sang song after song of comfort in beautiful a cappella four-part harmony. They also gave her fifty eggs, which amazed her in that most of them were poor subsistence farmers, so their gift represented great sacrifice.

Two other visits stand out. One woman, Ester, made a three-hour bus journey from a village eighty kilometers away, stayed about twenty minutes to pay her respects, and then took the long bus ride home again. The last visitor, the brother of her housekeeper Maria, came with her about five months later, apologizing that he had been so long delayed by his farming and work responsibilities but wanting Barbara to know that he and his family grieved with and for her, as she had also done with and for them when their younger brother had died the year before.

Barbara's account stirs new questions about discernment. My husband and I hope to develop new habits for visiting those who have lost loved ones. We would like to gain better skills for discerning more deeply how to comfort those who grieve. What choices might we make for gifts to bring to provide solace? The immense hospitality and sacrificial generosity of the Tanzanians inspire us all to greater care for those who need our soothing in times of sorrow. How could we participate in developing such a culture of welcoming and care among the people to whom we belong?

HOSPITALITY AND GENEROSITY AMONG THE MENNONITES

I like to jest that I joined the Mennonite church during the years I lived in South Bend, Indiana, because folks in other denominations didn't have cars. The truth of the matter is that I had called several churches, told them that I couldn't drive because of my visual handicaps, mentioned that the buses didn't run on Sundays and that their buildings were located too far away for me to walk, and asked if someone from the congregation could give me a ride. Because no one from those churches ever volunteered, what could I deduce but that they didn't own cars? Yet the Mennonites offered me a ride every Sunday morning and for special events. (I've been a big proponent of car hospitality ever since.)

Chapter Five described the discernment process which the Mennonite congregation followed concerning my membership. Here it is important to emphasize that the deep bond which I feel with that community is in large part due to the care with which they considered my request to belong to their community and the equal care they showed to me as a member in keeping the promises of their membership ritual. They continually provided transportation for me—not only for worship, but also to train stations and airports for my occasional speaking engagements. Members even drove me to their home to let me use their laundry facilities because my apartment in a big old house had none available, and they usually gave me dinner while I was there (and sometimes the leftovers because I was a graduate student with little time to cook).

That Christian community helped me see that it really is possible to be deeply hospitable and generous in the midst of our technologized, commodified culture. Out of their welcoming and magnanimous character—and the supportive culture of the whole community—they discerned numerous ways to help me.

Their tradition of care can inspire other Christian communities to discern new habits for welcoming and nurturing others. We and our churches could consider what kind of car hospitality we have for the elderly, the visually or physically impaired, or young children who would like to come but whose parents can't bring them to Sunday School and worship. Our congregations could offer sign language, large-print hymnbooks, space for wheelchairs, gracious hospitality for the mentally impaired. What kinds of assistance could we give to members or neighbors having hard times? What plans could we make for providing financial support for the un- or underemployed or for families in which the breadwinner is ill or between jobs?

The more we discern ways to be welcoming and caring, the more our individual and communal character will be formed into hospitality and generosity. The more that is our character, the more we will reflect the nature of the God to

Whom we belong and be able to discern the best choices for nurturing the well-being of others.

HOSPITALITY TO THE ENVIRONMENT

It is also important that we continually make our choices in light of the well-being of the whole earth and, thereby, of its citizens now and in the future. Usually, we speak of the hospitality of the environment for us, but present habits in various global cultures are so destructive to natural elements that we need to reverse that phrase and spend more time discerning how our choices affect the earth.

One good friend who grew up in a province in the middle of China said that his childhood community's practice for discernment put the sun, the land, the water, and the air into consideration. Regardless of the reason for that practice in earlier Chinese tradition, today that custom needs to be reinstated throughout the world as we make our personal, corporate, and community decisions.

In all our discernment processes, we could spend more time making sure that our choices do no harm to the air, the water, the land, and the creatures who inhabit them. Consider how it would affect our decisions about purchasing a car or food or choosing a method to heat our homes if we were more conscious of such issues as emissions, packaging, and waste products. Congregations could choose to use washable cups rather than Styrofoam. What other decisions might groups make in order to find better alternatives to many choices in our culture that are ecologically harmful? How could we as a people who belong to the God of all creation learn more thoroughly that we and all the other inhabitants of the earth belong together and are responsible for each other's well-being and the well-being of our surroundings?

Hospitality and generosity are desperately needed for the welfare of the earth and its people and creatures. How might that statement undergird all our personal and communal discernment processes?

A Culture of Reconciliation

My husband remembers a time long ago when two of his first-grade students were arguing and calling each other names. He said something to them like, "Do you really not want to be friends?" Surprisingly, one girl immediately apologized, and then the other did, too. They both began to cry and eventually returned to their activities together. Myron was startled that his simple words had led so quickly to reconciliation.

Once when I was angry with someone for his thoughtless and belittling treatment of me in a public setting, my brother Glen suggested, "Remember: he was doing the best he could at that moment." Then he counseled me to consider the other person's own emotional pressures and fears of failure. That new perspective led to understanding that made a healing of the relationship possible. My brother, who is the executive director of the Lutheran Peace Fellowship, is a master reconciler.

It seems most natural, after thinking about welcoming and hospitality, to move now to pondering issues of reconciliation, for once relationships are created, human beings have to stay constantly on their guard so that those relationships are not broken or, if they are fractured, so that they can be rebuilt.

The main question for our purposes here is whether or not it is possible to create the kind of culture in which seeking harmonization is our urgent habit. North Americans are not a people who generally make extra efforts to match our level of consumerism with our share of the resources of the earth, to reconcile our buildings with the environment, to attune ourselves to people with whom we disagree, to settle our disputes in a way that everybody wins, to integrate all the peoples of our nation, or to work in league with the other nations of the world.

I'm reminded of a little piece I encountered in another set of stories by the author of the "No. 1 Ladies Detective Agency" series to which I referred earlier. Alexander McCall Smith has also written a hilarious three-part spoof of academia featuring a Romance philologist from Germany named Professor Moritz-Maria von Igelfeld. In one of the books, while traveling, the professor lingered on a terrace

> and gazed out over the terracotta-tiled rooftops down below him, reflecting on how everything in Italy seemed to be so utterly in harmony with its surroundings. Even the modern works of man, buildings which in any other country would be an imposition on the landscape, here in Italy seemed to have a grace and fluidity that moulded them into the natural flow and forms of the countryside. And the people too— they occupied their surroundings as if they were meant to be there; unlike in Germany, where everybody seemed to be . . . well, they seemed to be so *cross* for some reason or another.[1]

What word would we use to describe the general attitude of people who live in the United States? Might we immediately think of words like *calm, courteous,* or *caring,* or would we more quickly suggest terms such as *aggressive, angry, arrogant,* or *anxious*? Consider what word you would use to describe your own overall bearing. How would you like to be perceived? Ponder the general demeanor of the people to whom you belong. Do they reflect the nature of the God to Whom we belong?

The general timbre of our life affects our discernment. The decisions we make would be adversely altered, for example, if our dispositions were, as von Igelfeld said, cross. How would we be different if our lives were shaped instead by the reconciliation of the cross? How are our habits of discernment changed by the eternal reuniting with God of resurrection Joy?

WHAKAHOANGA

Whakahoahoa is the Maori word that means "becoming friends" in a plural sense. Other people have adapted the word with the traditional Maori plural ending *nga* to make the word *whakahoanga* to signify "true reconciliation." One pamphlet that was given to me concerning *whakahoanga* told the story of how the killer of a young girl, through reading the Gospel of Luke which he took from her, sought reconciliation with the girl's father, and thereby their warring tribes ceased their conflicts. Reconciliation sometimes involves great cost, profound repentance, and phenomenal humility.

For the last few years I have been wearing a pendant that provides a beautiful symbol of such reconciliation. This Maori white bone carving was given to me by one of my students in a course on spiritual disciplines at Carey Baptist College in Auckland, New Zealand.

The symbol appears as Figure 1 here to stimulate your interest, thanks to my husband's artistic abilities. Perhaps I am reading more into the carving than is there, but symbols do that for us. They open up our memories of significant teachings to new reflections and insights. Four elements of the symbol stand out for me.

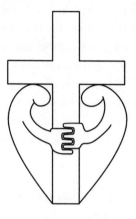

The first is that reconciliation takes place best under the cross. Because mortal beings have been reconciled to God through the cross of Christ (as we will contemplate more thoroughly later in this chapter), all of our human efforts at reconciliation have a sure foundation. Because at the end of time God will recapitulate the entire cosmos (which is to say, will bring all things—human beings, creatures, nature—together under the headship of Jesus Christ), we mortals can imagine and sample that future harmonization in our attempts at integration now. Thus, we can create among people the reconciling that characterizes the God to Whom we belong.

To understand the second aspect of the Maori symbol, we need to know that a prominent New Zealand emblem is the *koru,* the wound spiral that looks somewhat like the top of a violin and unfolds to make the fern frond. When the large *koru* of a tall fern plant in New Zealand is wound up, it can be about half a foot high. When that large *koru* unwinds, inside are numerous little ones that also unfold to make the

entire fern branch. You can see a striking illustration of the
koru painted on the tail of Air New Zealand airplanes.

The symbol on the pendant that was given to me looks
like two *koru* unfolding opposite each other to form a sym-
metry, and it thereby emphasizes that true reconciliation is
possible only if both parties unfold together and reach their
own fullness. Attempts at harmonization reach only a compromise if one or both parties have to give up something
of themselves or their goals in order to attain some sort of
equilibrium. Compromise, however, is not genuine reconciliation, for the latter requires that both sides come equally to
wholeness.

The third element that strikes me about the *whakahoanga* symbol is that the carver has etched the bone so that
it is also a striking rendering of two people in flowing robes
with bowed heads and clasped, interlocking hands. (The
block shape of the hands is a very traditional way of depict-
ing them and is used in almost all Maori carving.) The
symbol suggests that genuine reconciliation will lead to a
lasting friendship, a continuing relationship undergirded by
appropriate humility and repentance. Enduring friendship
cannot be built on arrogance.

Finally, the two *koru* together form a heart under the
cross. Only with the deepest of true love can genuine reconciliation take place. By the word *love* I mean not the senti-
mentalized Hollywood versions that make us feel romantic
giddiness. Nor do I use the word in the way we speak com-
monly about ice cream or some other favorite food. I use the
word with the meaning of the biblical noun *agapé,* that intelligent and purposeful love that always seeks the well-being of
the other—the kind of love that would make us ever welcoming and hospitable, generous and good to other people.

Only God is capable of such perfect love, but Christians believe that when Christ lives in us by the power of the Holy Spirit, we become more capable of the Trinity's absolute *agapé*. In fact, all the biblical commands to love one another use the verb form of this noun. We are to love each other not merely with friendship or familial, affectionate, or erotic love, but with the perfect love of the God to Whom we belong working through us to care for the holistic well-being, the complete *shalom* of the other person.

My goal for this chapter is that we would all be stirred more deeply to yearn to live out of a character—and through us, to develop a culture—of reconciliation, so that all our discerning will tend toward choices that lead to the greater wholeness of everyone involved. Beyond our immediate situations, furthermore, any act of reconciliation builds greater peace and harmony in the world. May all our processes of decision making lead toward the healing of the nations and of the earth.

WHAT PREVENTS THE DEVELOPMENT OF A CULTURE OF RECONCILIATION?

While I was in graduate school, one great privilege given to me was the opportunity to study with a Mennonite professor who lived and breathed, talked and walked reconciliation. The contrasts between his life and mine made it obvious what in me prevented the development of the manner of life conducive to reconciliation.

Perhaps you have also encountered such a person— either as a colleague or a friend or maybe even in literature— and that person has immeasurably raised your admiration.

When we meet reconcilers, we want to radiate peace in the same way, to develop the skills for reaching consensus as we glimpsed at the end of Chapter Five.

What gets in the way? Perhaps it is our lack of humility or an excess of fear. We can easily become afraid that there is a scarcity of what we need (whether that be love or tangible goods) and begin to think that we have a right to more than our share of attention or resources.

Such a case was revealed by two ballot measures in our city this past week. The majority of citizens voted to support an initiative to upgrade our community library system, especially with computers, but they voted against the legislation that would tax us slightly to pay for the upgrades. Basically, the voting said that yes, we deserve a better town library, but someone else should have to pay for it. Last year the ballot measure to fund the city bus system also failed, so that bus routes and times had to be curtailed—leaving many poor and handicapped people who work night shifts without transportation.

If ours were a culture of *whakahoanga,* then those who are blessed so much that they own property would be willing to be taxed (the amounts are so small it is astonishing!) to enable those less privileged also to have access to library computers and adequate, convenient transportation so that everyone in society can flourish. When will we realize that no one can truly thrive if everyone in the community is not given an equal opportunity to prosper? How might it affect our discernment with respect to our voting if we understood that we all belong to each other?

Perhaps some get arrogant about their abilities and accomplishments and think that they deserve better treatment or deserve to triumph in situations of competition. We see such behavior in famous and extremely well-paid ballplayers (sadly, in too many sports) who don't think that the ordinary rules of behavior apply to them.

But sometimes the inability to be a harmonizing agent arises simply from ignorance. Too often we might be guilty of a lack of awareness of the poor conditions under which others live. Hurricane Katrina in 2005 revealed an enormous gap between the rich and the poor and between the races in New Orleans, which opened the eyes of many in the United States to disparities of which they previously were (possibly blindly or prejudicially) oblivious.

On a larger scale, businesses or even church bodies fail to be a culture of reconciliation because of their emphasis on power and success. In more than one place overseas I have encountered missionaries whose welfare was threatened because the church bodies that sent them courted success in terms of numbers—not understanding the nature of the missionaries' role to "accompany" the people they served in the people's own issues and concerns. In one example, the North American church body wanted to see growth in terms of the number of "conversions," whereas the missionaries were first building the people's trust by helping them seek restoration of their family lands.

In such a case we recognize the importance of first "rectifying the names," as we discussed that practice in Chapter Three, for the missionaries were thinking in terms of incarnating the Good News of God's love and reign in the world in their location. Their home churches, in contrast, had lost the vision of the meaning of the Gospel in their struggle to survive in North America, where the influence of Christianity is shrinking, to some extent because of that very loss of vision.

Businesses similarly run into problems when they lose sight of their originating purpose and concentrate instead on surviving or thriving in terms of monetary success. The contemporary business-speak of a "bottom-line" mentality is inimical to building a culture of reconciliation because it fails to realize that a company can "do well" only if it truly cares about the flourishing of those it serves. How might a sense of the two figures holding hands in the *whakahoanga* symbol enable a business or a church to discern better the kinds of choices it should make?

On the largest scale, nation states often suffer from their arrogance in misunderstanding that their proper purpose is to care for the well-being of their own people *in correlation with* the welfare of their land and its resources and *in association with* the other peoples of the world. Empires rise on the backs of other nations, on the abuse and misuse of the global environment, or from all of these, and eventually they fall because of that arrogance. No earthly kingdom can last forever because ultimately other powers surmount it. We will see further on the example of three national leaders who envisioned their power differently and, as a result, built a culture of reconciliation that led to greater flourishing.

I mentioned the environment in the previous paragraph, and that subject can take us back to the personal level and a character of reconciliation. Each of us can build greater harmony by how we treat the earth and the things of this earth. You might wonder what this has to do with the larger subject of discernment which is the topic of this book, but how we care for our earthly possessions expands in a spiral with the development of our character to make us the sort of people who work toward the thriving of our neighbors as well as ourselves.

If we do not waste water because we are concerned that more people of the earth should have adequate and safe water, then our own acts of conservation build our character so that we become the sort of people who will more readily respond to requests for funds so that potable water is made available to those who need it. If we never acquire a new piece of clothing without giving away something we already possess so that our closet never gets more full, then we are more likely to develop further a character concerned that everyone in the world should be justly clothed and protected from the elements.

Even such little efforts as carrying our own grocery bags and reusing them to lessen the amount of plastics we dump into the earth is an act of reconciliation. Planting native species in our yards so that we don't spend so much on fertilizers or so that we don't waste precious water, working to preserve the wetlands in our communities, recycling, refusing to buy products with excess packaging—such simple things work toward the healing of the earth and illustrate why this chapter is calling for an entire culture of reconciliation.

The importance of environmental care became starkly clear with the devastation of Hurricane Katrina. People along the Gulf Coast realize as they look at the despoiled landscape how catastrophic it was to develop the former barrier lands which would have absorbed some of the tidal waves and some of the winds' furies. Similarly, victims of floods learn the hard way the calamitous effects of covering too much land with concrete.

I only introduce these subjects because I have no expertise to do any more, but these topics should be broached so that we can see that our little acts contribute one way or another to the care of the environment or to its devastation—and, in turn, to the well-being or harm of humankind. If our goal is *whakahoanga,* the full opening out of every *koru,* then we will practice choosing well, and, correlatively, our character will grow toward more godly discernment in this and other aspects of our lives.

THE BIBLICAL EMPHASIS ON RECONCILIATION

The Bible makes it very clear that the Triune God cares about the whole creation—especially human beings, but also every other created thing. God, indeed, designed all things and made them to be good. The great celebrative liturgy of Genesis 1 ends each day's creation with some variation of the grand proclamation "And God saw that it was good" (see vv. 4, 12, 18, 21, 25, and 31).

But when human beings rejected God's good purposes and the limits the LORD gave them (Genesis 3:1–19), the whole creation suffered the results of their fall. Now, the apostle Paul says, the whole creation groans in labor pains while it waits for God's recapitulation of the cosmos (Romans 8:19–23).

The Bible in this way underscores what we can see daily. We can recognize how much the earth suffers because of human selfishness and exploitation. We can notice the dangers of global warming, the loss of topsoil, the extinction of species, the reduction of the world's forests, and so forth. When we begin to comprehend the extent of human carelessness, we discover that the whole creation is in bondage to our sin.

What can't be readily seen in daily life, however, is the hope, the Good News that God is doing something about the whole mess, and the Joy that we can have because of that work. The apostle Paul makes this the most clear in 2 Corinthians 5.

I'll introduce a lengthy portion of that chapter here because it clarifies not only what God is doing, but why I feel compelled to write about it.

> 14For the love of Christ urges us on, because we are convinced that one has died for all; therefore all have died.
> 15And he died for all, so that those who live might live no longer for themselves, but for him who died and was raised for them.
> 16From now on, therefore, we regard no one from a human point of view; even though we once knew Christ from a human point of view, we know him no longer in that way. 17So if anyone is in Christ, there is a new creation: everything old has passed away; see, everything has become new! 18All this is from God, who reconciled us to himself through Christ, and has given us the ministry of reconciliation; 19that is, in Christ God was reconciling the world to himself, not counting their trespasses against them, and entrusting the message of reconciliation to us. 20So we are ambassadors for Christ, since God is making his appeal through us; we entreat you on behalf of Christ, be reconciled to God. 21For our sake he made him to be sin who knew no sin, so that in him we might become the righteousness of God.

Yes, the love of Christ for me—and my love for Him—spur me to write about this (v. 14) because it seems that if more people knew the hope that lies in Christ and the Triune God's care for us and for the world, then we would be more eager to develop a culture of reconciliation. But I get ahead of myself; let's look at that wonderful passage verse by verse and see the hope for the cosmos that it presents.

In verse 14 Paul emphasizes that Christ's love and our love for Christ compel us because He has died for all of us. As a result, we become willing to die to ourselves and our desires. We no longer wish to insist on our own ways and wants because we are caught up into the sacrifice that He made, and, by His grace, we become willing to enter into that same sacrifice.

The result is that we no longer live only to please ourselves (v. 15). Now we want to live for Christ. His resurrection invites us into the entirely new life of our own resurrection into selflessness.

Consequently, we even look at people differently. We regard everyone not from a human point of view (v. 16), but from God's perspective—and God's view of everyone is that each is loved perfectly. All this is because, though we once thought Jesus was merely human, now we know that He is God Himself, incarnate in a human existence for a time but reigning eternally as part of the Triune Godhead.

Therefore, if we are united with Christ, then everything is different! Not only do we become new, but there is an entirely new creation (v. 17). We regard everything from a new perspective, from the view of God's intimate and profound caring. We yearn for the wholeness of everyone and everything.

Of course, this isn't from us. All this is from God, Who brought us back to Himself through Christ and then commissioned us to do the same sort of reconciliation no matter where we go or what we are involved in (v. 18).

Do we realize how extraordinary God's work of reconciling is? Though we have rejected God again and again, though we have often turned away from the Trinity and have frequently violated God's best will for us, still in Christ God stooped to become One like unto us so that we could be reconciled to Him (v. 19). God never counts our evils against us but instead entrusts to us the same ministry—that we would be devoted to reconciling all things and all people to God and to each other.

We can consider ourselves ambassadors, citizens of God's Kingdom temporarily living in earthly kingdoms to teach everyone what God's Kingdom is like and to invite everyone to participate in the Joy of the Trinity's reign (v. 20). Everywhere we go, in words and deeds, we are entreating others through Christ to come back to God, Who is constantly waiting for us and eager to welcome us back.

Think of what Christ did for us! He was sinless, and yet He took all our guilt and wrongdoing, our evil thoughts and mistakes, and bore all this to the cross for us, so that in His grace, we might become newly created in His own righteousness (v. 21). Through Him, God sees us as holy, wholly set apart as participants in God's reign. No wonder we are compelled to tell everyone else this Good News! No wonder we want more than anything to live out of a character and a culture of reconciliation!

THE MONASTIC CULTURE OF RECONCILIATION

The New Testament epistles (letters) are full of examples of their writers seeking to reconcile members of various Christian communities, so that members of the Body of Christ would live in harmony with each other. The earliest Christians took seriously the lesson we saw in the previous biblical section that God's reconciliation of us through Christ commissions us also to be ambassadors of reconciliation in every dimension of our lives.

When Christians began to turn away from this ministry—largely through what is called the Constantinian Fall (in the fourth-century reign of Emperor Constantine), when Christians became aligned with the power of the Roman Empire and lost their vision for the distinctives of Christianity—the earliest monastic communities were formed to return to the basics of the faith, including the commission to be reconcilers.

Perhaps the most famous of all attempts on the part of monks to be reconcilers is the case of Francis of Assisi, who, during the Crusades, and probably because he was horrified by the monstrous violence and savagery of the crusaders, crossed the battle lines to speak to the Muslim caliph, Malik-al-Kamil. He made this visit with Brother Illuminato, one of his early companions.

Though scholars argue about why he went and what he did, there is no doubt that he made this visit. It is still possible to see some tokens which the sultan gave Francis, such as a mounted ivory tusk, which is now exhibited at the basilica of Saint Francis in Assisi. The most important aspect of this incident is how rare it was amidst the violence of the day that he should dare to "cross enemy lines at the risk of painful death in order to speak face to face with someone who was demonized by the crusaders."[2]

How might it change our choices in life if we went to such extremes to reconcile those who demonize each other, to protest against the violence of our times, to speak face to face with our supposed enemies? When we immerse ourselves in the biblical commission to be ambassadors of reconciliation, our character is more formed so that we will tend to make choices conducive to this harmonizing work. The more we exhibit such a character, the more perhaps we can influence others to be agents of unification so that we develop an entire culture of reconciliation.

Four of the Core Values of the sisters at St. Benedict's monastery in St. Joseph, Minnesota, function together to create there an integrated culture of reconciliation. Notice aspects in each item on the following list that contribute to the biblical vision sketched previously:

> *Prayer and Work* We are dedicated to a daily rhythm of prayer and work, as we praise God and witness to the dignity of work in God's creation
>
> *Listening* We strive to listen with the ear of our hearts, to hear the voices of all creation with compassion and reverence
>
> *Stewardship* We value simplicity and frugality as we reverence all of creation and care for the goods of the earth
>
> *Peace* We are committed to peace and to practicing justice locally and globally

Because of these values, Benedictine monasteries (and those of other orders) are known today worldwide as places of harmony and unity, welcoming homes to which broken people can go for reintegration and new wholeness, communities that work for reconciliation in the society around them and for better care of the earth. Those who belong to such communities are known as peacemakers.

Sister Joan Chittister highlights some of the virtues and attributes that make the Benedictine culture of reconciliation so prominent. Among them she underscores that humility which is such a lost virtue in contemporary North America and which is essential for those who seek the full opening of the *koru* of others.

She also presents to our attention "monastic mindfulness," which blends together a concern for harmony, wholeness, and balance in one's own life and in relation to others. This intentional care for integration within the self and for reconciliation with others enables everyone in the community, including visitors or outside groups with whom the sisters are working, to become attuned to each other and brought to their best selves in relation with one another.

The sisters are also consistently concerned for the environment and understand their own work as participation in creation so that nothing is harmed but everything and everyone can fully flower. Even the giftedness of the sisters is always inherently expressed in correlation with the skills and arts of others so that no one blooms in a way that prevents another from blossoming, too.[3]

In their humility, of course, the sisters would not want me to praise them too much here, but it is important for us to note the values and virtues they emphasize for our own formation into the character of reconciliation. Especially helpful to all of us is exposure to, or a period of residence in, such a culture of reconciliation so that we can be nurtured toward that end. Imagine how favorably it would affect our discernment if our habits naturally caused us to seek the full wholeness of everyone with whom we were in relation and we continually sought the harmony of all people in creation!

RECONCILIATION IN NEW ZEALAND

It is crucial, however, that we never lose sight of all the forces in ourselves and in society that work against the goal of genuine reconciliation. I had written to my Maori friend in New Zealand that I was very grateful for the idea of *whakahoanga* and all that it means, and I mentioned how much I loved the symbol that is on my gift pendant.

She replied with the Maori phrase *Kia kotahi tatou,* which means "Let us be one," and agreed that the symbol is indeed lovely and that the concepts behind it are beautiful and godly, but she also helped me to see that this wonderful idea has been all too frequently betrayed in New Zealand.

She wrote that Maori Christians have become fed up with this concept of reconciliation because it seems that they are always the ones striving for the wholeness and unity of both groups. Too often the *tauiwi,* or second (white) arrivals to Aotearoa (the Maori name for the land of New Zealand), have not cared very much for the wholeness of the Maori.

Of course, we who were second arrivals in the United States can recognize our own similar faults because we here have failed miserably to care for the well-being of Native Americans. Still today people from every ethnic group in the United States keep forgetting that our own wholeness is inextricably linked to the welfare of all the peoples who live in our country.

My Aotearoan friend noted that the Maori people must remember that if they try to pull away into themselves to work on their own wholeness separate from the *tauiwi,* it will be a doomed enterprise. The same is true everywhere in the world. As the great English poet and brilliant preacher John Donne (1572–1631) wrote during a severe illness, "No man is an Iland, intire of it selfe." Can we learn with him, as the poem continues, that every person's death also diminishes us because we are a part of humankind?

This is the poem that ends by reminding us that we need not try to find out for whom a tolling bell is chiming, for "It tolls for thee." The deaths of innocent victims of natural disasters or war diminish us all. When we remember this, we will pay more attention to discerning what we can do, how we can contribute to preventing such deaths in the future.

If North Americans and New Zealanders remember that the poverty and unemployment, alcoholism, and ill health of many of the first people in our lands damage all of us, surely we will try to make better choices for the sake of genuine *whakahoanga.* Can we learn to see again with the

Maori the godly beauty of pursuing the wholeness of others as a priority as we attend to our own health and well-being?

My Maori friend revealed a great example of her people seeking the wholeness of everyone in the land. She reported that New Zealand has a problem with drunk drivers killing people, but that sometimes the relatives of those who have died publicly forgive the drivers who killed their loved ones. She said that when these families doing the forgiving are Maori, their absolution is characterized by the noteworthy attitude that the guilty party needs forgiveness so that he or she has the chance to live a better life—and, if the guilty individual does so, then the loss of the treasured one will not have been in vain.

Recently on the radio a man spoke for the three families of three girls who were killed when a drunk driver crashed. He then ran away and left the girls to die. The families believed that it was right and good for the man to be punished by being sent to prison, but they also wanted him to know that they didn't conceive of him as a totally bad person. They distinguished between his character and some bad decisions he had made and some bad actions which he had committed. They hoped that he could turn his life around, and then their children's lives would not have been lost for nothing.

What a gloriously Christian attitude—and one that cannot be faked! If you were visiting in New Zealand and heard of such an act of forgiveness, you could safely assume that it was the gift of Maori people, for such a rich understanding of forgiveness uniquely characterizes the Maori of Aotearoa.

Prior to the early Christianization of the Maori, they were more characterized by the tradition of *utu* or "revenge."

However, the combination of Christian values and Maori collective thinking, in which the individual and the nuclear family are not considered the only consequential units in society, has led to the very strong sense the Maori have of the importance of acting for the common good by offering forgiveness.

Remember how the Maori introduce themselves, by naming not only themselves, but also their families and tribes and so forth. This is because the Maori know profoundly that they do not live solely for themselves. They are always aware that they live for the greater good of family, subtribe, tribe, nation, and so forth.

Also, we must note that the three families of the three girls who were killed gave a collective response to the media— that is, they spoke with one voice. No doubt they had gathered together for meetings, which are called *hui,* in which the families would have mourned and talked, yelled and talked some more, laughed and cried and talked still more over a period of time until they would have been able to offer forgiveness and would have reached a consensus about how they should proceed and what should then happen. The practice of the *hui* gives us a great model both of community care and of communal discernment.

Considering this Maori example makes me realize more forcibly why it is beneficial for us to learn the customs of other peoples. We each know too little and require the habits of other cultures to enable us to learn how better to live in the community of the world. In this case, it is especially important for us to see how valuable are the practices of communal grieving and discernment, of corporate forgiveness, and of decision making for the good of our own family, as well as for the healing of those who have wronged us and the

well-being of people in the nation and the world. Let us
handle the treasure of the Maori people's culture of reconciliation with care—not only to admire them, but to become
more like them, with humility and gratefulness for the model
they set.

RECONCILIATION IN BOTSWANA AND SOUTH AFRICA

Reading Alexander McCall Smith's novels about Mma
Ramotswe and the African leaders she mentions has made
me very interested in the history of those leaders and their
nations because of the gifts they give us. In *Tears of the Giraffe*,
Mma Ramotswe meditates on the importance of letting the
past alone, rather than dragging up events from a long while
before. People like to dredge up wrongs done to them, she
acknowledges, and the result is usually not to achieve reconciliation but only to poison the present.

As she ponders this, Mma Ramotswe thinks in particular of President Seretse Khama of Botswana and President
Nelson Mandela of South Africa, who both chose another
route.[4] Contemplating the lives of these two gentlemen,
along with the second president of Botswana, enables us to
consider three agents of reconciliation in the contemporary
world who show us what kind of character we need to discern well and what kinds of decisions will result for the sake
of healing in the world.

The best-known of the three men is Nelson Rolihlahla
Mandela, who, during the twenty-eight years of his impris-
onment, became an international symbol for resistance to
South Africa's white domination. But what should be pointed

out here is the change that took place in his own attitudes for how best to respond to that oppression.

Mandela, who was the son of an important tribal chief, first ran into trouble when he was expelled from a university for his social activism. He finished college, however, by correspondence and then studied law at the University of Witwatersrand in Johannesburg. Though the National Party had come to power in 1948 on a platform of white supremacy, which led to the institution of their policy of apartheid, nonetheless Mandela and his friend Oliver Tambo established the first black law practice in South Africa in 1950.

Meanwhile, in his continuing attempt to work for justice he had become involved in the African National Congress (ANC), a multiracial group seeking democratic political change; he became its president in 1951. Ten years later, largely in response to an outrageous massacre of nonviolent black protesters at Sharpeville, he founded *Umkhonto we Sizwe* (or Spear of the Nation), the military wing of the ANC.

After Mandela had gone to Angola for military training and returned to South Africa, he was arrested for treason in 1956 and endured a five-year trial. Again in 1962 he was arrested and sentenced to five years in prison, but in 1964 he was condemned to life in prison for sabotage, treason, and violent conspiracy. Eighteen years of his incarceration were spent at Robben Island, which is notorious for its harsh conditions; then he was moved to Pollsmoor Prison near Cape Town.

Mma Ramotswe puts a face on this story as she ruminates on the tragedy that Mandela had been sent to labor in a quarry, where he suffered permanent damage to his eyes from the rock dust.[5] Yet though he had lost nearly three decades of his life in prison and though the wrongful harsh treatment was exactly the kind of injustice he was trying to overcome, he forgave his oppressors when, due to both international and domestic pressure, he was released from prison.

When President F.W. de Klerk freed him on February 11, 1990, Mandela greeted all the people as friends, comrades, and fellow South Africans and spoke to them in the name of peace, democracy, and freedom for everyone.

Again, Mma Ramotswe lends tangibility to these facts. She remembers that when he finally was released "on that breathless, luminous day," he had no thought or word of vengeance or retaliation. He did not complain about the past—claiming that there were better things to be done—and, as she ponders, he had demonstrated over the course of time how seriously he took his own words "by hundreds of acts of kindness towards those who had treated him so badly."

Mma Ramotswe reflects that his behavior was truly the genuine way of Africa, the tradition closest to Africa's heart. If we all know that we are equally children of Africa, she muses, then no one will consider herself or himself more important or superior to anyone else. This, she thought, could be what Africa could teach the rest of the world; "it could remind it what it is to be human."[6]

International relations expert Peter Ackerman and television producer Jack DuVall report that when Nelson Mandela was sworn in as South Africa's president, he vowed that "'never, never, and never again shall it be that this beautiful land will again experience the oppression of one by another.' The last state bastion of racism had passed from the earth."[7] And Andrew Young, a former assistant to civil rights leader Reverend Dr. Martin Luther King Jr., as well as a former congressman, an ambassador to the United Nations, and the mayor of the city of Atlanta, recounted in his memoirs that "even now, after the harsh oppression of South African racism and his own imprisonment for twenty-seven years, Nelson

Mandela is able to say, 'There can be no revenge, reprisal, or retribution; we must move on together to build a non-racist South Africa.'"[8] What an amazing spirit of nonretaliation and, instead, reconciliation!

Imagine what the world would be like if all its citizens learned from Nelson Mandela the importance of his character of reconciliation in the midst of the African tradition—its culture of reconciliation. Could we become people who know that we all belong together?

What is most amazing about Mandela's story is that although he had in earlier years turned to violence, by the time of his release from prison he had embraced diplomacy instead as the best means for working toward reconciliation between blacks and whites in South Africa. He was part of the conversations that led to equal sharing of power by the various factions in South Africa (for which Mandela and F. W. de Klerk shared the 1993 Nobel Peace Prize) and also led to the first multiracial elections in the country on April 27, 1994, when he was elected the first black president of the unified nation.

Mandela continued his policies of reconciliation in his Reconstruction and Development Plan, which invested large amounts of money in projects to create jobs, housing, and basic health care for everyone. By this means the economy was turned to embrace a larger proportion of the citizens of the country. Then in 1996, under his leadership a new constitution was approved, which guaranteed free speech, free political activity, and the right to restitution for land seized under the apartheid regime.

Of course, not everything has gone smoothly, but throughout his presidency, which concluded in 1999, Nelson Mandela never retaliated against the whites who had imprisoned him for more than a quarter of a century. Instead, when he spoke to the Methodist Church of South Africa just prior to his eightieth birthday, he gave thanks for the Christian mission-school education he had received in his youth. Who knows how much that background led to his change of heart during his imprisonment as he progressed from plans for violence to choosing reconciliation as the means for ending white oppression, bringing justice to blacks, and reuniting South Africa?

Another Smith novel, *Morality for Beautiful Girls,* ends with Mma Ramotswe herself doing an amazing job of helping a divided family to reconcile. In the story, she thinks again of Mandela and Seretse Khama, who exemplify the African character of tending not to hang on to hatred.[9] Khama, who was born of royal parents just three years after Mandela, inherited the title of chief of the tribe that makes up more than one third of Botswana's population. He was exiled from his country by the British authorities in 1950 and deposed from his chiefdom in 1952 because he violated the color bar by marrying an Englishwoman in what was then called Bechuanaland.

Khama was allowed to return in 1956, and six years later he founded the Botswana Democratic Party (BDP), which was supported by a significant combination of whites, chiefs, and rural people. In 1965 the BDP campaigned on a multiracial platform and ascended to power, so that Khama became prime minister. The next year, after independence was achieved for Botswana, he was elected the first president of the country and later that year was knighted.

Notice again, as with Mandela, that Khama did not bear a grudge against his oppressors—in his case, those who had exiled him—but worked together with them to build democracy and achieve independence. His work to reconcile the peoples of Botswana was carried on perhaps even more thoroughly by his cofounder of the BDP, Quett Ketumile

Joni Masire, who served as the party's secretary general and publications editor.

Masire, who had grown up a herder of livestock, eventually became a teacher, an administrator, and a newspaper correspondent. After being elected in 1959 to a tribal council and then, two years later, to Bechuanaland's newly formed Legislative Council, he began serving as the deputy prime minister under Khama in March 1965, became very active in the negotiations for Botswanan independence, and then became vice president and minister of finance in 1966. Largely because of his work as minister of development planning (in 1967–1980), Botswana achieved economic stability, as Masire distributed the profits from government investment in mining into other sectors of the economy.

When Seretse Khama died in July of 1980, the National Assembly appointed Masire president. Though known primarily for his sage economic practices, he also demonstrated sensible foreign policy with neighboring powers. Reelected president by the National Assembly every five years thereafter, he served until 1998.

I am reporting so much about these three men because North Americans don't usually pay very close attention to Africans and their policies, and, as a result, we overlook, to our loss, significant models of reconciling practices. That Mandela, Khama, and Masire could overcome the racial tensions of southern Africa and build economic and development plans that served the poor and led to greater wholeness on the part of many more in their nations is noteworthy.

All three were men of enormous integrity and nobility. All three had a character of reconciliation and built in their nations more of a culture of reconciliation. Certainly, I am aware that Botswana and South Africa still have problems, and I am trying not to overstate the case for the models that these men present to us, but, indeed, most observers would agree that these three were agents of great healing, who discerned well (and at great cost) what needed to be done and how they should act to work for the restoration and well-being of all people, not just of their own tribes.

Their examples encourage all of us to engage more thoroughly in acts of reconciliation that spiral into building in us more of the character and culture of reconciliation. These, in turn, will result in even better discernment of how we can both participate and lead in harmonization and integration for the sake of the healing of the world. How can we more deeply learn and help others to learn that we all belong together? May we be formed by the God to Whom we belong to imitate the Trinity's character of reconciliation!

MORE THAN TWO OPTIONS

One aspect that perhaps you have observed, especially in the previous examples, is that better discernment for the sake of reconciliation involves more than two options. In the case of the African statesmen, they went beyond the choices of submission to oppression or violence against it to foster conversation and humility and forgiveness instead.

I accentuate this because many of our decision-making processes are hindered if we limit our choices to two options, usually conceived of as winning or losing. A culture of reconciliation will teach us instead to look for other alternatives by which means everyone can "win" (although such a term won't be necessary any longer).[10]

God, of course, is the best model of Someone Who chose a "third way" for the sake of the healing of the world. God could have simply rejected humankind when we rejected Him, or He could have said that our disobedience and evil don't matter at all, in which case all hell would break loose. Instead, God chose to enter into the evil and to take it into Himself in the person of Jesus Christ, Who became like us and bore all the evil that human beings could throw at Him through His passion and death. This is why the resurrection of Jesus changed the entire world: because it deals with our evil, not by dismissing it or by causing us to bear all its consequences, but by God taking it into Himself and triumphing over it.

Because of the resurrection, if we are in Christ, there is (as we saw in the biblical section) an entirely new creation. Everything is new, and we see everything from a new perspective. In the eschatological Joy of that perspective we can labor always as Christ did to find another option, a way to reconcile, a means to bring about harmonization and healing for the sake of the world.

RECONCILIATION IN A MONSTROUSLY DIVIDED WORLD

I believe that this chapter is crucially relevant as we try to learn better discernment in our atrociously discordant world. For the last several years the United States has been bitterly polarized, and the opposition between Democrats and Republicans has led to abusive animosity even in families and churches, as well as in local communities and national politics.

The world is also fiercely divided—between Muslim and Western nations, between the rich and the poor, between developed and developing lands, between different kinds of terrorists. The separations are so severe that we are often immobilized by their immensity.

What can we do? How should we live?

This chapter offers not an answer but a means. Let us all pay attention to each process of discernment so that the outcome leads to the well-being not only of ourselves, but of all those specifically involved in the decision and of all those who might be touched by its results.

We do not need to resort to hatred or violence. We do not need to give in to postmodern chaos. There is a very important place for us to stand—living with virtues and discerning actions of peacemaking and justice building for the sake of *whakahoanga*. It is a biblical position. It is the Joy-full way of Jesus.

8

A Willingness to Suffer

Perhaps the strongest tradition about Saint Martin of Tours (316?–397?) is that he was so charitable that he once divided his own cloak, gave half of it to a beggar, and later experienced a vision of Christ telling the angels about the merciful deed. But we should know him also for another characteristic of his noble life. Following his father's footsteps, he went into the Roman army as a teen. However, he had become a Christian at the age of ten and later discerned that his beliefs were incompatible with military service. Consequently, he was imprisoned—the first of his sufferings for his faith commitment.

After his release and discharge, he became a disciple of St. Hilary of Poitiers (a great scholar, writer, and bishop) and established the first monastery in Gaul. But then came another decision that caused him suffering. Though he hadn't wanted the office, he accepted being made the bishop of Tours and fulfilled it with distinction, yet humbly. Instead of sitting on the bishop's throne, he used a rude stool, and he lived as a simple hermit outside the city. He devoted his life to spreading the Gospel and to developing reconciliation between parties in conflict. A younger contemporary wrote admiringly of him in a widely circulated biography:

195

He judged none and condemned none and never returned
evil for evil. No one ever saw him angry. . . . He . . . presented
to everyone a joy of countenance and manner which seemed
to those who saw it beyond the nature of man. Nothing was
in his mouth except Christ, nothing in his heart but piety,
peace, and pity.[1]

Throughout his life, people gathered around Martin because of his godly character, and he continues to inspire
peacemakers who believe that it is more important to suffer
ourselves than to inflict suffering on anyone else. Saint
Martin has long been one of my heroes in the Christian faith
primarily because he so readily acted on his faithful discernments, though he knew that suffering would be the in-
evitable consequence.

Many early Christians who died as martyrs for their
faith could illustrate this chapter's theme of willingly accepting the suffering that comes to us because of our commitments, but I chose St. Martin of Tours to begin because
probably few of you reading this book will ever be forced to
choose between abandoning your faith and death. But all of
us will have to discern in various situations whether we are
willing to suffer in order to live out our highest passions. And
a growing willingness to pay the price of suffering often
makes certain matters of discernment easier.

By now, you are no doubt very aware that holding certain convictions and values might necessitate various degrees
of hardship. To be hospitable and generous and to work for
reconciliation (as discussed in Chapters Six and Seven) will
inevitably cost us. Consequently, the main questions in this
chapter fall into the same spiral that we have been noticing:
in the midst of discernment processes, do we have the character of persons willing to suffer for our commitments? How

would a readiness to suffer influence our decisions? Has our character been formed by the willing suffering of the community and the God to Whom we belong?

Let me hasten to add that I'm not a masochist or a sadist wanting to inflict suffering on myself or others. This chapter simply recognizes the facts that we live in a broken, sinful world; that we ourselves will suffer other people's hurts and our own illnesses and death; and that many goals for good in the world can only be pursued if we are willing to pay the price. Just as a world-class athlete, scholar, or artist has to suffer arduous training and various deprivations, so every noble commitment requires some expense to ourselves, some sacrifice of other things. These facts make us more careful in matters of discernment so that we seriously count the cost of our decisions. They also sometimes make us question whether God is truly sovereign *and* loving—whether the evils of the world have gotten out of control and whether God's grace really undergirds everything.

However, this chapter should not be read apart from the one that follows, for suffering and celebration go together. This is one of the reasons that I find the Christian Gospel so attractive—because the narrative of Christ's passion and cross, resurrection and ascension matches the shape of the world in its struggle and hope, adversity and victory. Just as a mother's pain in labor gives way to the delight of a newborn child, so many of our worst trials lead to some of our highest ecstasies. But even when the shape of the world doesn't point to celebration, Christ's resurrection and ascension assure us that ultimately God will bring to an end all sin and suffering, sorrow and death. Thus, we can claim eschatological Joy even in our struggles because we know that God is using them to transform us into Christ's likeness.

WHAT KEEPS US FROM DISCERNING WELL?

I am ashamed to admit that throughout my life there have been times when I have not chosen certain actions or directions because they might encompass some sort of suffering. For example, I was convicted by Sister Joan Chittister's comments in Chapter Six that to be hospitable requires that we go out of ourselves for someone else every day. Because it sometimes costs too much of me, I have not always been willing to go out of my way for others.

Our society is not in general a culture that fosters a willingness to go beyond our own comfort zones. We want the best of government services and say that we want the poor to be provided for, but we don't want to be taxed to pay for such things. The national level of indebtedness is evidence that as a society, we would rather put the burden on future generations.

Of course, no one wants to choose to suffer pain and loss. But would we willingly endure some expense to ourselves for a greater good or to keep a commitment to someone or something?

My favorite story on this issue concerns the extraordinary violinist Yehudi Menuhin. A great admirer once said to him in adulation, "I would give everything [or maybe it was "my life"] to play like you!" And Menuhin gently responded, "That's what it cost me."

For what are we willing to give everything? To what will we readily devote our lives—knowing well that sacrifice of some sort will be the accompaniment?

If a corporate leader chooses a direction for the company that will serve the workers well in the long run but requires some sacrifices in the short term, she has to be willing to pay the price of their anger. One who decides to write historical fiction must accept the requirements of an enormous investment of time and loneliness and exposure to the possibility of bad reviews. A politician or a public speaker risks the sufferings of public displeasure. When we discern our occupations, these costs must be taken into account. In this chapter we are adding a larger element to that discernment by asking what price we might have to pay to serve God not only through our occupations, but in all the other aspects of our lives.

The topic of this chapter ties in with the emphasis, introduced in Chapter Three, on focal concerns. Once we discern what is most important to us, we will make other decisions accordingly, no matter what the price. If, for example, we discern that we want to live in relationship with God by following Jesus, then we will choose intentionally to reject other gods. We might detect that we are enslaved to alcohol or that money gets in between us and the Trinity. I have recognized that sometimes my ambitions and my addiction to control are gods that must be renounced.

To forswear other gods *is* painful to us. All kinds of addictions are unhealthful and cause us struggle when we repudiate them. We might discern a necessity to live more simply so that prestige or being "number one" doesn't master us. We might suffer the anguish of abjuring our selfishness so that we can learn to love others with a more costly fullness. For example, because my medical regimens shortly after my kidney transplant sapped my energy and required an inordinate amount of hours, to spend more time helping a neighbor who had broken her ankle was costly to me, but it was necessary if I truly chose to love her more fully. It is a minor example and one which shows my selfishness, I realize, but I use it to point out that even the smallest choices of our daily lives usually entail some expense to ourselves.

It is essential that we each ask ourselves what hinders us from being willing to suffer for the sake of serving God and others. Have those things kept us from discerning various choices in connection with our noblest commitments? What, at our core, prevents us from discerning well?

The prodigious grace of the God to Whom we belong could form us instead to be a Joy-full people amenable to suffering and could thereby free us to make the hard decisions that will cost us for the benefit of others. The issue is whether we have erected stubborn barriers against God's formative work or whether we accept God's invitation to us to become more like Jesus through the Holy Spirit's work within us.

BIBLICAL INVITATIONS

It is essential for our biblical investigation that we remember that Jesus was not only submissive to suffering, but ready to embrace it for the sake of the Trinity's larger purposes. Chapter Five invited us to "keep house" in the midst of a great cloud of witnesses, including all the saints who have preceded us and Jesus Himself. We were encouraged there by Hebrews 12:1–2 to persevere in the challenges (and here we will underscore the sufferings) of our own lives. Remember this motivation from that text:

> Therefore, since we are surrounded by so great a cloud of witnesses, let us also lay aside every weight and the sin that clings so closely, and let us run with perseverance the race that is set before us, looking to Jesus the pioneer and perfecter of our faith, Who for the sake of the joy that was set before Him endured the cross disregarding its shame, and has taken His seat at the right hand of the throne of God.

If we recall all that Jesus endured to complete God's work to rescue us from ourselves, we can grasp more deeply the hope that the entire narrative of God's saving grace creates for us. When we contemplate the sweetness of knowing God's past, present, and future love in our lives and the immense Joy of experiencing the Trinity face-to-face eternally, we become more willing to undergo suffering for the sake of God's best purposes here and now. For example, if we keep remembering how thoroughly God loves both us and those to whom we speak, we are more able to be gracious when we have to tell the truth in a tense situation and to be willing to take the flak for doing so.

The phrase that is especially important for this chapter from the Hebrews text is *Who for the sake of the joy that was set before Him endured the cross.* What was the Joy set before Jesus?

Notice that I capitalized the word *Joy* because I want to emphasize that we are discussing a divine Joy, an eschatological one (as elaborated in Chapter Four). The Joy for Jesus was to be in perfect fellowship with His Father by the power of the Holy Spirit and thereby to fulfill the Trinity's purposes for *us!*

Isn't that astonishing? His Joy was to liberate and restore us—to free us from all our addictions, fears, and doubts and to reclaim us for relationship with God!

Derivatively, then, our Joy is to join in His work, to become part of all God's purposes for the cosmos and to know with assurance that we will participate in God's triune life throughout our limited earthly existence and eternally beyond. To choose, for example, to be a reconciler in a situation of conflict often causes us to be mocked or ostracized by both sides, but we can find greater courage for the task if we keep remembering that by working for peace and harmony we are participating in God's work.

On the deepest level, sometimes people wonder why it was necessary for Jesus to endure mockery, torture, and death on the cross so that we could be rescued. The more we study the Scriptures, the more we realize that it would not have been enough merely for Jesus to give us a model of someone willing to suffer. Suffering had to be, somehow, defeated.

It is a mystery that goes beyond our comprehension, but Christ's impenetrable intention was to kill evil by taking it into Himself, to swallow death by going through it, though He committed no sin to deserve it and became incarnate in real human flesh only for our sake. That design was perfected when the Father raised Jesus from the dead, by the same Holy Spirit power that releases us from death, so that new life springs from Christ to and through us.

The more we read the Bible's more expansive descriptions, the more our understanding grows, and the more we comprehend, the more we realize that the death and the resurrection of Christ for us are inexplicable marvels. In the following text from Romans, the word *sin* encompasses everything that bogs us down, including our awful mistakes, bad attitudes, outright evil actions toward others and ourselves, harmful habits, detestable desires, and corrupt motives. But this text also thrills us with possibilities that death to ourselves opens to us in Christ:

> Therefore we have been buried with him by baptism into death, so that, just as Christ was raised from the dead by the glory of the Father, so we too might walk in newness of life.
> For if we have been united with him in a death like his, we will certainly be united with him in a resurrection like his. We know that our old self was crucified with him so that the body of sin might be destroyed, and we might no longer be enslaved to sin. For whoever has died is freed from sin. But

if we have died with Christ, we believe that we will also live with him. We know that Christ, being raised from the dead, will never die again; death no longer has dominion over him. The death he died, he died to sin, once for all; but the life he lives, he lives to God. So you also must consider yourselves dead to sin and alive to God in Christ Jesus.

Therefore, do not let sin exercise dominion in your mortal bodies, to make you obey their passions. . . . Present yourselves to God as those who have been brought from death to life. (Romans 6:4–12, 13b)

This passage underscores death to sin and to ourselves because that is the source of our first suffering. We must get rid of a large measure of self-centeredness and pride to die to ourselves. We like to think that our own projects and interests are the most important things in life, but the Scriptures make it clear that loving God and others takes top priority. And look at the rewards sketched in this text for when we choose God and others over ourselves: resurrection freedom, newness of life, eternal Joy.

Out of the suffering of death to ourselves we become ready to undergo additional adversities, like changes in our priorities or in our spending habits, for the sake of others. We become willing to follow Jesus into afflictions, such as harassment or ridicule, as part of God's purposes for the larger world. We discern that when we take others' burdens and hardships into ourselves through actions of compassion and time-consuming care, we ease the grief of the world and become agents of God's healing.

Jesus told us plainly that we will suffer if we want to follow Him, but He also made it quite clear that thereby we gain real life. According to the Gospel of Mark, He said this to everyone, not just to the chosen apostles:

He called the crowd with his disciples, and said to them,
"If any want to become my followers, let them deny themselves and take up their cross and follow me. For those who
want to save their life will lose it, and those who lose their
life for my sake, and for the sake of the gospel, will save it.
For what will it profit them to gain the whole world and
forfeit their life?" (Mark 8:34–36)

Peter, who just before these verses had tried to dissuade
Jesus from pursuing His own path of suffering—perhaps
largely because he didn't like the implications of what
Christ's affliction might mean for him—demonstrates a
changed perspective when he later writes with Joy in his
own letter:

Blessed be the God and Father of our Lord Jesus Christ!
By his great mercy he has given us a new birth into a living
hope through the resurrection of Jesus Christ from the dead,
and into an inheritance that is imperishable, undefiled, and
unfading, kept in heaven for you, who are being protected
by the power of God through faith for a salvation ready to
be revealed in the last time. In this you rejoice, even if now
for a little while you have had to suffer various trials, so that
the genuineness of your faith—being more precious than
gold that, though perishable, is tested by fire—may be found
to result in praise and glory and honor when Jesus Christ
is revealed. (1 Peter 1:3–7)

When Peter talks about an inheritance "kept in heaven"
and a salvation "ready to be revealed in the last time," he does
not mean that throughout our human suffering we are just
waiting for some sort of "pie in the sky in the bye and bye
when we die." We know this because he goes on to say:

> Although you have not seen him, you love him; and even
> though you do not see him now, you believe in him and
> rejoice with an indescribable and glorious joy, for you are
> receiving the outcome of your faith, the salvation of your
> souls. (1 Peter 1:8–9)

Notice that last verb tense: "you *are receiving.*" We presently enjoy the benefits of joining Christ in His sufferings—the same Joy of obedience to God's best purposes that enabled Him to persevere.

Later in the same letter Peter invites us even to celebrate our sufferings. He encourages us not to be surprised if we have to submit to fiery trials (1 Pet. 4:12), but instead to "rejoice insofar as you are sharing Christ's sufferings, so that you may also be glad and shout for joy when his glory is revealed" (v. 13). When we become willing to enter into hardships by participating in the Trinity's works of compassion and care, then we discern the privilege that it is to share Christ's very own sufferings. Even adversities and pain become a source of divine Joy.

To be truthful, we don't always experience that Joy in the midst of participating in those hardships. St. Martin of Tours probably didn't enjoy being bishop. Eventually, though, we usually begin to perceive a deep contentment that we are right in the middle of God's will. I remember a particular speaking engagement that I really didn't want to go to because I knew I would have to be a reconciler between groups in conflict. By the end of the assignment, however, I had a deep sense that God had used me in spite of myself to bring the contentious parties together, and suddenly what had been quite difficult became a cause for Joy.

The apostle Paul says the same thing in his letter to the Colossians. After a glorious hymn describing Jesus Christ, he claims that he is a servant of His gospel and adds, "I am now rejoicing in my sufferings for your sake, and in my flesh I am completing what is lacking in Christ's afflictions for the sake of his body, that is, the church" (Col. 1:24).

When we share in Christ's sufferings, we do not complete anything lacking in His work of rescuing human beings, for that has already been totally accomplished in His death and resurrection. What we actually have is the privilege of completing His purpose of building the Church, the community of His people. By our investments of time and energy, skills and hardships, other people are brought closer to God. Every time we pay a price to help others, we are nurturing in them a sense of God's grace, whether or not they can name it at that time.

How might it affect our discernments if we realize that every choice of ours can bring others either less or more of God's grace? Most times, to endow them with more grace will cost us something of ourselves. Are we willing to pay that price?

When we consider all that God has done for us, when we notice all that the Trinity does for us each day, when we realize the Joy that is set before us, how can we not but choose the path of suffering and celebration?

Miles Coverdale (1488?–1569) was a great translator of devotional works and, in 1535, prepared the first complete translation of the Bible to be printed in English. Later in life he became known for his preaching and served as bishop of Exeter, but during the rule of Mary I he was imprisoned for his faith. Later released, he continued to suffer through the Catholic-Protestant controversies of the English monarchy. Yet he prayed:

> O Jesus Christ, the mirror of all gentleness of mind, the
> example of highest obedience and patience, grant me your

servant true devotion to consider how you, innocent and undefiled Lamb, were bound, taken, and hauled away to death for my sins, how well content you were to suffer such things, not opening your mouth in impatience, but willingly offering yourself unto death. O gracious God, how vilely were you mishandled for my sake! O Lord, let this never come out of my heart. Take away my heart's coldness and sloth, stir up love and fervency towards you; provoke me to earnest prayer and make me cheerful and diligent in your will. Amen.[2]

May we similarly be formed into the character of those willing to suffer because we remember the great humbling that the Trinity to Whom we belong undertook for us. Then may that cause us to discern how much more we could grow in love and diligence to fulfill God's purposes through death to ourselves and new life in God for the sake of others!

THOMAS À KEMPIS AND THE CALL TO SUFFERING

Thomas à Kempis (1380–1471), who was introduced in Chapter One, grapples thoroughly in his second book, *Consolations for My Soul,* with the issue of accepting suffering for the sake of growing in relationship with God and serving others. In the following excerpts from à Kempis' long dialogue between the Soul and God, God is the one quoted until page 210. First, the Soul realizes that some suffering is good for us so that we know whether we love God for Himself alone and not just because we hope to be rewarded with the Lord's good gifts. A modern paraphrase of *Consolations* underscores this when God says to us how much He wants us to love Him truly and not for any sort of "'temporal nicety'" or "'material perk'" or for anything we might be able to "'squeak out of the situation.'"[3] How often haven't we turned to God as to some sort of vending machine to give us what we want!

Suffering purifies our love. It shows us whether we love God and others with genuine *agapé* (see Chapter Seven), love that requires nothing back from the one loved. Suffering helps us to discern more clearly our true motives, both in relation to God and concerning those we are seeking to serve.

Second, à Kempis records God's promise that He knows our "'threshold of suffering'" and won't allow us to experience afflictions to the extent that they would crush us under their heaviness (p. 166). Meanwhile, we have prayer and the Scriptures to sustain us and to enable us to bear that weight. All along, we are comforted simply by realizing that a great proportion of our spiritual life is "'grunt and grind'" (p. 167).

Too many of us expect (probably because we are conditioned to think so by the technological and medical advances and wealth in our society) that life should be easy. If we discern instead from the outset that our path through this world will always involve travail and anguish, then when sorrows come we are more able to receive them by relying on God's grace.

Why do we constantly forget that the sovereign God is always in charge? Perhaps we think we know better than God what sufferings are good for us. I usually am sure that I need far fewer troubles. But remember our emphasis in Chapter One that the cosmos is created in, founded on, and sustained by grace. God continually wants to soothe and uplift us with the truth of His reign, that in the midst of the sufferings of this life God is constantly with us. And the Trinity really does know with infinite wisdom our threshold of suffering.

Though our infirmities or the sufferings that accompany our highest commitments might exasperate us to no end, they won't annihilate us. They will instead usher us into God's glory (p. 168). They will help us to notice the people and the events through which God's love and grace can be tangibly seen and felt.

Another gift of sufferings, God affirms in *Consolations,* is that we learn how completely reliant we are on the Trinity (p. 169). Where would we be without God? What could we be, besides nonexistent? We learn that our life has its deepest meaning and purpose in serving God.

Yet we sometimes give up on God. Every so often we become so exhausted by sufferings, by our inability to hear God's voice, by the struggles that confine and impede us that we walk away from God and pretend to get along without Him. In those times we usually begin to realize that help that is deep enough is nowhere else to be found. In those hardships in which we push God away, we increasingly notice that we can't get along without the Trinity.

I have never forgotten a bumper sticker that I saw thirty years ago or so which said, "If you are not feeling close to God, guess who moved." Jesus promised always to be with us (Matthew 28:20), but are we walking with Him in humility and grateful dependence?

At times, though, it seems that God has gone far away from us. In numerous places, however, the Scriptures assure us that God will never leave us or forsake us. And à Kempis shows us that even those feelings of abandonment can be good for us, for, in the seeming absence of God, we discover how much we long for the Trinity's presence (p. 170).

As the dialogue in *Consolations* continues, the Lord cheers the Soul by recognizing that it is good for us to weep when we experience a distance from God. In truth, "'THE LOVER'S SPECIAL DEVOTION is a gush of holy tears.'" In those instances we are nourished and soothed more than in luxuriant times. The Soul seems to recognize that and responds, "I CRY ALONE, but He wants to cry with me. Is that Consolation or what?" (pp. 191–192).

Not only do we want in this chapter to learn how much it changes our discernment processes if we are willing to undergo the sufferings that certain choices might involve, but we also need to learn to discern how much God grieves with us when we are afflicted, how much the Trinity shares our woes and stays beside us as we work through them. To emulate à Kempis, is that supreme solace or what?

Finally, in a chapter called "Crashing the Party," à Kempis brings to mind the cloud of witnesses and describes some of the saints in heaven, such as Mary, the patriarchs (Abraham, Isaac, and Jacob), the Hebrew prophets, the apostles, the disciples, John the Baptizer, the apostle Paul, John the Gospel writer, and Andrew the brother of Simon Peter (p. 200). As the Soul contemplates these "Martyrs galore, soldiers of Christ, purpled by their own blood, scarred by their own fidelity," he realizes that they inspire us with their steadfast trust through every imaginable adversity.

The Soul concludes, "THE JOY OF THE SAINTS! If only one could snatch a bit of it! That would make the great pilgrimage much less of a trudge!" (p. 201).

Thinking through all that à Kempis has taught us, we can ask ourselves whether we have set before ourselves that eschatological Joy that was before Jesus and the saints, so that we are willing to choose those options in our discernment processes that might involve suffering for the sake of others. Do we discern in our own afflictions that the God to Whom we belong is with us, grieving for us, and nourishing us? In the midst of what seems like the absence of God, past and present saints teach us to discern the importance of nourishing our spiritual life with prayer, meditation, and Scripture study and with the consolation of belonging to a community willing to suffer. Most important, do we love God for God's own sake, and not for what we might get out of Him?

VARIETIES OF SUFFERING

As the previous paragraph suggests, there are various kinds of suffering that have diverse ramifications for our discernment processes. Sometimes we simply suffer because we live in a world in which illness, arthritis, cancer, injuries, disabilities, and other evils befall us, and then the choice before us is how to respond, how to bear with the affliction.

In contrast, at other times evil comes from outside ourselves, from natural forces beyond our control. In the midst of such hardships, we might need to discern how to help both ourselves and others similarly distressed.

Perhaps another person or group of people decides to harm us. Then we are faced with the possibility to react with vengeance and retribution or to respond with grace and forgiveness, with attempts at reconciliation, and with trust in God's own vindication of us.

Sometimes pain and suffering are adjuncts to choices we want to make because of our specific commitments. Then we have to discern whether we are willing to pay the price to stand up for our values or to engage in actions that advance us toward our goals.

We have also previously in this chapter considered the suffering of giving up our self-centeredness and the price we sometimes pay to love our neighbors in tangible ways and work for their well-being. It would not be possible to list all the kinds of suffering we all endure during the course of our lives in this world, but all of them correlate with discernment processes—whether we are willing to undergo them, how we will respond, how best we can serve others so afflicted, or whether we still believe God is sovereignly caring for the world in the midst of them.

Contemplate also the spiral of character formation and habits of discernment. As we have seen in previous chapters, the more we willingly choose options that are accompanied by suffering, the stronger our courage becomes and the more likely it is that we will be inclined to discern for ourselves the harder choices. Furthermore, in an intertwining spiral, the more we are formed by the character of the God and the people (the saints) to whom we belong, the more our character will reflect their readiness to suffer and will, in turn, help to build a community willing to pay the price of godly love and commitment.

In his book on Celtic holy places, Daniel Taylor tells us about various kinds of martyrs in early Christianity. The red martyrs were those who died for their faith at the hands of persecutors, while the ones named green martyrs were persons, such as hermits, who elected to submit to deprivations they imposed on themselves.

A special kind of courage was required for the white martyrs, those who placed their destiny in God's hands and became what is called a *peregrinatio,* a "wanderer for God." These were the saints who got in their little boats called coracles and trusted that God, Who directs the winds and currents, would take them where they should serve.[4]

One of the best known of the white martyrs is Columba (521–597), who with twelve companions sailed to the island of Iona, on the west coast of Scotland, and established a monastery that is still an important retreat center today. Taylor comments that he admires the integrity and valor of such saints, but that such an ability to leave everything in order to pursue the biblical "pearl of great value" (Matthew 13:45–46) is "unsettling, frightening" (p. 31).

I'm grateful for Taylor's confession (in which you and I can join) that sometimes the saints unnerve us with their audacity and fortitude. It is important for us to acknowledge that it can be scary when we discern that a certain choice or a particular direction in life will cause us pain.

Taylor goes on to question why the spiritual life seems perpetually to involve ever higher levels of training and rigor and why every breakthrough in closeness to God seems too slight. He wonders why the saints on earth and in heaven unceasingly beckon us onward. Finally, he asks, "Why does our goal always move, mirage-like, just beyond reach?" (p. 135).

Of course, the simple answer is that we are longing for that intimacy with God that we shall someday know, when we are no longer hindered by our sinful, earthly selves. But we dare not be simplistic about the profundity of our yearning and the struggle that it is to put up with the various tribulations that we encounter at every stage in our spiritual quest.

Throughout this book I've been outlining skills, tools, and examples to help us think about our own discernment processes. In this chapter we admit that good and godly decisions are not easy, that our very discernment processes themselves might sometimes cause us suffering, even as they force us to ask whether we are willing to undergo more struggles because of the choices we might make.

What a gift it is also to acknowledge that God both goes with us and has gone on before us in the Person of Jesus, Who similarly faced difficult decisions. Our choices will be most free and gratifying if in the face of suffering we can say with Jesus, "My Father, if it is possible, let this cup pass from me; yet not what I want but what you want" (Matthew

26:39), and, again, "My Father, if this cannot pass unless I drink it, your will be done" (v. 42).

From Jesus we learn that if any suffering is our heavenly, holy Father's will, it shall be good—perhaps not until much later or in the end and probably not only for us. Through our readings of the Scriptures, through our own experiences and those of others we know, through other sources of spiritual nourishment, we can discern that our troubles are all held in the hand of God and that, as Paul declares in Romans 8:18, "the sufferings of this present time are not worth comparing with the glory about to be revealed in us." Even if our life now is full of troubles, someday they will seem very small in contrast to the overflowing fullness of eschatological Joy.

That Joy is set before us. The Scriptures and the saints help us see it and delight in it even now.

I do not write these things about suffering and Joy glibly. Certainly, the great destruction of such events as the Holocaust, the South Asian tsunami of 2004, the hurricanes and earthquakes of 2005, or the great pile of adversities that we ourselves might be experiencing make us question the sovereignty of a loving God. We must strongly assert that God does not cause such evils and that He grieves over them and is compassionately present with all those who suffer them.

People throughout time have questioned the meaning of suffering and its connection with God. For example, one of my friends in China told me about the great Chinese poet called Qu Yuan, who was born around 343 B.C.E. and in memory of whom, it is believed, the Dragon Boat Festival was started. Qu Yuan wrote a long poem called "Questions for the Heaven" because of his distress in wondering why good people suffer.

The more ancient biblical book of Job is perhaps the most famous form of the question of suffering in relation to

God. After the book wrestles with the subject through long discussions between Job and his friends, God answers the question primarily by responding to Job's request to meet with him. Thereby Job doubly recognizes that his mind is too small to comprehend the mysteries of God and that the world is founded not on retribution but on grace. Then Job repents for his arrogance and any evils he might have done and gladly submits to the God Who cares intensely about everything in all of creation.[5]

To discuss the whole issue of suffering and God's care in the midst of it would require much more space than we have here.[6] Let me simply affirm, however, that my own struggles with escalating handicaps over the past years, my study of the Scriptures in the midst of these trials, my work and friendship with others who are variously disabled and undergoing diverse tribulations, and my observations of suffering saints throughout time and space have convinced me that God's promised and fulfilled eschatological Joy is greater and more lasting than all of our calamities and distresses.

AN EXAMPLE OF JOY IN SUFFERING FROM ZIMBABWE

One recent saint, a Zimbabwean pastor who knew that Joy, expressed his confidence in it in this final journal entry before suffering martyrdom for his Christian faith and consequent actions.

> I am a disciple of Christ. I will not let up, look back or slow down. My past is redeemed, my future is secure. I am done with low living, small planning, smooth knees, mundane talking, chintzy giving and dwarfed goals. I no longer need pre-eminence, prosperity, position, promotion or popularity.

I don't have to be right, first, tops, recognized, praised or re-warded. My face is set, my goal is sure. My road is narrow; my way is rough, my companions are few. My God is reliable, my mission is clear. I cannot be bought, compromised, detoured, delayed or deluded. I will not flinch in the face of adversity, nor negotiate at the table of the enemy or meander in the maze of mediocrity.

I am a disciple of Christ. I must go until He comes, speak of all I know of Him and work until He stops me.[7]

This is a man who knows from his life experience that the Triune God to Whom he belongs is reliable. As a result of that knowledge, he can make the decision to endure suffering with confidence.

In both the regular sufferings of life and in the specific sufferings that are caused because we choose to live for God, we have a choice in the way we will respond to them. What discernments might we be able to make if we grow in our confidence that God is reliable and can be trusted for both our immediate and our eternal future?

WILLINGNESS TO SUFFER IN THE CZECH CHURCH

When we were in Prague, Czech Republic, we learned many stories and saw many memorials to Jan Hus (1372?–1415), the pre-Reformation Bohemian religious reformer, a professor at the University of Prague, and later a preacher at the famous Bethlehem Chapel in central Prague. His willingness to suffer burning at the stake because of his commitment to the Christian faith inspired other reformers and still today spurs us all to ask whether we have enough confidence in the Trinity to make choices for God's purposes that might necessitate affliction or even martyrdom. Having such a belief then frees us to discern more clearly the duties to which our commitment calls us.

One memorial plaque in Bethlehem Chapel pays tribute to a heroic example, which arose in Prague during the time of Hus, of willingness to suffer for the sake of one's highest commitments. Three courageous men stood up in a worship service and objected to the teaching that a person could buy forgiveness (a practice undertaken to help finance the Crusades) because it is a free gift from Christ. The men were immediately arrested and, in a speedy trial, condemned to death.

When the men were being taken to the execution block, the wagon was stopped by the large crowds protesting in the streets, so the men were beheaded right there on the sidewalk. The executioner then told the crowd that if anyone wanted to say the same things as those men, those individuals would suffer the same fate. Did anyone want to stand with the men who had been executed? Many hands went up all through the crowd; persons raising them were arrested and taken to jail. In the following days many more people willingly turned themselves in to the jail—all insisting that they stood by the same truth and would suffer the same fate. Soon there were more people than the jail could hold, and the town council decided to let them go because as many people as had come forward could not be executed without serious repercussions.

Ironically, just after I had written to our hostess in Prague that a restaurant we had visited together had grossly overcharged us on our credit card bill, she recounted that the story of these men was repeated in a recent worship service to encourage the Christians there to stand for truth in a culture filled with lies and compromises.

We might ask the same in our culture, for it is also filled with lies. What are we willing to pay to stand for the truth against our society's deceptions? What decisions might be easier to make if we have already discerned the importance of living at all times truthfully?

DIETRICH BONHOEFFER— A MODERN MARTYR

Probably the best-known modern martyr is Dietrich Bonhoeffer, who was executed at age thirty-nine by the Nazis on April 9, 1945, for his participation in a conspiracy to assassinate Hitler. But Bonhoeffer should also be recognized for other sufferings he endured.

A highly precocious and educated theologian, Bonhoeffer discerned when Hitler first rose to power that the leader's policies were contrary to the Christian gospel. Consequently, Bonhoeffer chose early in his career to align himself with what was called the Confessing Church, and that caused estrangement from the German state church.

During the time that he served as pastor for two German-speaking churches in London in 1933–1935, he worked extensively in ecumenism with the World Alliance of Churches, which sided with the Confessing Church instead of the state church, and he developed important contacts that later enabled him to inform the free world of the extent of Hitler's oppression of active Christians. Then he was called back to Germany to lead the Confessing Church's seminary at Finkenwalde.

Because of his opposition to Hitler, Bonhoeffer's appointment to the University of Berlin was terminated in

1936, and the Finkenwalde seminary was officially disbanded in 1937, but it continued underground until 1940.

When theologians at Union Seminary in New York learned of the danger to his life, they arranged for Bonhoeffer to come to the United States, but he stayed for less than two months. He discerned that he would have no right to speak to Germans after the end of Hitler's tyranny if he had not shared in their sufferings during it.

Eberhard Bethge, one of Bonhoeffer's closest friends, reports in his introduction to a collection of Bonhoeffer's *Letters and Papers from Prison* that Bonhoeffer suffered deeply when the plot of the resistance against Hitler in which he had been involved failed. He had already been imprisoned but was subsequently moved to another prison for greater confinement and torture. Nonetheless, though he then knew his end was near, he met that blow "with renewed dedication to the service of his people, and with steadfast determination to bear all the painful consequences."[8]

A fellow prisoner, English officer Payne Best, described Bonhoeffer during some of his last days as follows:

> Bonhoeffer . . . was all humility and sweetness; he always seemed to me to diffuse an atmosphere of happiness, of joy in every smallest event in life, and of deep gratitude for the mere fact that he was alive. . . . He was one of the very few men that I have ever met to whom God was real and close.

The day before he died, he held a worship service for his fellow prisoners "and spoke to us in a manner which reached the hearts of all, finding just the right words to express the spirit of our imprisonment and the thoughts and resolutions which it brought."[9] Bonhoeffer had barely finished the

prayers in that worship service when he was called by two
men who said, "Come with us"—words which certainly
meant his death.

Even in that death, nonetheless, Bonhoeffer chose to
trust his God. The prison camp's doctor recorded these observations of his final moments:

> On the morning of that day [after Bonhoeffer heard his
> sentence read] . . . I saw Pastor Bonhoeffer . . . kneeling on
> the floor praying fervently to his God. I was most deeply
> moved by the way this lovable man prayed, so devout and
> so certain that God heard his prayer. At the place of execution,
> he again said a short prayer and then climbed the steps to
> the gallows, brave and composed. . . . In the almost fifty
> years that I worked as a doctor, I have hardly ever seen
> a man die so entirely submissive to the will of God.[10]

Throughout his life, Bonhoeffer sought to discern God's will
and cooperatively—even Joy-fully—endured the suffering
that choosing it entailed.

As a result, we are all spurred to greater willingness to
bear whatever sufferings are involved in our best commitments and to greater openness to make choices that might
necessitate suffering.

Do we also discern what gifts we might receive from
adversities?

GIFTS OF SUFFERING IN
NIGERIA AND MADAGASCAR

One great gift of suffering, especially that which is not willingly chosen, is that it often deepens the victim's prayer life,

as we saw with Bonhoeffer. Bea Haagenson, who was introduced in Chapter Six, wrote that prayer is a very important part of Nigerian Christians' lives, and that their prayers "are far from routine."

She reported that their talking with God is very similar to their visiting with a friend. They sit down and take the time both to talk and to listen to God, and they look for answers in the Bible, as we stressed in Chapter Two. Bea noted her conviction that "prayer life [as] a guiding force in troubled times—of which there are many in a poor culture"—is "the key to the enormous growth of the Christian churches in Africa. The people need a loving God who is there for them no matter what happens."

Notice in Bea's account a very important spiral between discernment and character that is developed in the lives of those who suffer from poverty and oppression. In the midst of their sufferings, they discern that their best recourse is to turn to God. As a result, their prayer lives thrive, as do the Christian churches. In turn, these faithful people are more able to discern the presence of a loving God, Who enables them to keep choosing trust in the face of adversities.

Similarly, remember what we learned from Dr. Andry Ranaivoson and his wife, Bako Ramihaminarivo, in Chapter Four about the Malagasy Christians who suffered extreme persecution and martyrdom—how their obedience to God's Word was, in Andry's and Bako's words, "complete and total," even though that "brought them to a certain death." They had learned in their sufferings an absolute dependence on God and His Word that continues to inspire Malagasy Christians—and us.

THE FRUITS OF SUFFERING IN RUSSIA AND ETHIOPIA

Harold Kurtz, a pastor who served with his wife, Polly, for many years in Ethiopia, also founded Presbyterian Frontier Fellowship, under which he has traveled to many other places in the world to share his expertise in missions. From his report (dated March 16, 2002) of a trip to Siberia, to a place north of the Arctic Circle in the upper area of a district that in Russian is called "The Edge of the Earth," we learn of both past and present sufferings and their fruits.

Many of the scattered congregations in the region were begun in the Gulag camps, Harold relates,

> where faithful Baptist exiles maintained their witness and life through unimaginable hardships. Some congregations developed out of prayer meetings during those perilous times. These town and city congregations also find themselves bordering the vast wilderness and tundra areas where numbers of Aleut or Eskimo people live in scattered settlements herding their reindeer or hunting and fishing. When Jesus said, "Go and make disciples of all peoples," He was thinking of the Khanti, Nyensi, Komi and other people of this vast and forbidding region.

Churches grew from prisoners' witness and lives in the midst of their sufferings, and now from these churches spring missions to the native peoples.

In his report Harold describes the bitter cold encountered when he went to this far north region in the winter (so that driving would be easier). He traveled with a missionary working out of Moscow and two local Baptist leaders to an area called Samburg, near the Arctic Ocean. Their transportation was by airplane and then north as far as a van could go to a small east-west road junction called "Beyond the Arctic Circle" and from there by snowcat for three and a half hours to Samburg, a Nyensi settlement, and from there two hours by reindeer sled (pulled now by a snowmobile) to a village of six teepees, each housing an extended family of several generations. While there, Harold also had the opportunity to go for an actual reindeer sled ride to experience that common means of travel in the region.

His extended report recounts that the result of their labors was that several of the Nyensi people whom they met became interested in Christianity and made commitments to the faith, so that perhaps new house churches would be started. From the discernment of the missionaries that these unreached native peoples would be glad to hear the Gospel came their decision to undergo the rigors of the trip, and from that travail came the gift of new believers.

The woman who had taken Harold for his reindeer ride followed the missionaries back to Samburg to listen to the church gathering and became one of the new Christians. During that gathering Harold told the story of Esther, a young Dawro woman in Ethiopia, who had made a commitment to follow Jesus after seeing a vision of Him, even though the local witchdoctor threatened her with death. Now more than fifteen thousand of her people are followers of Christ, and she has been selected to represent her district in parliament.

We never know what effects our sufferings might have on others. Nor can we predict how our afflictions will change us. Do we trust God enough so that we are willing, in times of discernment, to choose a path that may involve adversity? How might our willingness to accept hardship affect our future decision making and, in turn, the growth of our character into steadfastness and endurance? How could our own distresses help the community to which we belong become more open to suffer difficulties? Do we believe the hope of God's eschatological Joy enough to accept suffering and to bear it with gladness—for our sake, the sake of others, and the glory of God?

9

The Wisdom
of Celebration

A dozen years ago during the months that I was battling cancer, I dreaded my birthday. What reason was there to celebrate when I felt so ill? Chemotherapy was wearing me out; it had rendered me bald, made me nauseous, and left me exhausted.

But as my birthday morning began, my husband, Myron, woke me with a bright smile and said, "Beautiful princess, your chariot ride awaits you." After I was dressed, he propelled me down the street in my wheelchair and around the neighborhood park while pointing out especially glorious summer flowers to make sure I wouldn't miss them because of my visual handicaps. We laughed most of the trip, partly because I was so surprised to begin the day that way.

When we returned to the house, I saw that long before awakening me Myron had set the kitchen table with special dishes and had gotten everything ready for breakfast. This included picking strawberries from the garden and setting a few wrapped packages near my plate.

The rest of the entire day continued with wonder after wonder—a picnic lunch, dinner in a restaurant, a surprise evening party (even though Myron claims that he doesn't know how to give parties). One special highlight was a wheelchair visit to the zoo—which required an enormous amount of energy on Myron's part not only to push me up-hill at several places, but even to get the wheelchair into the back seat of our 1968 Volkswagen "bug."

That special visit remains particularly memorable because the Portland zoo featured an exceptional glass house of African birds. While Myron pointed out to me astounding birds of radiant colors and remarkable songs, we tried to interest others in what we were seeing and hearing, but most of the people were in too much of a hurry to notice gifts that could be encountered with a little silence, some reflective waiting, and the sharing of a community. They missed the celebration.

The celebration for me, however, had long-lasting reverberations. It gave me courage and determination to persist in trying to do my work in spite of the debilitating effects of chemotherapy. And, still to this day, it reminds me that celebration is a good foundation for gaining a better life perspective, out of which better discernment is possible.

Several elements of that birthday bash spotlight themes for this chapter. Perhaps most important, celebration doesn't have to wait until sorrow is over. In fact, as we shall see further on, festivity, especially that based in eschatological Joy, provides a gift to help us deal with sadness and suffering.

Second, celebration is a choice that usually requires expenditure of energy, so it is a matter of discernment that leads to effort. But the result can be a great release from affliction, a renewed sense of meaning, and the ability to discern one's blessings in the midst of tough times.

Also, the gladness that resulted from the celebratory day's uplifting made it more possible in the days and weeks that followed for me to pursue my work and to make the kinds of decisions that were necessary, in spite of how I felt.

Finally, our experience in the bird house reveals part of the reason that North Americans do not seem to be as good at revelry as are people in other cultures. Our habits of busy-ness and efficiency or perhaps even our wealth and possessiveness may blind us to delights that could change our perceptions and bring us gladness. Celebration is a matter of discernment as we focus on what is good in the midst of sorrow, and, in turn, it leads to better choices. What wisdom are we missing if we don't take time for festivity?

WHAT KEEPS US FROM DISCERNING WELL?

Today again I am moving around my house in the wheelchair. A bad fall injured my good leg in the knee, and my crippled leg isn't strong enough to support me very well on crutches, so I can use them only for short periods of time. I still don't have much energy because of immunosuppressants and other medications, and I'm sitting at my computer awkwardly now with the swollen leg up on another chair.

Meanwhile, one of my favorite piano concertos is playing on the radio. A sun break in our usual dismal Washington winter weather is splaying brilliant beams of light across the walls of my study; soon my husband will be home from his morning meeting and we'll enjoy lunch together; and the topic of this chapter interests me immensely.

On which will I focus—the aggravation and inconvenience of the first paragraph or the beauties and blessings of the second?

I confess that yesterday, when there were no sun breaks, I was as gloomy as the sky. I know my guilt: thinking only of my frustrations and hurts keeps me from discerning all the gifts that God continually pours into my days.

Just at this point my writing was interrupted by a telephone call from a woman who suffers from constant pain. She called to discuss a church matter but then asked how I was doing. When the attention shifted to her health, she reported on her situation and then said, "I'd rather focus on the positive things."

Do we make that conscious choice?

More deeply, do we take the time to notice the elements of our lives that call for celebration?

More deeply still, do we realize that in all the cosmos, the good outweighs the bad? Do we remember that eschatological Joy is always possible because the God to Whom we belong has triumphed over evil in Christ?

This chapter is a corollary to Chapter One, in which we considered the Triune God's grace as the basis for the world. If we realize that grace is also the foundation particularly for our lives, that God and good have triumphed over evil in Christ, and that someday God will bring the Trinity's purposes for the cosmos to completion at the end of time, then we know that we can live in eschatological Joy (see Chapter Four), and we will make our decisions accordingly.

We have already considered in Chapter One what keeps us from receiving grace, but each of us should ask what prevents us personally. What hinders us from believing that Christ has triumphed over evil? What obstructs our acceptance of God's assurance that the Trinity is at work in us, even in struggles, to form us into Christ's likeness? What deters us from trusting God's promises for the end of time and the consummation of eschatological Joy?

When we have pondered our own particular answers to those questions, then we will acknowledge what hampers our celebration. Perhaps we are too busy to take time to notice all the goodness in our lives. Maybe we are too overwhelmed by struggles to remember God's undergirding care. Possibly we can't imagine that God is really in control when so many catastrophes have befallen the world. It could be that we are blaming God for evils that human beings have caused. Perchance we have been so richly blessed that we expect only good things and take them for granted. Maybe we are not part of a community that keeps focusing on eschatological Joy.

Whatever distracts us from discovering the fullness of God's Joy can only be repelled by a fuller sense of the all-pervading grace of the Triune God and a sense of how truly we don't deserve it. If we consciously focus our lives on God's gracious character, then gradually His love breaks through the fog of our struggles or pride.

I write this as a person who regularly has to make that conscious choice. It is an act of will, and I'm not promising that it is easy, but the Scriptures repeatedly assure us that rejoicing is possible if we learn ever afresh to depend on God in humility and trust.

It helps if we belong to a community that is willing to enter into our suffering and to enfold us in its celebrations. I'm regularly encouraged by worship services, the support of friends, readings from the Scriptures, and the model of the saints throughout time and space to claim the Joy that is definitively ours in Christ's decisive victory over death and all the evil powers.

Also, as we have seen especially in Chapter Six, the celebrations of the community in various cultures' practices of care for the bereaved in times of loss enable the bereaved better to discern how to go on because they have been enfolded in a company of embracing nurture. How might we all begin to discern better ways to surround suffering people with eschatological celebrations of enduring hope?

BIBLICAL INVITATIONS TO
ESCHATOLOGICAL CELEBRATION

I am writing this in the season of Advent, the four weeks of preparation before Christmas in which the Sunday Scripture readings recount for us the strange stories of Jesus' coming. One of the most unthinkable is that of Jesus coming into Jerusalem and being hailed by the bystanders as a king—though He rides not an elegant war horse but a humble donkey (see Luke 19:29–40 and John 12:12–19) to fulfill a prophecy in Zechariah 9:9–10.

It's not how we would expect God to come, just as it is another of God's jokes that the world's Messiah should come first as a baby in poverty and then as a refugee (see Luke 2:1–24 and Matthew 2:1–15). But God seems to like showing up in a way that understates Who He is, so that we can learn to recognize Him and the fullness of His love in all things, especially the simple, and even in the midst of our struggles in this world. Can we see the Triune God in every modest delight of our lives? Do we have the eyes to see Him and the ears to listen to His voice of grace in times of trial?[1]

The apostle Paul certainly did. Even though he was in prison when he wrote his letter to the Philippians, he could say, "Finally, my brothers and sisters, rejoice in the Lord" (3:1) and "Rejoice in the Lord always; again I will say, Rejoice" (4:4). These are but three of the seventeen times he uses forms of the verb *rejoice* in that prison letter. The secret is that our Joy comes from focusing on the Lord instead of on ourselves.

That is one of the reasons that I so love the biblical commands to keep a Sabbath day holy and wholly. By setting aside one day a week to focus more on God and to rest in His grace and love, we learn better to discern and celebrate

God's presence in the other days of our week. (Perhaps we should add, to discern God's presence in our weak-nesses.)

Elsewhere in the Scriptures we are invited to step away from our own paths to learn to recognize God's goodness, to rest in it, and thereby to celebrate it. For example, ponder this passage from the prophet Jeremiah:

> Thus says the LORD:
> Stand at the crossroads and look,
>   and ask for the ancient paths,
> where the good way lies; and walk in it,
>   and find rest for your souls. (Jeremiah 6:16)

But Jeremiah (and the LORD) perceived that the people of Israel would not walk in God's good ways, would not listen to the sentinels warning them. They were too stubborn.

Do we sometimes banish celebration and Joy from our lives because we are too stubborn and would rather wallow in our own self-pitying? Certainly that affects our discernment of grace. How does it change our choices?

Might our lack of celebration—and the repercussions of that for our skills of discernment—be due to our need to be in charge of our own integrity and destiny?

In the previous chapter we glanced at the book of Job. When we look at its ending, God's magnificent speech from the whirlwind to Job changes the way we see our human attempts to define our own lives. First Testament scholar and professor at Duke Divinity School Ellen Davis offers this brilliant description of Job's new perception of his life after he witnesses God's "guided tour of the creation":

> It means fitting into a design vastly bigger and more complex than Job ever imagined. What God says, in effect, is this: "Look away from yourself, Job; look around you. For a moment see

the world with my eyes, in all its intricacy and wild beauty.
The beauty is in the wildness, Job; you cannot tame all that
frightens you without losing the beauty." God calls this man
of integrity to take his place in a ravishing but dangerous
world where only those who relinquish their personal
expectations can live in peace. The price of peace is the
surrender of our personal expectations, which are always
too small for the huge freedom built into the system.

The great question that God's speech out of the
whirlwind poses for Job and every other person of integrity is this: Can you love what you do not control?[2]

Ah, there's the issue! Perhaps our lives lack celebration because we try too hard to control them ourselves.

When we learn dependence instead, we will know true
Joy. We can gladly submit to God's control, for, as the great
English mystic Julian of Norwich (1343–1413) so famously
records, God pledges, "I may make all things well; I can make
all things well, and I will make all things well, and I shall make
all things well; and you shall see for yourself that all manner
of things shall be well."[3]

Julian's vision bears witness to God's promises in the
Scriptures. The biblical psalms especially keep reminding us
of this truth that we know highest elation when we turn our
lives over to God. For example, Psalm 37 promises this:

> Take delight in the LORD,
> and he will give you the desires of your heart.
> Commit your way to the LORD;
> trust in him, and he will act. (Psalm 37:4–5)

Trusting in God has been made so much easier for us
because God has come so near to us. Rather than staying dis-

tant in stupendous magnificence, God has condescended in Jesus to become one with us so that we might know Him.

The living out of God's grace in Jesus Christ demonstrates God's majesty in His humility, His transcendence in His immanence (that is, His closeness to us), His mighty power in His choosing to submit to limitation, His eternal love in His stooping to surrender for our sake to time, His all-sufficient life in His subjection to death. Because of all Christ's choices, He has defeated our limitations and confusions, our sufferings and death for all time and eternity.[4]

Christ's completed work is the source of our eschatological Joy, which changes forever how we make our decisions. That is our reason for celebration, which unceasingly affects our discernment.

We can rejoice every day not only because God is eternally victorious over our sorrows, but also because God desires an intimate relationship with us now, each moment. Imagine this: the Lord of the cosmos wants to be our friend!

The Scriptures affirm this in many ways and places. See, for example, Exodus 29:43–46 and 33:11, Psalm 23, Isaiah 41:8–10 and 49:13–16a, John 15:13–15, and Hebrews 13:5–6. Just as Jesus was a friend to many in his day, so He extends that love to us—see such texts as Mark 10:21, Luke 12:4–7, John 11:5, 11 and 13:1, and Galatians 2:20.

The Bible makes it clear that no matter what takes place in our lives, we can live out of Joy. (Remember that Joy is a fact, not necessarily a feeling. It is the knowledge of the truth of God's reign through Christ.) The letter of James affirms:

> My brothers and sisters, whenever you face trials of any kind, consider it nothing but joy, because you know that the testing of your faith produces endurance; and let endurance have its

full effect, so that you may be mature and complete, lacking
in nothing.

    If any of you is lacking in wisdom, ask God, who gives to
all generously and ungrudgingly, and it will be given you.
(James 1:2–5)

It strikes me that James moves immediately from the
subject of Joy in our trials to the topic of wisdom. What is the
connection? Why should we consider celebration as a necessary skill for discernment?

FESTIVITY AS A BASIS FOR DISCERNMENT

Of course, in this chapter I am not using the idea of celebration in a loose sense—I don't mean revelry as mindless par-
tying, gluttony, dissipation, or acquisitiveness, which actually
negate genuine festivity. Rather, I'm especially referring to
Joy-full celebration of Who God is, who we are in God, and
what God's present and eternal gifts to us convey.

    All of our decisions will be better made if we ponder
them on a foundation of confidence in God's goodness to
and through us. Celebration or praise precedes discernment.
As University of Southern California professor of philosophy
and author Dallas Willard says, "Our concern for discerning
God's voice must be overwhelmed by and lost in our worship
and adoration of him and in our delight with his creation and
his provision for our whole life."[5]

    When we become "lost in wonder, love, and praise," as
Charles Wesley's hymn expresses it,[6] we are more open to
hearing God's directions for our choices because we are more
knit to God in devotion and reverence. When we more as-
suredly trust the Trinity, we are more able to make bold de-

cisions without fear. When we are filled with eschatological Joy, we believe that God wants what is best for us and for the world, and we more readily rely on God to direct us to discern it.

GLADNESS AS A SIGN OF GOD'S CALL

The inverse is also sometimes true. Often when we are faced with choices, the one which stirs us the most and brings us the greatest exhilaration is the best decision for us. Here I want to stress the words *sometimes* and *often* because our selfishness could derail the process. Also, occasionally the best decision does not excite us because it might involve suffering or might seem impossible or be risky or too costly. However, on further reflection we might realize that it is even more costly to deny our true selves.

But our optimum decisions will always prove to be what is best for us as individuals, even as they also reveal themselves to be what is best for the wider world. Presbyterian pastor and author Frederick Buechner captures this felicitously in his well-known line "the place God calls you to is the place where your deep gladness and the world's deep hunger meet."[7]

Buechner's insight fills us with awe. Isn't it astounding that God has so formed us that what gives us the greatest pleasure is also what best serves the world?

It seems that frequently we are too afraid to choose what is most appealing to us. What we then fail to realize is that the God to Whom we belong has lovingly created our deepest desires, and that He is enormously pleased when we live according to our truest selves.

Besides, we have several other tests to make sure that our gladness is pointing us in the right direction. Is the decision in keeping with other skills we have considered in this book? Does it increase our awareness of, and does it depend on, God's grace? Does it follow the Scriptures or contradict them by perhaps obeying the habits of the culture around us? Have we defined all the terms of the decision accurately? Does it build our character in godly directions and strengthen our moral values? Did the community help in the discernment process, and does the community affirm our decision? Does our choice build hospitality, generosity, and reconciliation in the world? Have we turned away from a better decision because we are afraid of the suffering that might be involved or have we been able to look adversity boldly in the face to make the best choice according to our noblest commitments?

Our deepest Joy is an eternal one. When we discern choices that have eternal consequences in bringing grace to us and the world around us, we will experience a deep gladness, the ecstasy of God Himself.

JOY-FULL SAINTS

One of the most notable aspects of the saints throughout history has been their Joy. Not only do they rejoice in the promises of God's future life, but they also typically are people who take special delight in the beauties of earth and the simple pleasures of life. Let us look at an example of each kind of rejoicing and notice the saints' ability to endure suffering and how their eyes are open to make good decisions because of their Joy.

First, let us savor an exalted outpouring of praise by a saint looking forward to the rejoicing of heaven. The previous chapter introduced St. Columba (521–597), who founded the Iona monastery. A very popular hymn with the medieval Church, *Altus Prosator,* might have come from Columba himself or from someone at Iona in the following century. Based on the sublime biblical visions in Revelation 4:1–11, 5:1–14, and 7:9–17, this hymn displays an exquisite, divine perception undergirding eschatological Joy:

> By the singing of hymns eagerly ringing out,
> by thousands of angels rejoicing in holy dances,
> and by the four living creatures full of eyes,
> with the twenty-four joyful elders
> casting their crowns under the feet of the Lamb
>   of God,
> the Trinity is praised in eternal threefold exchanges.[8]

Praise is the secret of the saints' Joy because praise shifts our attention away from ourselves to the character of the God Whom we laud.

In her book subtitled *Rediscovering the Spiritual Art of Attentiveness,* noted Benedictine commentator and retreat leader Esther De Waal cites these lines of the Austro-German poet Rainer Maria Rilke (1875–1926):

> O tell me, poet, what do you do?—I praise.
> But how can you endure to meet the gaze
> Of deathly and of monstrous things?—I praise.[9]

To praise in the face of evil and death is a conscious decision, but it is also the means by which we are delivered from our fears of them. How would it affect all our processes of discernment if we enfolded them in the Joy of praise?

Probably the saint with the best reputation for Joy is Francis of Assisi. One of the best-known biographers of Francis, Father Cuthbert, describes the irresistible delight of the saint that caused him to speak "as one looking intently upon a vision of beauty, and asserting its claim upon men's lives, and sorrowing for the blindness which made a man unseeing." Francis always wished to share with others the treasures from God, including God Himself, that he found surrounding him. His compelling leadership attracted followers because "he was so manifestly happy in himself and in his message."[10]

Felix Timmermann's book *The Perfect Joy of St. Francis* describes Francis' preaching and life further from the perspective of his brothers in the order. For them, "when it was Francis speaking, everything seemed so clear, so beautiful, so young and fresh. It was as if he were storming their hearts with love, attacking them with bursts of divine fire. It was useless to try and give it a name; it was just beauty, pure and simple." His secret was that "his soul was ablaze. He had made room for God, and with God he was filled."[11]

Being so saturated with God, Francis knew that the greatest Joy in life is to love God and accept from His hand whatever God wills. He counseled his followers, "Love Him! There you have it all. . . . The essential, the only thing that matters is that we should always be pleased with whatever He chooses to give us. And that is love."[12]

Think how different our discernment processes might be if we were ready to receive gladly whatever God brings our way. How might that change our choices, our attitudes, our character?

Certainly we would live more wholly, more exuber-antly, more freely.

One modern saint who rebukes us for living so pas-sively, so routinely, when all the Joys of heaven surround us is Annie Dillard. In her Pulitzer Prize–winning book *Pilgrim at Tinker Creek* she writes:

> There is always an enormous temptation in all of life to
> diddle around making itsy-bitsy friends and meals and
> journeys for itsy-bitsy years on end. It is so self-conscious,
> so apparently moral, simply to step aside from the gaps where
> the creeks and winds pour down, saying, I never merited
> this grace, quite rightly, and then to sulk along the rest of
> your days on the edge of rage. I won't have it. The world
> is wilder than that in all directions, more dangerous and
> bitter, more extravagant and bright. We are making hay
> when we should be making whoopee; we are raising
> tomatoes when we should be raising Cain, or Lazarus.[13]

Are we listening to the creeks and winds, or ignoring them? Are we shouting with them, "I never merited this grace" and therefore rejoicing more deeply in that grace? Or do we "sulk along" and wonder what is the source of our hidden rage?

This book ends with celebration and eschatological Joy because it is an invitation to seize the moment to live for God, to discern God's presence in, with, and through us in every instant of our lives. Imagine how much more delight-ful our decision processes will be when they are enfolded in confident conviviality. Envision how much our lives will be changed if we more clearly discern the divine Joy that under-girds them.

CELEBRATION IN
INDIA AND LATIN AMERICA

I first learned about choosing to celebrate in the midst of sorrow from a close friend of mine who served for a period of time as a doctor in India. The custom there is to throw a large party when a baby is born. When my friend delivered a baby for a very poor family, she wondered if she could pay for the party in order to help the family. However, the family members responded, "Would you deprive us of the privilege?"

It was a conscious decision on their part, and one they did not regret. The celebration might cost them all that they possessed, but it was worth it to them to honor their newborn child.

Their story reminds me of a lovely little Christmas tale called "The Well of the Star" in which David, a young tattered shepherd boy with an ailing father, a despairing mother, and hungry brothers and sisters, follows three kings to a stable in Bethlehem. When he sees the Christ Child in the manger, he responds with utter adoration and with Joy gives to the Baby his shepherd's pipe, his dearest and only treasure. On his way home, he realizes what he has done and weeps in despair because now he has lost all he had and has to return to his destitute family empty-handed. But he is rescued by one of the kings and discovers that his unconditional offering of his very life to the Child is honored by God.[14]

In the midst of struggles and poverty of spirit, do we realize the importance of celebration, of utmost adoration and dedication of all that we are and have, of naming and expressing God's Joy? Choosing to celebrate, in a continuing spiral, lessens our woes and frees us for more festivity.

Long ago I read an account of a North American missionary doctor who was serving in a Latin American refugee camp. The work was extremely difficult because the odds against the refugees were overwhelming. When a beloved small child died the day before Christmas, the doctor was surprised that the preparations for the Christmas fiesta proceeded almost as if nothing had happened. The men continued to prepare the pit for roasting a pig, and the women persisted with their cooking and other arrangements.

When the doctor asked a fellow health worker how the people could go on in this way, the native nurse replied that the doctor could only question it because she was from a wealthy place. "If you lived here always," the nurse continued, "you would know that we have to celebrate in order to survive."

This has been my experience throughout the world. Those who live in more difficult circumstances seem to have developed a culture of celebration in which the people know much more thoroughly the power of celebration to ease our sorrows. Those who are more affluent often seem less capable of choosing Joy in the face of trials.

JEAN VANIER AND L'ARCHE COMMUNITIES OF EQUALS

In 1964, the French-Canadian philosopher Jean Vanier created a covenant community in which he deliberately lived with some handicapped men. Today there are l'Arche (the Ark) homes, which pair the supposed able with the mentally and emotionally handicapped, not only in Europe and North America, but also in the Two-Thirds World.

Perhaps the best-known commentator on the meaning of life in these communities was the spiritual leader and writer Henri Nouwen, a former professor at Harvard who left academia to live with, and serve as a priest for, Daybreak community in Toronto until his death. Nouwen discovered, as do all who participate in such l'Arche communities, that those considered "deficient" teach us important lessons about life.[15]

I learned, when I visited Daybreak, that one of the most important lessons they can teach us is the significance of celebration and its power to lighten our afflictions. L'Arche community members commemorate everyone's birthday, prominent events in each other's lives, and particular blessings that come to the "family." If they have no specific cause for revelry, they invent one.

The biographer Michael Downey underscores that l'Arche celebrations prevail "no matter how deep the suffering." In truth, the celebration "intensifies as the suffering is recognized and appropriated" and it "flows very easily into prayer."[16]

The festivities at l'Arche communities highlight the point we made before that we do not need to wait until suffering is over to frolic. I experienced a festive birthday celebration at Daybreak for and with a resident who could not talk, shift her position, or feed herself. Nonetheless, her revelry was palpable.

Furthermore, we learn from Downey that the celebration itself nourishes our relationship with God. Moreover, we notice in l'Arche communities that the decision to live by Joy is made easier because residents belong to a people who party deliberately.

Downey accentuates that festivity is not a *compensation* for suffering. Rather, "Joy born of deep suffering is nourished by moments of celebration. . . . Celebration properly understood is the acceptance of life in an ever growing recognition that it is so precious."[17]

That is why it is essential that we highlight celebration in this last chapter. Do we comprehend how precious life is? We would certainly take all our little decisions much more seriously if we unceasingly remembered what a treasure life is—not only ours, but also the lives of all those whom we might serve.

And can we accept our own lives, no matter what befalls us, in the profound perception that they are undergirded by the grace of the God to Whom we belong and, therefore, that we can live each moment in eschatological Joy?

CELEBRATIONS, FESTIVALS, SABBATH DAYS

What kinds of celebrations might we want to add to our lives and our community's life to keep reminding us of these truths? We can gain some hints for the types of festivities that will be nourishing for us from this definition in the Mennonite Sara Wenger Shenk's book *Why Not Celebrate?*

> Celebration is the honoring of that which we hold most dear. Celebrating is delighting in that which tells us who we are. Celebration is taking the time to cherish each other. Celebration is returning with open arms and thankful hearts to our Maker.[18]

Her clarifications help me name some of the festivals that are important for my life so that I keep remembering who I am in relation to God and others. These times of commemoration include not only the birthdays and anniversaries of loved ones, but also, for me, festival days and seasons in the Church year. For example, the season of Lent—the forty days in which we ponder all that Christ did for us through His passion and cross to rescue us from sin, death, and evil—is very important for me to put aspects of my life into perspective and to help me realize much more thoroughly how rich is the Joy of Easter, when we celebrate the fulfillment of God's promises in Christ and the assurance of our own resurrection from the dead.

I have also occasionally mentioned Sabbath keeping in this book. The Sabbath day (which we observe on Sunday in honor of Christ's resurrection, which changed everything in the cosmos!) has become a very important weekly celebration for my husband and me. Over the course of almost twenty-five years that I have ceased working in an entire Sabbath day of resting and feasting, I have noticed how much it affects my processes of discernment because every week it turns me back to remember more thoroughly all that God has done for me and is doing in my life. It undergirds my weeks with Joy so that I can make better choices for the mundane elements of daily life.

Sabbath keeping provides us with an incomparable opportunity to praise, for what we commemorate is God's unchanging and unfailing grace, His unwavering steadfastness and commitment to us, the preciousness of life under His loving reign. Unlike spectacular events which we solemnize because they happen so rarely, the Sabbath is observed every seven days because God's grace endures always.

At one time I suspected that a weekly celebration of the Sabbath would become too mechanized and thereby meaningless. Greatly to the contrary, each Sabbath has proved to be unique in itself; each week it has brought its own singular revelry and delight in God's provision. Each week, it has brought rest and grace—though it is true that some Sabbaths have been more beneficial than others in restoring my perspectives and in fitting me for better discernment. Nonetheless, to keep that special day has been a good practice for me to remind myself regularly of the Joy that can buttress my life.

The Sabbath has also become a special day of hospitality and generosity and of building a community of Joy. Because there is no work to do on the Sabbath, we are liberated on that day to spend more time with others, to remember more deeply to whom we belong (both people and God). Also, because of the day's celebration and feasting with special foods, we are set free to live more simply the rest of the week and to share our resources more generously with those in need.

What habits and customs might you choose to remind you regularly of the Joy that undergirds your life? Contemplate in what practices you might engage so that you can frequently renew your perspectives and remember the fullness of God's grace. How might these habits and practices affect your everyday discernment processes? How might they deepen the Joy of the community to which you belong?

THE IMPORTANCE OF RITUAL

Because of the abuses of ritual*ism* when ceremony becomes empty show, the word *ritual* has sometimes gotten a bad press in our society. However, we actually need rituals in our lives. Otherwise, all time is the same. Rituals make some moments more special than others, and thereby they give high points to our lives.

Such things as Sabbath keeping and observing religious rites and church holy festivals help us to give some ordering and differentiation to our days. I have discovered that I find

more meaning in following the church calendar than in keeping our society's substitute rituals for Halloween, the Super
Bowl, the World Series, and the Final Four.

It seems that if people don't have religious rituals, they
will make up others to give some sense of rhythm to their lives.
Our need for them is demonstrated by children's insistence
that birthday and bedtime rituals be followed meticulously.

In his book on prayer, former pastor and author Robert
Hudnut points out that the word *ritual* comes from the same
root as "arithmetic," a root that means to "fit together." We
can see that our religious ceremonies fit together elements of
our lives—events, people, good and bad times. Hudnut fo-
cuses our attention on the connection of rituals and discernment when he writes, "With ritual we can begin to see how
things are adding up and how we are being moved toward a
potential listening point,"[19] a juncture at which we can hear
God's directing voice.

One major value of celebratory observances is that they
remind us of God by their very existence. However, the
ritual, Hudnut cautions, "has to be habitual or it will not be
strong enough to bring you to God in bad times as well as
good."[20]

That is why the practices of Sabbath keeping and
weekly participation in worship services have been such
treasures for me. Every Sunday I see art and candles and liturgical colors, sing anew hymns and liturgies, and hear afresh
Scripture texts and sermons that remind me of the fullness of
God's grace. I taste the assurance of Christ's love in the Eucharist. I gather with and touch Christian saints who enfold
me in the abundance of the Trinity's Joy.

These celebrations place us more firmly on the foundation of God's reign so that throughout the following week we
can make better decisions accordingly. We remember more

deeply the community and the God to Whom we belong, and the Trinity and the saints form our character for more godly discernment.

CELEBRATION THROUGHOUT THE WORLD

When I first visited Japan as part of the college choir tour mentioned in this book's introduction, one of the most startling experiences for me was a conversation with a young Christian woman whose Joy was tangible, even as she explained that she had been disowned by her family because of her newfound faith. In the midst of that pain, she was confident that her decision had been the right one because she believed that God's reign in her life would enable her to become reconciled eventually with her family. In the meanwhile, she said, God's grace to her was so rich that she could not help but choose to live in Joy.

We have seen many other stories of Joy and celebration and their relationship with wise discernment throughout this book. In Chapter One (and in this chapter), for example, we saw the effects of his Joy on Francis of Assisi and his community. We also perceived heavenly Joy in George Evans when he received his father's teaching in his threefold dream and was thereby led to discern an avenue of ministry for those still in the refugee camps.

In Chapter Two we witnessed the Joy of Chinese and Indian people in memorizing Scripture, and we observed in Chapter Three the way the Bambemba tribe of South Africa celebrates the return of a person who has acted wrongfully. We learned in Chapter Four about the Joy of obedience from Malagasy and Chinese people, and in Five we encountered

the Joy of the Celts in the Trinity and their resultant emphasis on community life. We also glimpsed Mennonite celebrations of processes to discern the Spirit.

We recognized the celebration of choices for hospitality
and generosity in the Maori people's custom to welcome
others with a *powhiri* (Chapter Six) and of decisions for reconciliation (Chapter Seven) in the people's *whakahoanga* and
in African leaders' discernment for their nations. In the chapter prior to this one we remembered the Joy of Jesus, Who
fulfilled all of God's purposes on our behalf because of it, the
Joy of St. Martin of Tours as he constantly worked for reconciliation, and the Joy of a Zimbabwean pastor who went to a
martyr's death confident in the God Who had guided his decision to remain faithful.

To all these examples, let us add one more. During a
time of drought and food shortage in Tanzania, the church at
Iberoda dedicated its new building. The people had painted
the church beautifully with bright colors and had made decorative streamers of small pieces of fabric strung on ropes
across the entryway of the church compound. There was a
guest choir from the nearby village of Getanyamba. Four pastors and the head of the church district were there. The
building was packed to the rafters, Barbara Robertson wrote,
with congregation members, visitors, and neighbors.

The most striking element to me of their celebration is
that after the worship service everyone present was served a
wonderful lunch—even those who had come simply because
they'd heard there was a party going on with free food. Alto-
gether the people cooked 150 pounds of rice alone, as well as
meat, potatoes, beans, maize, and other treats. It is truly a Joy-
full celebration when, especially in times of shortage, members of a church discern that it is important to invite their

hungry neighbors to share their food, even though the people are strangers wandering by.

In all these instances we have perceived the intertwining of festivities and wisdom. Often it is a choice to celebrate—and that choice leads to other fresh discernments. Frequently, commemorations of festal days grant new perspectives out of which better decisions can be made. In many cases we have noted specifically that eschatological Joy—that Joy which has been made possible because of what Christ has done for us and which will be brought to its culmination when God brings the triune purposes for the cosmos to completion—has freed people to make tough decisions for faithfulness, in spite of the sufferings which then ensued.

THE SOURCE AND THE OUTFLOW
OF SUPERB DISCERNMENT

At its beginning, we noted that this chapter correlates with Chapter One. Present and eternal Joy are available to us now because of the immensity of the grace of the God to Whom we belong. May these two chapters be the ribbon that ties up the package of all the skills for discernment we have considered in this book, for when we are enfolded in grace and Joy, all our decisions will flow for good.

Throughout this book we have learned these skills from a global and timeless community to which we belong. Because we are part of the community of saints, our decisions will be different and will be made differently from those of the world around us. Because we, together with all the saints, belong to God, we will discern choices from God's perspective, which we will know more deeply through the saints that surround us.

We will want to know more about the God Who so enfolds us, so we will base our decisions more thoroughly on
the Scriptures that teach us about the Trinity and God's ways.
We will rectify the names of our choices so that we perceive
each component clearly in light of Who God is and who we
are in relation to the Trinity. We will be formed with godly
virtues and moral values out of which better decisions will
necessarily emanate. We will specifically seek the counsel of
the community to which we belong, and all our decisions will
be formed by the character of that community in which we
are immersed. In imitation of God, we will make better
choices for hospitality, generosity, and reconciliation, which in
turn will build our character so that we more easily make such
choices. Finally, we will be formed with a character more willing to suffer for the sake of our noblest commitments.

All of our best discernments will spring from this astounding source: the overflowing stream of the Triune God's
illimitable grace for us and the Joy which is our eternal pos-
session because of that copious grace.

EPILOGUE

We have explored many cultural habits that make us more receptive to hearing God speak, to knowing how we shall live in light of God's good will. But, as has been obvious, there are no surefire methods to know precisely how we ought to proceed. The key is a deepened trust that the God to Whom we belong really cares about what is best for us and leads us along graciously through many whisperings and confirmations, friends and counselors, tests and practices, habits and prayers.

Perpetually, there is a sense of mystery and awe.

Our decisions are always bigger than we are, for they affect far more than we realize. That is why our very discernment processes make us more aware of our need for a Christian community, for God, and for the Trinity's guidance in our lives.

Sometimes God speaks to us directly. Sometimes God makes a decision so very clear to us that we are exceedingly glad to obey.

I don't usually experience God's guidance so free of doubt, but I am the enormously grateful recipient of a gift from someone who did.

Usually, I realize God's will in hindsight; as I look back on life, I can tell that I was led in certain ways for very good reasons that I did not completely know or understand when those directions were first chosen or accepted. But some people hear God's voice as clearly as did Moses.

I'm tempted to be jealous. I wish God spoke to me so clearly. But I realize that the struggle to discover God's word is to me an important element in the overall process of the Trinity's drawing me closer and transforming me into Christ's likeness.

But I have been the stunned recipient of a clear message from God to a friend of mine. When I asked Connie Johnson, to whom this book is dedicated, why she decided to offer me her kidney, her short answer was, "It was a God thing." She acknowledged that she didn't know *why* she knew, but she simply knew that she would be the one to give me the transplant. It remains sheer mystery.

It is a mystery all glorious. Twelve hours after the transplant surgery I woke in the middle of the night and realized, to my utter surprise, that I didn't feel full of toxins and waste for the first time in a dozen years. When I was roused by a nurse the next morning, I actually wanted to be awake instead of, as before, wanting to go back to sleep in order to ignore how rotten I felt. It was deliriously exhilarating.

Connie heard God's will clearly and offered me the greatest sign of God's grace possible (besides the cross and the resurrection!): a chance to experience fresh, new life, an unprecedented possibility to do my work.

It is not easy, for God's will isn't without costs. The struggles to balance all my handicaps with all the new medical regimens have been depressing and demanding. But these are petty problems compared to this freedom from being poisoned by myself.

And that freedom has taught me more about God's will than anything. What God wants, more than we can imagine, is to deliver us from the poisons of our own selves—our frivolous desires, our selfish ambitions, our narrow visions of what life can really be, our trivial pursuits. God wants to give us new blood, a whole new life, His Triune purposes.

I had been on a severely restricted diet for the last twelve years. Imagine what consummate delight it was the fifth day after the transplant to be given an entire banana all for myself! Since then I've tasted all sorts of wonderful delights for the first time in a long while. Do we realize how amazing are the possibilities God has created for us? I don't think I will ever take our immense variety of food for granted. And that is just a reminder of the infinitely prodigious gifts of God's creation.

Have we tasted God's fullness? Or have we narrowed the possibilities of grace too much? Do we know how to celebrate every sign of the goodness of God? Are we aware of the holy in a banana?

God's love is a magnificent mystery, and I am an astonished adorer.

This kidney is sheer gift, a sign of the immense treasure of God's life through us all. Taste and see how good the Lord is. How could God's will for us be anything less?

How can we not but gladly obey it when we discern it?

CONNIE'S STORY

Connie's account of what led up to her decision to become a transplant donor shows that God often leads us through many previous experiences and practices to come to the point when a matter of discernment becomes clear.

She had had a rough childhood. A victim of abuse and family alcoholism, she "escaped" into a marriage that proved to be equally destructive when her husband abruptly left her. She felt that she had "lost" herself, that she had become only somebody's mother or wife and didn't know what to do with herself.

Through all of this, however, she had a strong faith. The Church (the saints to whom she belonged) had held her tightly throughout her childhood and continued to uphold her as she began to discover who she was. God gave her strength through her trust, her children, friends, and a superb counselor as she started an entirely new life. She told me, "I love this life the most. This is *me!*"

That led her into a new discernment process. She thought, "I need to find out why I am here. Why am I so healthy? For whose sake is this?"

It was at this point that Connie's life and mine began to intertwine. Her mother-in-law heard a presentation I gave and told Connie my name and, as she reported, "that name went straight into my heart." Who could have known in what way our lives would converge?

For a few years, she and I and our husbands belonged in the same congregation, and she heard my sermons and Bible classes there. She and her husband came to our home during the congregation's stewardship program, and we four resonated with our attitudes about it. After she and her husband relocated to the Midwest when he accepted a pastoral call, a mutual friend sent her tapes of my sermons.

Our lives, Connie said, were like "a braided river." She had continued to pray for my work and for my health situation with its multiple handicaps. Then the minute she read my Christmas letter notifying friends and family of my need for a kidney, she said to herself, "I'm going to give a kidney to Marva." And she knew in her deepest self that she would be the one to do it. Even though the transplant coordinator told her that several other people had volunteered to be donors, Connie believed and told her husband, "I know that this is mine to do."

All through the path of testing for a match, through her own temporary setback with an infection, through all of the preparations for the transplant, Connie never worried. She knew that she was the one and that everything would go well for the surgery.

I asked Connie how she knew that she was going to be the one or that God had directed her to do this, and she replied, "I don't know; I just did. It's a God thing."

Connie had in the past experienced some frustration that she didn't clearly have a call such as her husband's to be a pastor, but that had led her continually to ask, "Why am I here?" In response, she always knew that she would be a gift for someone else. Because she had frequently asked, "For whom am I to share?" she knew immediately when the call for a kidney came that this was her "thing to do." "It's a God thing," she repeated when people asked her later about her choice to donate a kidney.

Connie laughed when she told me about being questioned by the transplant hospital psychologist for forty-five minutes to see if her motives in offering a kidney were "right." How can you tell someone in public health that you know "it is a God thing"?

The congregation that Connie's husband serves as a pastor had my name on its prayer list for months, but the members never knew until after the surgery that their own pastor's wife would be the one to give me a kidney; Connie hadn't wanted them to worry or give her undue praise. She knew that God had given her this as her work to do, and she wanted the glory to go to God.

Isn't her story amazing? I'm sure you can understand why I am so awed not only by her gift, which prevented my needing dialysis, but also by the mystery it is that she discerned it was her "work to do." God be praised! And thank you, Connie, for your generous gift and for your faithful listening!

No matter what skills of decision making we acquire, let us stay open to the mysteries of God's grace. Do we believe that God has ways of working far beyond our human comprehension? Do we participate in a community that enfolds us in God's grace and wisdom? Do we trust that God will direct us and transform us, and in the eternal Joy of that confidence can we proceed boldly in life?

Grace. Community. Discernment. Joy. The Triune God. Mysteries all, worthy of our wildest celebration.

NOTES

CHAPTER ONE

1. Several good studies of the Trinity are these: Colin E. Gunton, *The Promise of Trinitarian Theology,* 2nd ed. (Edinburgh: Clark, 1997); Catherine Mowry LaCugna, *God for Us: The Trinity and Christian Life* (San Francisco: HarperSanFrancisco, 1991); Roger E. Olson and Christopher A. Hall, *The Trinity* (Grand Rapids, Mich.: Eerdmans, 2002); and Allen Vander Pol, *God in Three Persons: Biblical Testimony to the Trinity* (Phillipsburg, N.J.: Presbyterian and Reformed, 2001).

2. See, for example, the artwork and sample prayers in Michael Mitton, *Restoring the Woven Cord: Strands of Celtic Christianity for the Church Today* (London: Darton, Longman and Todd, 1995). This wonderful book describes the fundamental characteristics of the Celtic church in the British Isles and beyond in the fifth through ninth centuries.

3. For deeper study of the pronouns and the names for the Three Persons of the Godhead, see Marva J. Dawn, *Talking the Walk: Letting the Christian Language Live Again* (Grand Rapids, Mich.: Brazos Press, 2005).

4. For a Chinese perspective on the Trinitarian basis of spiritual discernment, see Herrick Ping-tong Liu, *Towards an Evangelical Spirituality: A Practical-Theological Study of Richard Baxter's Teaching and Practice of Spiritual Disciplines with Special Reference*

to the Chinese Cultural Context (Hong Kong: Alliance Bible Seminary, 2000), pp. 17, 22, 197.

5. Thomas à Kempis, *Consolations for My Soul: Meditations for the Earthly Pilgrimage Toward the Heavenly Jerusalem,* trans. William Griffin (New York: Crossroad Carlisle, 2004), p. 34 (translator's emphasis).

6. Opening Prayer for Thursday of the Week of Pentecost 11, as cited in *For All the Saints: A Prayer Book for and by the Church, Vol. IV: Year 2: The Season After Pentecost,* compiled and edited by Frederick J. Schumacher with Dorothy A. Zelenko (Delhi, N.Y.: American Lutheran Publicity Bureau, 1996), p. 378.

7. See John Piper, *The Legacy of Sovereign Joy: God's Triumphant Grace in the Lives of Augustine, Luther, and Calvin* (Wheaton, Ill.: Crossway Books, 2000).

8. Thomas à Kempis, *Consolations for My Soul,* pp. 136 and 137.

9. The R. S. Thomas poem is quoted in Daniel Taylor, *In Search of Sacred Places: Looking for Wisdom on Celtic Holy Islands* (Saint Paul, Minn.: Bog Walk Press, 2005), p. 49.

10. James Mulholland, *Praying like Jesus: The Lord's Prayer in a Culture of Prosperity* (San Francisco: HarperSanFrancisco, 2001).

11. Anselm (1033–1109), Closing Prayer for Thursday of the Week of Pentecost 7, as cited in Schumacher, *For All the Saints,* IV, p. 252.

12. Thomas Aquinas (1225–1274), Eucharistic hymn, *Adoro te devote, latens deitas,* translated by Gerard Manley Hopkins, as cited in Schumacher, *For All the Saints,* IV, pp. 371–372.

13. F. Eppling Reinartz sermon, "If I Only Knew," broadcast on the ABC radio network, April 14, 1948, quoted in Schumacher, *For All the Saints,* IV, pp. 1025–1026.

14. Taylor, *In Search of Sacred Places,* p. 53.

15. Taylor, *In Search of Sacred Places,* p. 60.

16. Taylor, *In Search of Sacred Places,* p. 88.

17. For example, consider the fine craftsmanship and the contemplative life demonstrated by the works of Solrunn Nes in *The Mystical Language of Icons* (Grand Rapids, Mich.: Eerdmans, 2004).

18. Gernot Candolini, *Labyrinths: Walking Toward the Center,* trans. Peter Heinegg (New York: Crossroad, 2003), p. 45.

19. Desiderius Erasmus (1466?–1536), as quoted in *For All the Saints: A Prayer Book for and by the Church, Vol. I: Year 1: Advent to the Day of Pentecost,* compiled and edited by Frederick J. Schumacher with Dorothy A. Zelenko (Delhi, N.Y.: American Lutheran Publicity Bureau, 1994), p. 95.

20. See, for example, Lawrence S. Cunningham, *Francis of Assisi: Performing the Gospel Life* (Grand Rapids, Mich.: Eerdmans, 2004), p. 131. The best compilation of texts by and about Francis are these four volumes edited by Regis Armstrong, Wayne Hellmann, and William Short: *Francis of Assisi: The Saint; Francis of Assisi: The Founder; Francis of Assisi: The Prophet;* and *Francis of Assisi: Index* (New York: New City Press, 1999, 2000, 2001, and 2002, respectively).

CHAPTER TWO

1. See Augustine, "Confessions," in William C. Placher, ed., *Callings: Twenty Centuries of Christian Wisdom on Vocation* (Grand Rapids, Mich.: Eerdmans, 2005), pp. 83–103.

2. To learn more about Global Health Ministries or to participate in its mission, you may contact the organization at 7831 Hickory Street NE, Minneapolis, MN 55432; telephone (763) 586-9590; e-mail: ghmoffice@cs.com; Internet: www.ghm.org.

3. See Todd Lake's article on how much it would increase denominations' care for the poor if they would follow the practices of the Salvation Army (which holds Isaiah 58 as its "charter") in the Fall 2005 issue of *Prism,* cited in Martin E. Marty's *Context,* January 2006, Part B, *38*(1), 5–6.

4. Michael Mitton, *Restoring the Woven Cord: Strands of Celtic Christianity for the Church Today* (London: Darton, Longman and Todd, 1995), p. 30.

5. *The Daily Texts* is available from the Department of Publications and Communications, the Moravian Church, P.O. Box 1245, Bethlehem, PA 18016; telephone (215) 867-0594; fax (215) 866-9223.

6. For example, for the last few years I have been using *For All the Saints: A Prayer Book for and by the Church,* compiled and edited by Frederick J. Schumacher with Dorothy A. Zelenko, and published in Delhi, N.Y., by the American Lutheran Publicity Bureau in 1994–1996. This set is available in four volumes that cover two years. In the past I have found the following very helpful: John W. Doberstein, ed., *Minister's Prayer Book: An Order of Prayers and Readings* (Philadelphia: Fortress Press, n.d.); Rueben P. Job and Norman Shawchuck, eds., *A Guide to Prayer: For Ministers and Other Servants* (Nashville, Tenn.: Upper Room, 1983), which follows the *Revised Common Lectionary* with daily biblical texts and readings as well as psalms, hymns, and prayers that match the week's theme (there is also a version for nonprofessionals); and Bob Benson Sr. and Michael W. Benson, *Disciplines for the Inner Life* (Nashville, Tenn.: Nelson, 1989), which contains the same weekly elements but builds a progression of themes from disciplines for the inner journey, through obstacles, patterns, and graces, to outward fruits of the inner life.

7. Jean Bethke Elshtain, "Abraham Lincoln and the Last Best Hope," *The Second One Thousand Years: Ten People Who Defined a Millennium,* ed. Richard John Neuhaus (Grand Rapids, Mich.: Eerdmans, 2001), p. 106.

8. *Moments of Delight: Inspirational Bible Verses for Each Day* (Grand Rapids, Mich.: Baker Book House, n.d.).

9. C. S. Lewis, ed., *George MacDonald: An Anthology* (London: Bles, 1946), p. 39.

CHAPTER THREE

1. T. R. Reid, *Confucius Lives Next Door: What Living in the East Teaches Us About Living in the West* (New York: Random House, 1995), p. 102.
2. Randy Alcorn, *Safely Home* (Wheaton, Ill.: Tyndale House, 2001), p. 105.
3. Alcorn, *Safely Home*, p. 88.
4. That is why the name is printed with every letter capitalized, to clarify that this refers to the Hebrew name *YHWH* rather than to the word that means "lord" in the sense of a sovereign ruler. The name LORD is used in the Bible to rectify the names, to call readers to remember that this means Israel's covenant God, the Promising One Who always keeps commitments.
5. For a deeper discussion of spiritual gifts, see Chapter Eleven, "Gifts from the Fullness of Grace," in my *Truly the Community: Romans 12 and How to Be the Church* (Grand Rapids, Mich.: Eerdmans, 1992; reissued 1997).
6. Albert Borgmann, *Technology and the Character of Contemporary Life: A Philosophical Inquiry* (Chicago: University of Chicago Press, 1984).
7. See Marva J. Dawn, *Unfettered Hope: A Call to Faithful Living in an Affluent Society* (Louisville, Ky.: Westminster/John Knox, 2003).
8. Donald McCullough, *If Grace Is So Amazing, Why Don't We Like It? How God's Radical Love Turns the World Upside Down* (San Francisco: Jossey-Bass, 2005), p. 170.
9. See George E. Ganss, *The Spiritual Exercises of Saint Ignatius: Translation and Commentary* (Chicago: Loyola University Press, 1992). Protestants might find it necessary to modify slightly some of Ignatius' terminology and directions, especially for penance, but may still discover that the exercises provide very helpful tools for prayer and discernment.

CHAPTER FOUR

1. It is interesting to me that my book on that subject, *Keeping the Sabbath Wholly: Ceasing, Resting, Embracing, Feasting* (Grand Rapids, Mich.: Eerdmans, 1989), was the first of my works to be translated into Chinese, and this was the subject requested for two series of lectures I presented in Hong Kong and Singapore. See also my book *The Sense of the Call: A Sabbath Way of Life for Those Who Serve God, the Church, and the World* (Grand Rapids, Mich.: Eerdmans, 2006).

2. Robert H. Frank and Philip J. Cook, *The Winner-Take-All Society: How More and More Americans Compete for Ever Fewer and Bigger Prizes, Encouraging Economic Waste, Income Inequality, and an Impoverished Cultural Life* (New York: Free Press, 1995).

3. Robert Kegan, *In Over Our Heads: The Mental Demands of Modern Life* (Cambridge, Mass.: Harvard University Press, 1994), p. 6.

4. David Tomlins, "The Meaning and Value of Silence in Christian Living," *Cistercian Studies,* 1982, *17*(2), 173, 175, as cited in Esther De Waal, *Lost in Wonder: Rediscovering the Spiritual Art of Attentiveness* (Collegeville, Minn.: Liturgical Press, 2003), p. 46.

5. Karl Rahner, *Encounters with Silence* (South Bend, Ind.: St. Augustine's Press, 1999).

6. Richard Baxter, *A Christian Dictionary,* as cited in Herrick Ping-tong Liu, *Towards an Evangelical Spirituality: A Practical-Theological Study of Richard Baxter's Teaching and Practice of Spiritual Disciplines with Special Reference to the Chinese Cultural Context* (Hong Kong: Alliance Bible Seminary, 2000), p. 78.

7. Liu, *Towards an Evangelical Spirituality,* pp. 22, 96, 125–127.

8. Joan Chittister, *Wisdom Distilled from the Daily: Living the Rule of St. Benedict Today* (San Francisco: HarperSanFrancisco, 1991), p. 195.

9. Wil Derske, *Spirituality for Daily Life: The Rule of Benedict for Beginners,* trans. Martin Kessler (Collegeville, Minn.: Liturgical Press, 2003), p. 41.

10. T. R. Reid, *Confucius Lives Next Door: What Living in the East Teaches Us About Living in the West* (New York: Random House, 1999), p. 14.

11. Reid, *Confucius Lives Next Door*, p. 16.

12. Reid, *Confucius Lives Next Door*, p. 62.

13. Reid, *Confucius Lives Next Door*, p. 129.

14. Alexander McCall Smith, *Tears of the Giraffe* (New York: Anchor Books [Random House], 2000], p. 226.

15. Smith, *Tears of the Giraffe*, pp. 177–178.

16. Alexander McCall Smith, *Morality for Beautiful Girls* (New York: Anchor Books, 2001), pp. 77–78.

17. Smith, *Morality for Beautiful Girls*, p. 77.

18. Alexander McCall Smith, *The Kalahari Typing School for Men* (New York: Pantheon Books, 2002), p. 157.

19. A recent news report on global health issues demonstrates how important this attribute of respect for the elderly is in Nepal. There Ram Shrestha, a chemist and health expert, has enlisted forty-nine thousand grandmothers, who have the most influence in the family, to distribute vitamin A to 3.5 million Nepalese children every year. As a result the infant mortality rate has been cut in half, and the rate of eye disease has plummeted. See Jeffrey Kluger, "Vitamin Sherpa," in "18 Heroes," *Time*, Nov. 7, 2005, pp. 93 and 95.

CHAPTER FIVE

1. See my *Truly the Community: Romans 12 and How to Be the Church* (Grand Rapids, Mich.: Eerdmans, 1992; reissued 1997). See also Tod E. Bolsinger, *It Takes a Church to Raise a Christian: How the Community of God Transforms Lives* (Grand Rapids, Mich.: Brazos Press, 2004).

2. Howard Baker, *Soul Keeping: Ancient Paths of Spiritual Direction* (Colorado Springs, Colo.: NavPress, 1998), p. 145.

3. Charles Pinches, *A Gathering of Memories: Family, Nation, and Church in a Forgetful World* (Grand Rapids, Mich.: Brazos Press, 2006), p. 31.

4. Patrick Thoms, *A Candle in the Darkness: Celtic Spirituality from Wales* (Llandysul, Wales: Gomer Press, 1993), p. 11.

5. Some suggestions for building deeper and more caring Christian communities are offered in my *Truly the Community.*

6. Concerning gadgets and the influence of our technological milieu on our sense of humanity and community, see my *Unfettered Hope: A Call to Faithful Living in an Affluent Society* (Louisville, Ky.: Westminster/John Knox, 2003).

7. Alexander McCall Smith, *Tears of the Giraffe* (New York: Anchor Books, 2000), pp. 216–217.

8. Michael Battle, "Penitence as Practiced in African/African-American Christian Spirituality," in Mark Boda and Gordon T. Smith, eds., *Repentance in Christian Tradition* (Collegeville, Minn.: Liturgical Press, 2006).

CHAPTER SIX

1. David G. Benner, *The Gift of Being Yourself: The Sacred Call to Self-Discovery* (Downers Grove, Ill.: InterVarsity Press, 2004), p. 97.

2. Nancy Gibbs, "Saving 1 Life at a Time," *Time,* Nov. 7, 2005, p. 55.

3. This might be deduced from the progression of events in John 13 in correlation with the other Gospels.

4. Ancient Celtic poem quoted in Daniel Taylor, *In Search of Sacred Places: Looking for Wisdom on Celtic Holy Islands* (Saint Paul, Minn.: Bog Walk Press, 2005), p. 28.

5. A lovely book for children (and adults) about Ciaran by Gary D. Schmidt and illustrated by Todd Doney is *Saint Ciaran: The Tale of a Saint of Ireland* (Grand Rapids, Mich.: Eerdmans, 2000).

6. See Mary Forman, *Praying with the Desert Mothers* (Collegeville, Minn.: Liturgical Press, 2005), pp. 38–46.

7. Joan Chittister, *Wisdom Distilled from the Daily: Living the Rule of St. Benedict Today* (San Francisco: HarperSanFrancisco, 1991), pp. 121–132, especially pp. 132 and 127.

8. Chittister, *Wisdom Distilled from the Daily,* p. 126.

9. Alexander McCall Smith, *Tears of the Giraffe* (New York: Anchor Books, 2000), p. 206.

10. For the Hebrew understanding of time, see my *Keeping the Sabbath Wholly: Ceasing, Resting, Embracing, Feasting* (Grand Rapids, Mich.: Eerdmans, 1989) and *The Sense of the Call: A Sabbath Way of Life for Those Who Serve God, the Church, and the World* (Grand Rapids, Mich.: Eerdmans, 2006). See also Abraham Joshua Heschel, *The Sabbath: Its Meaning for Modern Man* (New York: Farrar, Straus & Giroux, 1951).

CHAPTER SEVEN

1. Alexander McCall Smith, *The Finer Points of Sausage Dogs* (New York: Anchor Books, 2003), pp. 55–56.

2. Lawrence S. Cunningham, *Francis of Assisi: Performing the Gospel Life* (Grand Rapids, Mich.: Eerdmans, 2004), p. 63.

3. See Joan Chittister, *Wisdom Distilled from the Daily: Living the Rule of St. Benedict Today* (San Francisco: HarperSanFrancisco, 1991).

4. Alexander McCall Smith, *Tears of the Giraffe* (New York: Anchor Books, 2000), p. 62.

5. Smith, *Tears of the Giraffe,* p. 63.

6. Smith, *Tears of the Giraffe,* p. 63.

7. Peter Ackerman and Jack DuVall, *A Force More Powerful: A Century of Nonviolent Conflict* (New York: St. Martin's Press, 2000), p. 367.

8. Andrew Young, *A Way Out of No Way: The Spiritual Memoirs of Andrew Young* (Nashville, Tenn.: Nelson, 1994), p. 131.

9. Alexander McCall Smith, *Morality for Beautiful Girls* (New York: Anchor Books, 2001), p. 78.

10. See, for example, how the Mennonite culture of reconciliation leads to more choices than to kill or be killed when an intruder enters your house in John Howard Yoder's *What Would You Do?* (Scottdale, Pa.: Herald Press, 1992).

CHAPTER EIGHT

1. Anonymous early biographer quoted in Kenneth Scott Latourette, *A History of Christianity,* Volume I: Beginnings to 1500, rev. ed. (New York: HarperCollins, 1975), p. 231.

2. Miles Coverdale, Opening Prayer for Thursday of the Week of Pentecost 7, as cited in *For All the Saints: A Prayer Book for and by the Church, Vol. IV: Year 2: The Season After Pentecost,* compiled and edited by Frederick J. Schumacher with Dorothy A. Zelenko (Delhi, N.Y.: American Lutheran Publicity Bureau, 1996), p. 247.

3. Thomas à Kempis, *Consolations for My Soul: Meditations for the Earthly Pilgrimage Toward the Heavenly Jerusalem,* trans. William Griffin (New York: Crossroad Carlisle, 2004), p. 163. Page references to this book in the rest of this section are given parenthetically in the text.

4. Daniel Taylor, *In Search of Sacred Places: Looking for Wisdom on Celtic Holy Islands* (Saint Paul, Minn.: Bog Walk Press, 2005), p. 29. Page references to this book in the following paragraphs are given parenthetically in the text.

5. For further comments on the book of Job, see Chapter Nine, "Joy in Our Weakness: Embracing the Cost of Discipleship," in my book *The Sense of the Call: A Sabbath Way of Life for Those Who Serve God, the Church, and the World* (Grand Rapids, Mich.: Eerdmans, 2006).

6. This issue is partially addressed in my *Joy in Our Weakness: A Gift of Hope from the Book of Revelation,* rev. ed. (Grand Rapids, Mich.: Eerdmans, 2002).

7. This journal entry has been passed around so much that, I apologize, I cannot attribute the quotation to a specific source. If you know the original source, I would be very grateful to learn it.

8. Eberhard Bethge, "Editor's Preface," in Dietrich Bonhoeffer, *Letters and Papers from Prison,* rev. ed. (Old Tappan, N.J.: Macmillan, 1967), p. xxi.

9. Payne Best, *The Venio Incident,* as quoted by Bethge, "Editor's Preface," *Letters and Papers from Prison,* p. xxii.

10. Wolf-Dieter Zimmermann and Ronald Gregor Smith, eds., *I Knew Dietrich Bonhoeffer,* trans. Käthe Gregor Smith (New York: HarperCollins, 1966), p. 232, as cited in Dallas M. Roark and Bob E. Patterson, eds., *Dietrich Bonhoeffer: Makers of the Modern Theological Mind* (Waco, Tex.: Word Books, 1972), p. 27.

CHAPTER NINE

1. These two paragraphs were inspired by a meditation I read a few years ago by Edmund A. Steimle (1907–1988), *From Death to Birth* (Philadelphia: Fortress Press, 1973), quoted in *For All the Saints: A Prayer Book for and by the Church, Vol. II: Year 1: The Season After Pentecost,* compiled and edited by Frederick J. Schumacher with Dorothy A. Zelenko (Delhi, N.Y.: American Lutheran Publicity Bureau, 1995), pp. 11–12.

2. Ellen F. Davis, *Getting Involved with God: Rediscovering the Old Testament* (Boston: Cowley, 2001), p. 140.

3. Julian of Norwich, *Revelation of Love,* ed. and trans. John Skinner (New York: Image Books/Doubleday, 1996), p. 60.

4. This paragraph builds on some ideas in Donald McCullough, *If Grace Is So Amazing, Why Don't We Like It? How God's Radical Love Turns the World Upside Down* (San Francisco: Jossey-Bass, 2005), p. 39.

5. Dallas Willard, *Hearing God: Developing a Conversational Relationship with God* (Downers Grove, Ill.: InterVarsity Press, 1999), p. 211.

6. This line is from Wesley's glorious 1747 hymn "Love Divine, All Loves Excelling."

7. Frederick Buechner, *Beyond Words: Daily Readings in the ABCs of Faith* (New York: HarperCollins, 2004), p. 405.

8. Thomas Owen Clancy and Gilbert Markus, *Iona: The Earliest Poetry of a Celtic Monastery* (Edinburgh: Edinburgh University

Press, 1994), pp. 52–53, as cited in Esther De Waal, *Lost in Wonder: Rediscovering the Spiritual Art of Attentiveness* (Collegeville, Minn.: Liturgical Press, 2003), p. 145.

9. De Waal, *Lost in Wonder,* p. 149.

10. Father Cuthbert, *Life of St. Francis of Assisi,* 3rd ed. (London: Longmans, Green, 1921), pp. 60–61.

11. Felix Timmermann, *The Perfect Joy of St. Francis,* trans. Molly Bird (London: Mowbray, 1954), pp. 110 and 151.

12. Timmermann, *The Perfect Joy of St. Francis,* p. 159.

13. Annie Dillard, *Pilgrim at Tinker Creek* (New York: Harper Perennial Classic Edition, 1998), p. 274. (Originally published 1974)

14. Elizabeth Goudge, "The Well of the Star," in *Behold That Star: A Christmas Anthology,* ed. the Bruderhof (Farmington, Pa.: Plough, 1996), pp. 29–63.

15. See, for example, Henri J. M. Nouwen, *In the Name of Jesus: Reflections on Christian Leadership* (New York: Crossroad, 1989).

16. Michael Downey, *A Blessed Weakness: The Spirit of Jean Vanier and l'Arche* (San Francisco: HarperSanFrancisco, 1986), p. 85.

17. Downey, *A Blessed Weakness,* p. 83.

18. Sara Wenger Shenk, *Why Not Celebrate?* (Intercourse, Pa.: Good Books, 1987), p. 3.

19. Robert K. Hudnut, *Call Waiting: How to Hear God Speak* (Downers Grove, Ill.: InterVarsity Press, 1999), p. 155.

20. Hudnut, *Call Waiting,* p. 154.

FURTHER READING

Baker, Howard. *Soul Keeping: Ancient Paths of Spiritual Direction.* Colorado Springs, Colo.: NavPress, 1998.

Benner, David G. *The Gift of Being Yourself: The Sacred Call to Self-Discovery.* Downers Grove, Ill.: InterVarsity Press, 2004.

Benson, Bob, Sr., and Benson, Michael W. *Disciplines for the Inner Life.* Nashville, Tenn.: Nelson, 1989.

Blackaby, Richard, and Blackaby, Henry T. *Hearing God's Voice.* Nashville, Tenn.: Broadman & Holman, 2002.

Bolsinger, Tod E. *It Takes a Church to Raise a Christian: How the Community of God Transforms Lives.* Grand Rapids, Mich.: Brazos Press, 2004.

Brackley, Dean. *The Call to Discernment in Troubled Times.* New York: Crossroad, 2004.

Chittister, Joan. *Wisdom Distilled from the Daily: Living the Rule of St. Benedict Today.* San Francisco: HarperSanFrancisco, 1991.

Dawn, Marva J. *Joy in Our Weakness: A Gift of Hope from the Book of Revelation,* rev. ed. Grand Rapids, Mich.: Eerdmans, 2002.

———. *Keeping the Sabbath Wholly: Ceasing, Resting, Embracing, Feasting.* Grand Rapids, Mich.: Eerdmans, 1989.

———. *The Sense of the Call: A Sabbath Way of Life for Those Who Serve God, the Church, and the World.* Grand Rapids, Mich.: Eerdmans, 2006.

———. *Talking the Walk: Letting the Christian Language Live Again.* Grand Rapids, Mich.: Brazos Press, 2005.

———. *Truly the Community: Romans 12 and How to Be the Church.* Grand Rapids, Mich.: Eerdmans, 1992; reissued 1997.

———. *Unfettered Hope: A Call to Faithful Living in an Affluent Society.* Louisville, Ky.: Westminster/John Knox, 2003.

De Waal, Esther. *Lost in Wonder: Rediscovering the Spiritual Art of Attentiveness.* Collegeville, Minn.: Liturgical Press, 2003.

Farrington, Debra K. *Hearing with the Heart: A Gentle Guide to Discerning God's Will for Your Life.* San Francisco: Jossey-Bass, 2003.

Ganss, George E. *The Spiritual Exercises of Saint Ignatius: Translation and Commentary.* Chicago: Loyola University Press, 1992.

Griffin, Emilie. *Clinging: The Experience of Prayer.* San Francisco: HarperSanFrancisco, 1984.

Hansen, David. *Long Wandering Prayer: An Invitation to Walk with God.* Downers Grove, Ill.: InterVarsity Press, 2001.

Houston, James. *The Transforming Power of Prayer: Deepening Your Friendship with God.* Colorado Springs, Colo.: NavPress, 1996.

Hudnut, Robert K. *Call Waiting: How to Hear God Speak.* Downers Grove, Ill.: InterVarsity Press, 1999.

Julian of Norwich. *Revelation of Love.* (John Skinner, ed. and trans.) New York: Image Books/Doubleday, 1996.

à Kempis, Thomas. *Consolations for My Soul: Meditations for the Earthly Pilgrimage Toward the Heavenly Jerusalem.* (William Griffin, trans.) New York: Crossroad Carlisle, 2004.

Mitton, Michael. *Restoring the Woven Cord: Strands of Celtic Christianity for the Church Today.* London: Darton, Longman and Todd, 1995.

Peterson, Eugene H. *Answering God: The Psalms as Tools for Prayer.* San Francisco: HarperSanFrancisco, 1991.

Placher, William C. (ed). *Callings: Twenty Centuries of Christian Wisdom on Vocation.* Grand Rapids, Mich.: Eerdmans, 2005.

Taylor, Daniel. *In Search of Sacred Places: Looking for Wisdom on Celtic Holy Islands.* Saint Paul, Minn.: Bog Walk Press, 2005.

Waltke, Bruce K. *Finding the Will of God: A Pagan Notion?* Grand Rapids, Mich.: Eerdmans, 1995.

Wangerin, Walter, Jr. *Whole Prayer: Speaking and Listening to God.* Grand Rapids, Mich.: Zondervan, 1998.

Webster, Douglas D. *Finding Spiritual Direction: The Challenge and Joys of Christian Growth.* Downers Grove, Ill.: InterVarsity Press, 1991.

Willard, Dallas. *Hearing God: Developing a Conversational Relationship with God.* Downers Grove, Ill.: InterVarsity Press, 1999.

Williams, Rowan. *The Dwelling of the Light: Praying with Icons of Christ.* Grand Rapids, Mich.: Eerdmans, 2003.

THE AUTHOR

A n internationally renowned theologian, author, and educator, Marva J. Dawn has served the worldwide Church for the past twenty-seven years through her affiliation with Christians Equipped for Ministry of Vancouver, Washington. She also serves as Teaching Fellow in Spiritual Theology at Regent College in Vancouver, B.C., Canada. She teaches and lectures on a wide array of topics, most often on themes of worship and community life, Christian ethics, homiletics, pastoral ministry, spiritual formation, and the relevance of the Bible for everyday life. She has been a presenter at seminaries, clergy conferences, churches, assemblies, and universities throughout the United States and Canada and in Australia, China, England, Hungary, Japan, Madagascar, Mexico, New Zealand, Norway, Poland, Singapore, and Scotland. A scholar with four master's degrees and a doctorate in Christian ethics and the Scriptures from the University of Notre Dame, Dawn is also well known and highly appreciated as a preacher and speaker for all ages.

Dawn is the author of twenty books (all royalties from which are donated to ministries of education, community building, and care for the poor). Her book on money and the technological milieu, *Unfettered Hope,* was cited as one of the American Academy of Parish Clergy's top ten books of 2003, and the Independent Publishers Association selected it as a runner-up to the Religion Book of the Year. Three of her other books—*Reaching Out Without Dumbing Down, A Royal "Waste" of Time,* and *The Unnecessary Pastor* (cowritten with Eugene Peterson)—were listed by the Academy of Parish Clergy among the academy's ten top recommended books in their year of publication, and her *Powers, Weakness, and the Tabernacling of God* was honored with the 2002 *Christianity Today* Book Award in the category of "The Church and Pastoral Leadership."

Dawn has translated two books, and many of her own books are being translated into Chinese, Korean, Portuguese, and other languages. She has also written numerous articles and has served on several advisory boards, especially in relation to her major concerns for economic justice and comprehensive peacemaking.

Dawn is joyfully married to Myron Sandberg; they reside in Vancouver, Washington.

INDEX

Ascension of Jesus, 4
Asian culture: and communal discernment, 125–127; demographics of, and church leadership, 111; perspective in, 37, 60–63; and public schools, 96; virtues and morality in, 94–96. *See also specific countries of Asia*
Attentive listening: emphasis on, 157; learning, 123–124; time for, 221; virtue of, 93, 102, 181
Attitude, 167–168
Augustine, St., 15, 34, 36, 49
Australia: and communal discernment, 127–128; idea of mateship in, 128, 133
Australian and New Zealand Army Corps (ANZAC), 128
Authority: communal, issue of, 113–114; higher, 111–112
Awareness, 93

B

Baker, H., 107
Ballplayers, behavior of, 172–173
Bambemba tribe, 75–76, 247
Bamboo stands, 66
Bantu tribe, 12
Baptism, 129, 130
Baptist exiles, 222
Barnabas, 117, 118
Barrera, C., 12, 83, 112, 122, 155–156
Bats, 66
Baxter, R., 87
BBC news report, 139
Bechuanaland, 190, 191
Bedtime rituals, 246
Benedict, St., 92, 93, 149, 150
Benedictine monasteries, 27, 52, 93, 120–121, 180–181
Benner, D., 138
Bergquist, J., 52
Bernard of Clairvaux, 35, 39
Best, P., 219
Bethlehem Chapel, 216, 217
Bible reading and study: attentive,

93; basis for, 40; habit of, 51; immersion in, examples of, 51–53; method for, 54–55; nurturing our spiritual life with, 210; surprises found in, 56–58; time for, 48, 49–50; in welcoming and generosity, 158
Bible, the, foundational word of. *See* Foundational words
Bible translation, 206
Biblical Christian eschatology, meaning of, 88–89. *See also Eschatological entries*
Biblical emphasis: on celebration, 117, 230–234; on communal discernment, 115–118; on reconciliation, 117–118, 176–179; on truth and rectifying the names, 63–66; on virtues and morality, 87–92; on welcoming and generosity, 117, 141–144; on willingness to suffer, 117, 200–207
Biblical literacy, 53
Biblical perspective, 37
Biblical remembrance, 68
Biblical verses. *See specific biblical passages*
Biblical virtues, 87–92, 87–92
Birthday celebrations, 225–226, 242, 243
Birthday rituals, 246
Blaming, 229
Blessing: practice of, 147, 148; symbol of, 66–67
Blessings, ability to discern one's, 226
Boaz, 143
Bonhoeffer, D., 218–220
Borgmann, A., 73
Botswana: and communal discernment, 124; reconciliation in, 186, 190–191; virtues and morality in, 97–98, 99–100; welcoming and generosity in, 154–155
Botswana Democratic Party (BDP), 190–191

Chinese gardens, 25–26
Chinese people, serving, in Hong
  Kong, 74–75
Chinese proverbs, 37, 52, 62, 67, 125
Chittister, J., 92–93, 150, 181, 198
Choice, 15, 47, 116
Choosing, two ways of, exercise
  involving reaction to, 79
Christ. *See* Jesus Christ
Christian banners, 67
Christian character, 88, 89–90, 106
Christian communities: deeply con-
  nected, lack of, 106; wisdom of,
  value of gaining, 116–117. *See also*
  Communal discernment
Christian martyrs. *See* Martyrs
Christian schools, 54–55, 190. *See
  also* Seminary schools
Christianity: distinctiveness of, loss
  of vision for, period of, 179–180;
  extraordinary gift of, 41; and
  monasticism, 120; nature of the
  God of, 5; shrinking influence of,
  in the United States, 173; suspicions about, addressing, 39–45
Christians: aligned with the Roman
  Empire, 179–180; call to, 117, 138;
  in China, under communism, diffi-
  culties of, 109–110; faith and life
  of, in the United States, 106; the
  God of, 1; persecution of, 7-8,
  61–62, 102, 221; reconciliation
  between Muslims and, attempt at,
  31–32; seriousness of, about biblical knowledge, 48
Christians Equipped for Ministry
  (CEM) board, 132–133
Christmas, 70, 230, 241
Christmas tale, 240
Chua, H. C., 101–102, 126–127
Chua, K., 102, 126
Chung Ming Kai, 51, 66
Church calendar, following the,
  245–246
Church, the: building, privilege of
  completing His purpose of, 206;

lectionaries of, 50, 260n6; rebuild-
  ing, 35
Church year, festival days and sea-
  sons in the, 243–244
Churches: in Africa, enormous
  growth of, 221; developed out of
  suffering, 222; growth of, emphasis
  on, problem with, 173; leadership
  of, 111–112; trust in, 42; web of
  relationships in, 124–125. *See also
  specific churches*
Ciaran of Saighir, St., 146
Circumcision, 117–118
Civility, 100–101
Clans, people divided into, 105
Clare, 120
Class separation, 95, 154, 173, 193
Collective visiting, 152. *See also*
  Communal discernment
Colossians 1:8b–10, 47
Colossians 1:24, 206
Colossians 3:12–13, 101
Colossians 3:12a, 89
Colossians 3:12b, 90
Colossians 3:13–17, 90
Colossians 3:16, 48
Colossians 4:10, 143
Colossians, letter to the, 205–206
Columba, St., 212, 237
Commandments, the, 74, 89, 95
Commands, 53, 147, 230
Communal consensus, 118,
  129–130, 132, 133, 134, 152, 185
Communal counsel, 120, 121, 250
Communal discernment: in African
  communities, 122–125; among the
  Achí, 121–122, 155; Asian patterns
  of, 125–127; Australian emphasis
  on, 127–128; biblical emphasis on,
  115–118; celebration of, 248; in
  Celtic and monastic communities,
  118–121; concluding thoughts on,
  134; in Maori culture, 104–105,
  113–114, 185; in Mennonite culture, 128–134; and new habits for
  welcoming and generosity, 163;

biblical virtues, 89; and celebration, 226, 228, 233–234, 235, 237, 239; effect of, 249; and reconciliation, 193; and willingness to suffer, 197, 201, 210, 214, 215, 224. *See also* Joy

Eskimo people, 222

Ester, 161

Esther, 223

Eternal hope, 88

Eternal Joy, 89

Ethics, situation, pitfall of, 98

Ethiopia, 222, 223

Eucharist, 18, 246

European culture and traditions, and biblical knowledge, 48. *See also specific countries of Europe*

Evangelical Lutheran Church of America, 8

Evans, C., 11

Evans, G., 7–11, 12, 17, 97, 247

Evans, M., 11

Evans, V., 11

Evil, 14, 178, 211, 214, 228, 229, 238. *See also* Sins

Exodus 3:1–14, 22

Exodus 18:21–23, 63

Exodus 20:2a, 89

Exodus 20:2b, 89

Exodus 29:43–46, 233

Exodus 33:11, 233

Expanding spiral, 174

Exploitation, 176

External obstacles, 81–84

Eye disease rate, 263*n*19

Ezekiel, 55

Ezekiel 1, 55

Ezekiel 2, 55

F

Failures, repentance for, 78

Faithfulness, remembering, 68

False selectivity, 41

Family: pressure from, 110; significance of, 107

Family groups, people divided into, 105

Family honor and shame, 108–115

Family meetings, 185

Father, Son, and Holy Spirit. *See* Trinity; Triune God

Fear, 86–87, 88, 139, 172, 235, 238

Fellowship group, for international students, 9

Fern plant, wound spiral of the. *See* Koru

Festivity, as a basis for discernment, 234–235, 249. *See also* Celebration

Fielding, B. (fictional character), 62

Fieldwork, sharing in, 159

Filipinos, serving, in Hong Kong, 69, 74–75

Final Four, the, 246

Finkenwalde seminary, 218, 219

Finland: and grace, 32; seminary faculty from, 51

First Testament, the: and the captive experience, 69–70; and communal discernment, 117; Jewish practice of learning, 51; living in the company of saints from, 119–120; and practice of providing a Watchword, 49, 50; prayer featuring lessons from, 14; promise in, 45; prophet in, 55; and remembering faithfulness, 68; and understanding who is the Triune God, 3. *See also specific books*

Fisher, A., 29

Focal concerns, 73, 74–77, 85, 98, 199

Focus time, setting aside, 81

Fools, 115

Forgiveness, 2, 39, 41, 88, 90, 109, 184, 185, 188, 217

Formation: and being welcoming and generous, 137–138, 139, 141, 145, 149, 163; and communal practices, importance of, 106; concern for, 110; individualistic, 112;